Endorsements

This beautifully written festschrift represents the triple crown of missiological scholarship. Its subject, diaspora missiology, represents the greatest mission challenge and opportunity of our time. Its object, Dr. Enoch Wan, represents the epitome of Christian scholarship and discipleship. Its globally representative authors emulate their teacher in their own pioneering research, their ever-expanding body of work, and their motivating missionary passion. Thank God for the life and work of Dr. Enoch Wan and for the vision and tenacity of his disciple, Joy Tira, to gather his brilliant friends to scatter abroad new paradigms and strategies for getting the Good News to everyone, everywhere.

Douglas Birdsall, Ph.D.
Honorary Chairman of the Lausanne Movement

As a young theologian shaped by global conversations, MAP is inspiring and deeply grounding. Dr. Enoch Wan's life and work embody what it means to follow Jesus across cultures—with conviction, humility, and academic depth. His voice has helped many over the years see the importance of diaspora communities and rethink how theology is lived, not just taught. This book is a tribute to a man whose legacy isn't just in books and classrooms, but in the lives and ministries of those he's mentored around the world. If you care about mission, theology, or learning from those who've walked faithfully ahead of us—MAP is for you.

Micaela Braithwaite, B.Th.
Communications Strategist, Lausanne Movement

With deep respect and honor to Dr. Enoch Wan—a man who has lived multiple lifetimes in one, faithfully shaping missiology through scholarship and relationship. His life and teaching have multiplied through generations of students now ministering across dimensions and cultures. The results are astounding impact that defies measurement now but will echo and reverberate in eternity.

Rev. Samuel E. Chiang, Ph.D.
Deputy Secretary General, World Evangelical Alliance

Dr. Enoch Wan's scholarship has consistently led the way in shaping the field of Intercultural Studies—especially through his innovative work in Diaspora Missiology and the Relational Paradigm. *MAP: Missionary, Anthropologist, Professor* honors this legacy with intellectual rigor and heartfelt gratitude. The essays collected in this volume reflect the global breadth and theological depth of Dr. Wan's influence, offering a resource that is as much a guide for future missiological engagement as it is a tribute to a life well lived. Readers will find in these pages a rich conversation at the intersection of academic excellence and missional passion.

Charles J. Conniry, Jr., Ph.D.
President, Western Seminary, Portland, Oregon

Dr. Enoch Wan has consistently and tirelessly advocated for reflection and engagement of the mission of God. From my early days as his student to more recent years as a colleague, Dr. Wan's curiosity has never waned. This festschrift captures well the breadth of his contribution to mission studies and the significance of intentionally building into successive generations of missiologists through his work in the academy. May his example of faithfulness and innovation inspire a new generation of scholars.

Charles A. Cook, Ph.D.
Professor of Global Studies and Mission,
Executive Director of the Jaffray Centre for Global Initiatives,
Ambrose University, Calgary, Canada

The mission of God in Scripture is often played out among peoples on the move. And in our present world, with increased migration, the Christian faith is good news for diaspora peoples, which requires a diaspora missiology. Enoch Wan has been a pioneer in the study of diaspora missiology, teaching us to think about mission amid these realities. This volume celebrates his work and continues this essential task in missiological reflection and practice.

Edward L. Smither, Ph.D.
Past-immediate President, Evangelical Missiological Society
Dean & Professor of School of Missions and Intercultural Ministry,
Columbia International University

Professor Enoch Wan has enjoyed a stellar and impactful career across local church ministry, academia, and the global mission world. As a fellow seminary colleague, Enoch was an encourager and supporter. As an educator, he was deeply admired by his students. As a missiologist, he was the primary architect of Diaspora Missiology and advanced the Relational Paradigm. As an author, he was remarkably articulate and prolific. As a pastor, he served as a compassionate shepherd. And as a Christian leader, he has consistently set an exemplary standard. This festschrift serves as a fitting tribute to the incredible journey of Enoch's life—a life marked by purpose, perseverance, and profound contribution.

Rev. Dr. T.V. Thomas
Director, Centre for Evangelism & World Mission
Chair, Global Diaspora Network, Lausanne Movement

This festschrift honors the life and works of Dr. Enoch Wan. Each chapter provides important glimpses of how his life and writings have impacted these authors. The book is an important example of recognizing those who are diligently "paving the way for others" as Dr. Jacky Lau writes. Wan's zeal for diaspora missiology, relational paradigm, and other areas in anthropology and missiology continues to spread not just among his mentees but even beyond, of which I am one of those. When I first met Wan back in 2010, he graciously gave me a copy of *Scattered and Gathered* that inspired me to focus on diaspora missions for my dissertation.

Juliet Lee Uytanlet, Ph.D.
Chair of the Intercultural and Urban Studies Department
Asian Theological Seminary in Quezon City

This Festschrift is a powerful tribute to the life and legacy of Dr. Enoch Wan, capturing his pioneering contributions to diaspora missiology, relational theology, and global missions. This carefully curated volume reflects not only his academic brilliance but also his deep personal impact as a mentor, pastor, and servant-leader. Through scholarly essays and heartfelt reflections, it honors a man whose vision, humility, and faithfulness continue to inspire and equip a new generation of Kingdom workers around the world.

Jura Yanagihara, Ph.D.
President of Alliance World Fellowship

MAP
Missionary, Anthropologist, Professor

A Festschrift for Dr. Enoch Wan

Editors
Jacky Lau, Mark Hedinger, Sadiri Joy Tira

Copyright © 2025
Jacky T. K. Lau

Jacky T. K. Lau hereby assert his moral rights to be identified as Author of the Compilation in the Work in accordance with the Canadian Copyright Act (R.S.C., 1985, c. C-42).
Individual writers have the right to reproduce or use portion of their own papers in the book

All rights reserved. No part of this book may be reproduced or transmitted in any form by any means without permission in writing from the publisher, except by a reviewer, who may quote brief passages in a review.

Scripture quotations taken from The Holy Bible, New International Version® NIV® Copyright © 1973 1978 1984 2011 by Biblica, Inc. ™. Used by permission. All rights reserved worldwide.

Cover Design by Nikitha Sushma
Photo by Karen R. Hedinger
Images by Michal Parzuchowski & Christian Lue on Unsplash.com

ISBN:
Paperback: 978-1-77354-705-3
ebook: 978-1-77354-706-0

MAP: Missionary, Anthropologist, Professor
A Festschrift for Dr. Enoch Wan
Editors: Jacky Lau, Mark Hedinger, Sadiri Joy Tira

Key Words: Theology and Missiology, Diaspora Missiology, Diaspora Missions, Relational Paradigm, Church Planting, Hybridity, Orality.

Publication assistance by

PageMaster.ca

Dedications

This book is dedicated to Dr. Enoch Wan and his family:

Dr. Fung Ling Mary Wan, faithful wife, dear friend,
trusted advocate, and consistent ministry supporter.
"She is a wife of noble character."
(Proverbs 31:10)

Samuel and William, dedicated and loyal sons.
"Sons are a heritage from the Lord; Children are a reward from Him."
(Psalm 127:3)

Elijah and Jonah, grandsons and torch bearers of
their grandfather's godly life and rich legacy.
"Children (*and grandchildren*) are a reward from the Lord."
(Psalm 127:3)

Acknowledgements

"Let everything that has breath praise the Lord." (Psalm 150:6)

The ultimate purpose of this festschrift is to glorify God by honouring His good and faithful servant Dr. Enoch Wan who "keep(s) the Message alive (and) do(es) a thorough job as God's servant." (2Tim 4:5, MSG)

Praise our Lord, this book was completed on a tight schedule by a dedicated team of kingdom collaborators. We would like to express our sincere gratitude for their contributions.

- To the authors of the fifteen chapters in this volume – thank you for your thoughtfully composed articles addressing topics relevant to Dr. Wan and the global church,
- To the endorsing Christian organizations – Lausanne Movement, World Evangelical Alliance, Evangelical Missiological Society, Alliance World Fellowship, Chinese Coordination Centre of World Evangelization Canada, Canadian Centre for World Mission, Western Seminary, and Supper Club – for permitting us to use your logos as your endorsements to this book to honour God and Dr. Wan,
- To the endorsers, for your encouraging and inspiring endorsements,
- To the contributors of Tributes, for sharing your insightful and earnest testimonials,
- To Dr. Nelson Jennings, for writing the Foreword for this festschrift,
- To Dr. Karen Hedinger, for assisting us to write Dr. Wan's biography and bibliography,
- To Dr. Miriam Adeney, for her thoughtful Afterword,
- To Dale Youngman and staff of PageMaster Publishing, for assisting us to publish this book,
- To Nikitha Sushma, for your exceptional artistic design of the book cover,

- To churches, donors, and sponsors of the editors – for your encouragements, financial contributions, and prayer support which helped make this project possible,
- To Dr. Sadiri Joy Tira, for your dedication and leadership as Project Coordinator while facing a health crisis,
- To Sadiri Tonyvic Tira, for your professionally designed poster for the Official Book Launch to be held in Edmonton, Canada on October 18, 2025,
- To the management and staff of MAX's Restaurant in Edmonton, for hosting the Official Book Launch of this festschrift in your facility,
- To the guests and volunteers who will attend the Official Book Launch – thank you for joining us to celebrate with Dr. Enoch Wan and his wife, Dr. Mary Wan, for their contributions in the Kingdom of God.

Finally, we would like to thank Lulu Tira, Dr. Karen Hedinger, and Anne Lau (wives of the editors), for their encouragement and unwavering support for this book project.

Glory to God Alone!

Foreword

Breathtaking changes have characterized the life and the times of Dr. Enoch Wan. Given his tumultuous life experience, it is no wonder that Professor Wan spearheaded the development of Diaspora Missiology. His cross-cultural missionary service and urban church-planting work built a foundation for Wan to ably lead intercultural studies programs for theological students and institutions. Studying and living in North America, with his Chinese background, helps explain Wan's formulation of his Relational Paradigm that challenges conceptual Western theology. Moreover, Enoch Wan's eventful life has played out against the backdrop of numerous dramatic events of the latter half of the Twentieth Century and first quarter of the Twenty-First, including war-torn China, Cold War relations, and multidirectional migrations. Divine Providence has unmistakably been at work in the life and times of Dr. Enoch Wan.

I first met Enoch in the late 1990s. He was teaching at Reformed Theological Seminary in Jackson, Mississippi, USA. Here was a Chinese-North American professor, experienced as a church-planter and trained in anthropology (and other fields), teaching at a primarily white US-Southern theological institution known for its staunch defense of Reformed orthodoxy. Unknown to me at the time was Enoch's displacement as a child with two siblings from China to being raised in an orphanage in Hong Kong, other family members having been scattered to Burma and to Cuba. His formal education in the US, missionary service in Australia and the Philippines, and pastoral leadership among Chinese diaspora communities in major North American cities were also unseen components of this fascinating gentleman's makeup.

A few years later Enoch asked me and a few others to serve on the editorial board of a new multilingual journal he was establishing, *Global Missiology*. That open access e-journal has been producing valuable material for over two decades; remarkably Wan still edits the Chinese portions of the journal. He soon served two influential terms as President of the Evangelical Missiological Society. Over the years, Wan has mentored numerous doctoral students from a vast array of linguistic, cultural, and national backgrounds, particularly during his lengthy tenure as Research Professor of Intercultural Studies and Director of Intercultural Studies and Education Programs at Western Seminary in Portland, Oregon, USA. Enoch Wan's servant heart is no more clearly seen than in the fruit born by his students as he has equipped them to flourish in their own research, writing, and ministries of evangelism, discipleship, and teaching.

Diaspora Missiology has become a familiar area within Evangelical Missiology thanks to Wan's teaching, speaking, and voluminous publishing. Wan's 2011 book Diaspora Missiology: Theory, Methodology, and Practice (revised in 2014) was a seminal work in the field, although Dr. Wan had been speaking and publishing articles on the subject much earlier. Wan's multidisciplinary approach—using biblical studies, anthropology, missiology, and other areas—helps explain how his writings have played such a significant role in developing Evangelicals' understanding of missions to, through, and by diaspora peoples. At the same time, Wan's anchoring of Diaspora Missiology in concrete examples involving not only Chinese but also Filipino, Vietnamese, Pakistani, and numerous other migrating people—including of course his own and his family's set of personal experiences—provides the substance that enlivens the academic excellence that Wan's teaching and writing has provided.

The engrained Chinese background and makeup of 溫以諾 (Enoch Wan) has given him the instinctive insights to see blind spots in the English-language, Western theological world in which he has researched, taught, and written throughout his adult life. Wan's development and promotion of Sino-Theology and his Relational Paradigm have undoubtedly emerged from the crucible of his ongoing wilderness experience as a migrating Chinese in North America—where as a young adult, in his own words, he "learned to trust God for provision and protection and began walking in the Spirit"—as well as in other contexts. Wan's kindness and humility have enabled him to communicate effectively his Chinese-rooted insights to his colleagues in the [North American] Evangelical Missiological Society and theological institutions, who could not have been as contextually self-aware as the cultural wanderer Enoch Wan necessarily has been. The Providential gift of 溫以諾 (Enoch Wan) to the Evangelical missiological world, including English-speaking, Chinese-speaking, and other linguistic sectors, has been immense.

Thanks be to God for the life and ministry of Dr. Enoch Wan! Thanks be to God as well for the authors of this festschrift and their insightful contributions offered in Enoch's honor. I must also express my personal thanks for the privilege of contributing this foreword, which I hope adds at least a bit to readers' understanding of, and heartfelt appreciation for, the fruitful service of a dear friend, brother, and father in Jesus Christ, Professor Enoch Wan.

Hallelujah!

Rev. J. Nelson Jennings, Ph.D.
Editor of *Global Missiology – English*

Preface

The title of the book is self-explanatory. This volume is designed as a festschrift or tribute to a missionary, anthropologist, and professor, Rev. Dr. Enoch Wan.

In the publishing world, a festschrift is not a money-making book. It is not written by a single bestselling author but rather is a collection of essays written by the students, colleagues, co-workers, and friends of the honourable and distinguished person. In this case, Professor Wan is honoured and recognized by his former students and co-workers. It is their individual expressions of gratitude and respect for his impact in each one's life, career, and ministry.

As the book project coordinator, I am inspired to personally acknowledge Dr. Wan's life-time influence in my life, academic journey, and ministry. The Bible urges that we "honour our leaders" (Heb 3:27). "Dr. Wan is a close personal friend, brother in Christ, ministry partner, counsellor, and my "Academic Father".

I first met him in the hallways, cafeteria, and classrooms of the Canadian Theological Seminary in Regina, Saskatchewan. I had the privilege of observing him relate to both students and co-workers. I witnessed his humility, simplicity, and godliness. He became my professor in missiology and anthropology courses. At the beginning of each class, he led a devotional and prayer time. For three years I benefited from his knowledge, wisdom, and scholarship.

In 1999, He surprised me with a personal letter. He wrote: "Joy, enroll in the Ph.D. Program (here) at the Reformed Theological Seminary (RTS) in Jackson, Mississippi. I will make sure you receive a full tuition scholarship". After much prayer and consulting with ministry partners, I decided to accept the generous offer and kind invitation of Professor Wan. Every time I was in Jackson, he let me stay in his house, he cooked my meals and he lent me his car. Of course, I offered to help pay the bills. He did not let me wash the dishes; instead, he would tell me to go to the library, and study, study, study. He told me, "Joy, if you do not meet the RTS academic standard, they will not hesitate cutting your scholarship." From that time on I labelled him as my "academic mentor and tormentor." He is a gentle brother, gracious, and generous. Due to serious health issues, I did not finish the rigid Ph.D. requirements, but he encouraged me not to drop out altogether. By his guidance and the grace of God, I graduated with a Doctor of Ministry in Intercultural Studies.

In 2001, when he became Director of the Doctor of Missiology program at Western Seminary in Portland, Oregon, once again he recruited me to study and offered a full tuition scholarship. I started in the Doctor of Missiology program in 2005. He emphasized studying international migration and diaspora studies under his supervision. He challenged me to become an expert in this field and to see this global trend through the lens of the Great Commission and the Global Church. At that time, diaspora missiology was not a major focus of missiologists because international migration and diaspora are in the domain of social sciences, i.e., history, sociology, geography, political science, law, etc. It was not carefully studied in the Protestant Evangelical seminaries. Dr. Wan understands current global events of our times like the sons of Issachar (1 Chronicles 12:32ff).

Providentially, in 2006, I met Rev. Dr. Douglas Birdsall in Macau, China, and Dr. Tetsunao Yamamori in Portland, Oregon. These two men were Lausanne Movement (LM) leaders, Birdsall being the Chairman and Yamamori the International Director. They appointed me to be the first LM Senior Associate for Diasporas/Catalyst for Diasporas. LM leaders, in partnership with Dr. Enoch Wan, launched the Diaspora Mission Studies program at Western Seminary and hosted a historic gathering of select mission practitioners to chart the future of diaspora missions for the Lausanne Movement. In 2006, Enoch Wan and I taught Diaspora Missiology at the Cebu Theological Seminary in Cebu City, Philippines. This was followed by the Diaspora Missiology course at Western Seminary leading to the founding of the Institute of Diaspora Studies (IDS) at Western Seminary. The first IDS publication in partnership with the Filipino International Network was the book *Mission in Action in the 21st Century* (Editors, Tira and Wan. Ottawa, Canada, 2008). I must note that it is in this book that I first read Relational Theology and Missiology. Dr. Wan inspired me to write short articles and a blog. This was followed by the publication of my D.Miss.

dissertation by the Evangelical Missiological Society (EMS). I observed that Dr. Wan was laying the groundwork for diaspora missiology to become a new field or discipline in missiology and intercultural studies. Clearly, Professor Wan has been a thinker and visionary leader for world evangelism and global missions.

I am privileged that these three giants, Dr. Birdsall, Dr. Yamamori, and Dr. Wan, allowed me to "stand on (their) shoulders." Professor Enoch Wan in particular led me to understand my contextual theology, which had been a blind spot of the western missiological framework because of its emphasis on task instead of building relationships. He let me stand on his shoulders so I could see further into future global trends and respond to these issues to advance the Kingdom.

In 2020, at the height of the COVID-19 pandemic, I became the victim of a cruel and debilitating stroke. These three men reached out to me while I was in hospitals for six months. One day, as I was looking at the sunset from my window, God assured me that after the sunset there is a sunrise. I prayed, "Lord, see the sunrise and extend my life so that I can honour these three leaders."

In 2022, I assembled a team to assist me in publishing the volume *Missionary, Statesman, Strategist, and Servant: A Festschrift for Tetsunao (Ted) Yamamori* (Langham Global Library, U.K. 2023).

In 2024, the book *Tides of Opportunity: Missiological Experiences and Engagement in Global Migration* was published by William Carey Publishing (USA). This compendium was dedicated to Rev. Dr. Stanley Douglas (Doug) Birdsall.

In December 2024, Dr. Jacky and Anne Lau visited me in my apartment. I shared with them the idea of publishing a festschrift to honour our beloved brother and distinguished professor, Dr. Enoch Wan.

Now, *MAP: Missionary, Anthropologist, Professor - A Festschrift for Dr. Enoch Wan* has been published by PageMaster Publishing (Canada) and is presented in recognition of Dr. Enoch Wan's contribution to theological education and missional training of Kingdom workers. This book is not a product of one person but a collaboration and partnership of friends and former students of Professor Enoch Wan.

The contents of this book honour the landmarks of Enoch Wan's expertise and research. Specifically, from this volume readers will be informed, inspired, and instructed about Relational Missiology, Diaspora Missiology, Orality in Global Missions, Cross Cultural Church Planting, Racial Hybridity in families and communities, and Intergenerational Discipleship.

We are thankful for all the editors, contributing writers, book endorsers, the graphic designer, and publisher, PageMaster, for taking this book project to the finishing line.

Soli Deo Gloria

Sadiri Joy Tira, D.Min., D.Miss.
MAP Project Coordinator,
Edmonton, Alberta, Canada, June 10, 2025

Contents

Foreword - J. Nelson Jennings..11
Preface - Sadiri Joy Tira...15
Contents..19

Introduction..21

Theology & Missiology...23
1. "An Introduction to Diaspora Theology
   as a Form of Scriptural Reflection" - Ria Llanto Martin....................24
2. "Diaspora Missiology or Migration Theology: A Creative
   Tension between Two Perspectives." - Tereso C. Casiño...................33

Diaspora Missions..43
3. "Chinese Diaspora Mission: A Reflection on Dr. Wan's
   Kingdom Contributions" - Jacky Lau..44
4. "The Vietnamese Alliance Church in Edmonton:
   A Case Study of Diaspora Congregation" - Thanh Trung Le.............51
5. "Engaging the 5th Largest Religious Block:
   Sikhs and Sikhism" - Sadiri Joy Tira..59

Relational Paradigm...67
6. "Unmerited Grace in Relationships:
   A Reflection on the Influence of
   Enoch Wan on My Life and Ministry" - Juno Wang..........................68
7. "The Relational Teacher -
   The Theory and Practice of Relational Interaction
   by Educators" - Mark R. Hedinger & Karen R. Hedinger.................75
8. "Missiology for the 21st Century:
   The Point-Line-Plane Perspective of
   Relational Interactionism" - Elton Siu Lun Law................................83

Church Planting..91
9. "Cross-Cultural Church Planting in Latin America:
   Reflections by an American Missionary
   Fifteen Years Later" - Matt Cook..92
10. "Diaspora Missions and Church Planting:
    Three Lasting Lessons Learned by Greenhills
    Christian Fellowship Canada" - Narry Santos 100
11. "One Meal, One Prayer, One Neighborhood at a Time.
    A Case Study of Relational Mission" – Sadiri Tonyvic Tira............114

Hybridity and Home..123
12. "Jewish-Gentile Intermarriage and Family:
    A Perfect Missiological Opportunity" - Tuvya Zaretsky................124
13. "On Hospice, Home, & Host"
    - Lorajoy Tira-Dimangondayao...133

Orality in Global Mission...143
14. "Will the Three Orality Movements Intersect?"
    - Tom Steffen...144
15. "The Journey from Concept to Story:
    Orality Comes Full Circle" - Danyal Qalb........................155

Biography of Dr. Enoch Wan...165

Bibliography of Dr. Enoch Wan's Writings........................175

Tributes 205
   John Baxter, Ronald Brown, Sharon Wai Man Chan,
   Charles J. Conniry, Jr., Rev. Sirgisberto de Costa,
   Wonsuk Ma, Rev. Francis Tam, Mandy Tao.

Afterword - Miriam Adeney..217

Editors & Contributors..221

Introduction

"Different is Different not Better or Worse." (Professor Enoch Wan)

A Festschrift is a collection of writings published in honour of a scholar. In academia, it is a book honouring a respected person, especially an academic, and presented during his/her lifetime. It contains original contributions by close colleagues of the person being honoured, including his doctoral students and others.

MAP: Missionary, Anthropologists, Professor - A Festschrift for Dr. Enoch Wan is a collection of articles and essays. The contents are written by former students, ministry partners and colleagues of Dr. Enoch Wan. They are multi-cultural and multi-generational writers, multi-disciplinary contributors and Kingdom-collaborators who have been influenced by Enoch Wan. Authors were given the freedom to write and articulate their research findings and views but those are not necessarily the views of the Editorial Team nor Dr. Enoch Wan himself. Every writer used their own writing style and each was given equal space. Some of them portrayed themselves as authoritative - practitioners while others are scholars and researchers. However, everyone who contributed to this book project including the book endorsers are committed to the mission of God (Matthew 28:18-20).

The articles are clustered in the following groups:
1. Theology and Missiology
2. Diaspora Missions
3. Relational Paradigm
4. Church planting
5. Hybridity and Home
6. Orality in Global Mission
7. Biography and Bibliography of Dr. Wan
8. Personal Tributes by selected colleagues and friends of Dr. Wan

May this book inform, inspire and instruct the readers to help fulfil the Great Commission.

The Editorial Team

Theology & Missiology

"In Him we live and move and have our being."
(Acts 17:28)

Chapter 1

An Introduction to Diaspora Theology as a Form of Scriptural Reflection

Ria Llanto Martin, D.I.S.

> *"A real life turning point was coming to New York as a lonely foreign student in 1970 when I learned to trust God for provision and protection and began walking in the Spirit. Those were formative years in lifestyle and academic pursuit. - Dr. Enoch Wan's Defining Moment."*

I met Dr. Enoch Wan on my first day of class at Western Seminary in Portland, Oregon, USA. He approached me when he saw me walk into the classroom, as I nervously looked for an empty seat. I was struggling with doubt and impostor syndrome, wondering to myself, "Should I even be here?"

He handed me the book, *Scattered: The Global Filipino Presence,* and said, "This is my personal copy, and I am now giving it to you." That short interaction calmed the apprehension that I felt.

Enoch Wan, a Chinese diaspora, has been in the vanguard of what we call today the "diaspora missions movement."[1] His book, *Diaspora Missiology: Theory, Methodology, and Practice* was the first full-length exposition of the discipline.[2] That book developed an appropriate contemporary missiological response to the shifting center of Christianity to the southern hemisphere.[3]

My experience in diaspora ministry is parallel to the experience of countless others. It was hard and lonely. My sense of belonging was

---

[1] Enoch Wan, *Diaspora Missiology: Theory, Methodology, and Practice* (Portland, OR: Institute of Diaspora Studies, 2011), viii. "Foreword to the First Edition" by Michael Pocock.
[2] Wan, *Diaspora Missiology*, viii.
[3] Wan, *Diaspora Missiology*, 3.

challenged, and my identity was shaken. The juxtaposition of feeling lost yet certain of God's call in my life was so apparent, and I have learned to live with those two tensions of identity and belonging. Those same two questions continue to excite scholars in the pursuit of reconciling the tensions of being a person of faith on the move.

Even though the diaspora missions movement was actualized at the height of globalization and migration, Wan claims that both scattering and regathering are Biblical realities. Numerous books on diaspora and its implications[4] have been accounted for by scholars from the majority world, but so far, none has considered diaspora as a theological framework.

Diaspora Contributions to Theology
Teologia del Balcon and *Teologia del Camino*

Two concepts that are relevant to diaspora study were written in 1889 by Scottish Missionary Juan (John) Mackay: The *teologia del balcon* (Theology of the Balcony) and *teologia del camino* (Theology of the Road).[5]

In the Philippines, as in Latin America, homes often have a balcony. It is a small extension from the second floor that lets us see onto the streets. It is a perfect spot to be a spectator: close enough to see, but far enough away not to be involved. Theology of the Road is the antithesis of the Theology of the Balcony. It means more than being down to earth, "but something *en route, en marcha*, theology that is going somewhere; indeed, a theologian who is going somewhere... where life is intensely lived, where thought has its birth in conflict and concern, where choices are made and decisions carried out...where concern is never absent from the wayfarer's heart. On the Road, a goal is sought, dangers are faced, life is poured out..."[6] It is too easy for pastors and church leaders to speak of God without considering the life experiences of their community. The preaching of the Scriptures is oftentimes detached from the daily reality (the *camino*) of diaspora communities[7] living with abuse, poverty, injustices, and marginalization. Maria recounts, "Here in

---
[4] See the Western Seminary's Center for Diaspora and Relational Research resources for Dr. Wan's list of diaspora books.
[5] Hays, *Eight Million Exiles*, 23.
[6] Hays, *Eight Million Exiles*, 23.

Bogota, I attended a lot of churches, but I'd never heard of a Christian church that was with the victims."[8]

There is nothing more truthful and authentic than theology as lived experience. Diaspora theology is a Scriptural reflection, an authentic way to view the Scriptures and understand God as fellow road travelers where tensions, conflict, concerns, and life happen. "Theological reflection – that is, the understanding of the faith – arises spontaneously and inevitably in the believer, in all those who have accepted the gift of the Word of God."[9] Diaspora theology helps the Church (diasporas or not) to understand Christian faith in the middle of crisis, displacement, marginalization, injustices, powerlessness, and feelings of homelessness. My working definition of diaspora theology[10] is understanding God from a minority or marginalized perspective.

Theology of Redemption and Restoration

God's call to Abraham to leave his homeland is attached to him being a blessing and a great nation. This promise is extended to all the families of the earth, right after the scattering in the Tower of Babel. Jacob received reaffirmation of God's covenant to Abraham and the promise that he would be a blessing to all nations. Joseph, sold as a slave to the Ishmaelites, became a blessing to Egypt and its neighbors. Moses, disoriented about where to place his loyalty as an Israelite raised in the Egyptian royalty, left power, comfort, and royalty to free the Israelites from slavery.

God revealed himself through Jesus Christ, a diaspora from heaven to earth, a person of faith on the move, an immigrant and a refugee whose family was forced to seek refuge from King Herod's wrath. Jesus Christ, our Messiah, carries a long history of diasporas (Fourteen generations from Abraham to David, fourteen from David to the

---

[7] Enoch Wan and Michael Pocock wrote *Diaspora Missiology: Reflections on Reaching the Scattered Peoples of the World.*
[8] Hays, *Eight Million Exiles* 28.
[9] Gustavo Gutierrez, *A Theology of Liberation* (Maryknoll, N.Y.: Orbis, 1998).
[10] See Wan, Enoch. *Diaspora Missiology: Theory, Methodology and Practice.* 2nd ed. Pp 1 – 8 "definitions of key terms" and Chapter 4, "Exploring Major Dispersion Terms and Realities in the Bible" by Narry F. Santos (pp 35 – 42).

Babylonian exile, and fourteen from the Babylonian exile to the Messiah. see Matthew 1:17).

In the New Testament, Simeon the Cyrene (Luke 23:14) or the Niger (Acts 13:1), a diaspora missionary, carried the cross of Jesus at the crucifixion. He has a Jewish name with a dark complexion.[11] Mark recounts Simeon's journey with his two sons, on their way to celebrate Passover at the temple. A Roman soldier who probably saw his dark skin demanded that he carry the cross. "…like so many migrants living in the shadow of an empire, he was obligated to obey despite the humiliation of being treated like a pack of animals in front of his sons on what should have been a celebratory day."[12] When the persecution broke out, Simeon was one of the missionaries who traveled to Antioch. Fluent in Greek, he was able to share the good news about the Lord Jesus Christ. "The Lord's hand was with them, and a great number of people believed and turned to the Lord." (Acts 11:21)

Today, we have a plethora of diaspora academic literature, recounting stories of how individuals outside of their homeland have become a blessing to their new home. Katia Adams and Jesus De Paz's stories are both diasporas and leading a church in America.[13]

Finke and Stark observed, "From 1965 to 2000, over twenty-three million immigrants arrived in the United States and…the vast majority of the new immigrants involved in religion are forming Protestant and Catholic congregations. Joseph Castleberry argues that these statistics give evidence that immigrants in America guarantee a strong American faith in the future.[14] However, there is an equally overwhelming barricade from xenophobia, anti-Asian hate, and the marginalization of

---

[11] "…the meaning of Simeon's Latin nickname suggests a dark complexion and allows for the possibility that he was descended from proselytes from the Romanized coast of North Africa. Cyrene, on the North African Coast, had a large Jewish population and a large Greek population. Craig Keener, The IVP Bible Background Commentary New Testament 2nd Ed (Downers Grove, Illinois, IVP Academic, 2014), 357.

[12] Hays, *Eight Million Exiles*, 160.

[13] See Katia Adams and Jesus De Paz's stories from Joseph Castleberry. *The New Pilgrims: How Immigrants Are Renewing America's Faith and Values*, 51.

[14] Joseph Castleberry. *The New Pilgrims: How Immigrants Are Renewing America's Faith and Values*.

immigrants and refugees in their new home countries. "The diasporic communities have played a strategic role in the creation and advancement of Christianity from its inception. Just as the Jewish diaspora of the first century helped Christians to scatter and resulted in the diffusion of Christianity to the Gentiles, today's diasporas--including refugees are renewing and advancing Christianity in unanticipated ways."[15]

Theology of Identities in Tension:
Who am I, or Who is the GREAT I AM?

In my doctoral research, I had a conversation with a Filipina woman in Germany, married to a German. They have two beautiful sons, and the whole family interact beautifully, shifting from German to English to Tagalog. She told me that she is not naïve to the challenges and marginalization she faces despite being married to a German. However, her identity is deeply rooted in how God sees her, "I see myself how God sees me," "at the end of the day, I am a child of God."

Like Hagar, the Egyptian slave who served Abraham's household even to the point of fulfilling Sarah's desire to have their children through her. When Hagar became pregnant, she was despised and humiliated. She ran away, which led to one of the most beautiful scenes in the Bible. In her pain, an angel of the LORD appeared to her (Gen.16:6) and told her she would have a son named Ishmael, meaning God hears. In the middle of distress and injustice, Hagar said, "I have now seen the One who sees me" (Gen. 16:13).

Moses was conflicted about his identity, and in his confusion an angel of the LORD appeared to him as a burning bush. Jacob, who fled home to avoid his brother Esau's anger, met the LORD in his dream. God reminded Jacob of His promise to bless all peoples through him. Sam George and Miriam Adeney wrote, "Displacements can uproot our false sense of security until we have to sink our roots deeper into God. There is so much pain in displacement, but there are also blessings."[16]

---

[15] Sam George and Miriam Adeney, Refugee *Diaspora: Missions Amid the Greatest Humanitarian Crisis* (Littleton, CO: William Carey Publishing, 2018), xxii.

[16] George and Adeney, *Refugee Diaspora*, 169.

Diaspora identity is unique: loyal to our roots and yet living in our new home. Timothy Smith said, "Migration is fundamentally 'a theologizing experience' because displaced peoples ask questions about identity, purpose, meaning, worldviews, and ultimately God." [17]

Minority Does Not Always Mean Powerless

Anthropologists Charles Wagley (1913-1991) and Marvin Harris (1927-2001) in their 1958 volume, *Minorities in the New World: Six Case Studies,* presented the term of "minority."[18] One of the characteristics that they identified is that minorities are frequently powerless in comparison to the dominant culture in which they live.

Sometimes minorities are treated with persecution and violence, like the Israelites under the bondage of Egypt. Besides that kind of persecution, minorities can suffer marginalization. In contemporary usage, the term minority has been loosely affiliated with specific racial or ethnic backgrounds, like Black or Hispanic Americans. In diaspora literature, many Filipino scholars have written about the marginalization and oppression of Filipino diasporas in other countries.[19] But a minority does not always mean powerlessness.

Daniel, Esther, Ruth, and Rahab are some of the diasporas in the Old Testament who were minorities yet lived influential and powerful lives. David Valeta, a scholar of the book of Daniel, observed that "Martin Luther King Jr. references a parallel story in Daniel chapter three where Daniel and his friends were thrown into the fiery furnace for refusing to obey the laws of King Nebuchadnezzar on the grounds that the higher moral law was at stake… Daniel's refusal to obey the king's law and his willingness to suffer the consequences help expose illegitimate use of political authority and the need for subversive behavior to change unjust laws."[20] Martin Luther King Jr., a leader in the civil rights movement in

---

[17] Timothy Smith, "Religion and Ethnicity in America, from the American Historical Review," 83.
[18] https://www.ebsco.com/research-starters/social-sciences-and-humanities/minority-and-majority-groups accessed June 22, 2025.
[19] See Chapter two of *Diaspora Missions Engagement in the Global North Through Intercultural Campus Ministry: "By and Beyond" Filipinos* by Enoch Wan and Ria Llanto Martin.
[20] David M. Valeta, https://www.bibleodyssey.org/author/david-m-valeta/The SBL Study Bible NRSV Updated Version

America, an African-American minister, was a minority but surely not powerless.

Christianity Is a Minority Religion.

In the story of Daniel chapter 2, the minority kept their identity. In a different story from Daniel chapter 3 a minority came into power and used it for self-exaltation. British evangelical biblical scholar Joyce Baldwin explains that Daniel 3 represents an ideology. "It represents the conflict between worship of the true God and the humanistic use of religion to boost the power of the rulers of this world."[21] We can trace this pattern by thinking of the image of a golden bull starting from the Egyptian bull gods that were wrongly credited with leading Israel out of Egypt (Exodus 32:4). Aaron and the Israelites merged their commitment to the God of Israel and the god of Egypt. Walter Brueggemann's (2025) *Prophetic Imagination* outlined Solomon's attempts to secure his dynasty by committing a harem, taxing to the point of state control, creating bureaucracy like those of other nations, forced labor (slavery), gluttonous daily provisions, and thousands of military personnel. Is this the reality of God's promise to Abraham? A state-sponsored syncretism and, according to George Mendenhall, the paganization of Israel.[22] Advancing our religious belief to political power is a form of syncretism; it resembles the golden bull.

As a diaspora from the majority world, it is hard for me to imagine an affluent Christian nation while half of the people on the other side of the planet are in poverty and starving. When economics, affluence, and satiation become the agenda, it is countercultural to become a blessing to all nations. "It is nonetheless reasonable to conjecture that the affluence and prosperity so attested is not democratically shared. The menu report of 1 Kings 4 just cited most likely represented only the eating habits and opportunities of the royal entourage, which at best, was indifferent to the plight of the royal subjects…eating that well means food is taken off the

---

[21] Joyce G. Baldwin, *Daniel: An Introduction and Commentary*, vol. 23, Tyndale Old Testament Commentaries (Downers Grove, IL: InterVarsity Press, 1978), 110.

[22] Walter Brueggemann, *Prophetic Imagination 40th Ed.* (Minneapolis, MN: Fortress Press, 2018), 24.

table of another."[23] Human nature tells us that with such an exploitive and wasteful appetite, there will never be enough. Satiation and affluence dull passion for Jesus, compassion turns into consuming and promises to compromise. "The Solomonic establishment embodies the loss of passion, which is the inability to care or suffer."[24] Solomon, a diaspora, became the very empire that God had freed them from. Daniel and Jonathan Boyarin point to the Jewish diaspora as a model for others and an important lesson for the world. "Jewish Diaspora can be a prophetic voice warning us of both the tyranny of universalism and the violence produced by cultural nativism. Diaspora allows for the acceptance of difference and the creative interaction across communities, one that can be taught only from the position of a minority out of power."[25]

Scriptural Reflection

John Mackay expanded the Theology of the Road as a "symbol of first-hand experience of reality where thought, born of a living concern, issues in decision and action."[26] Diaspora reality leads to real life questions we have seen in this chapter: the IDPs (internally displaced persons) struggles to understand their suffering, diasporas' questions about their identity and the feeling that "I don't belong." Diaspora theology forces us to ask how to respond as a person of faith when injustices and marginalization occur. The need to understand Christian faith from a diasporic lens is becoming more apparent. It bridges the gap between life experiences and Christian doctrines.

Diaspora theology invites Christians to reflect on our collective purpose and meaning, the Abrahamic covenant of blessing all peoples. Our identities might be shaken, and we may be unsure how to answer the question of "Where are you from?" But in these times, God continues to choose to reveal Himself as the great I AM. We question our value when we experience marginalization and dehumanization. Yet we remember

---

[23] Brueggemann, *Prophetic Imagination*, 26.
[24] Brueggemann, *Prophetic Imaginaton*, 41.
[25] Jennifer Saunders, Elena Fiddian-Qasmiyeh , and Synder, Susanna, *Intersections of Religion and Migration: Issues at the Global Crossroads* (New York, NY: Springer Nature, 2016), 183.
[26] John Mackay, *A Preface to Christian Theology* (New York, NY: The Macmillan Company, 1946),44.

that a minority does not mean powerless because we have God as our source of strength. Diaspora theology takes us back to our call to love God and our neighbors. It warns us of the allure of a self-serving empire. Hay quotes Graham on reflection as "a means of ensuring the authenticity and discernment by which we come to know ourselves but also … to know the reality of a God who continues to be revealed and encountered in the empirical world."[27] Reflection is that pause, that breathing space that helps us align our breathing with the LORD. How we answer these questions as a Christian community will have significant consequences for this world and future generations. Diasporas need theological reflection not just for themselves but for the good of the Christian community.

---

[27] Hays, *Eight Million Exiles*, 210.

Chapter 2

Diaspora Missiology or Migration Theology: A Creative Tension between Two Perspectives

Teresa C. Casiño, Th.D., Ph.D.

Introduction

Diaspora and migration represent the realities, processes, and intricacies of people's geographic and spatial movements since the rise of human civilizations. Academically, viewing these phenomena through the lens of m*issio Dei* (mission) as embodied by the church's participation (missions) is relatively novel. From the onset of the third millennium, attempts have been made to codify diaspora missions practice as a distinct missiological discipline. This innovative approach has rocked the traditional field of missiology, resulting in what is currently known as *diaspora missiology*. Ironically, unlike other traditional disciplines, diaspora missiology developed out of *praxis* where *theory* emanates from *practice*. On the educational front is Enoch Wan who is acknowledged as a pioneering "lead scholar,"[28] while on the practical side is Sadiri Joy Tira, serving as the main "catalyst" for diaspora missions who tirelessly promoted diaspora missiology intercontinentally.[29] In 2010, Tira, alongside others, launched Global Diaspora Network (GDN), in collaboration with the Lausanne Movement.[30]

Although diaspora missiology is advancing, "migration missiology" still lacks the traction to develop it as another discipline.[31] Connections between the two perspectives exist but not without *creative tensions*.

---

[28] See Enoch Wan, ed., *Diaspora Missiology: Theory, Methodology, and Practice,* 2nd ed. (Portland, OR: Institute of Diaspora Studies, 2014).

[29] Sadiri Joy Tira, "Preface," in *Scattered to Gather: Embracing the Global Trend of Diaspora*, Lausanne Diaspora Leadership Team (Manila: LifeChange Publishing Inc., 2010), 4-5.

[30] See https://globaldiasporanetwork.org.

This essay identifies the tensions between diaspora and migration and how both nomenclatures could inform and enrich each other amid perceived dissonance.

The Great Objection

In May 2009, Tira convened the "Lausanne Diasporas Strategy Consultation" in Manila, Philippines hosted by Greenhills Christian Fellowship (GCF). The gathering was part of the preparation for the Third Lausanne Congress to be held in Cape Town, South Africa the following year. Participants comprised mostly of practitioners, missiologists, educators, and missions executives. Presentations focused on diaspora missions—a combination of academic papers and regional reports--with a special feature on the role of theological institutions in equipping diaspora leaders. After two days of lively discussions, the mood in the room slowly changed when a migration scholar, Jehu Hanciles, politely voiced his objection to the use of diaspora as a nomenclature. Hanciles argued patiently that "migration" would be the proper terminology, which, if accepted by the participants, would pave the way for "migration missiology." He noted the limitation of the term "diaspora" to account for geographic mobility in human history, contending, as he wrote in his earlier publication, that "not only is migrant movement crucial to the unfolding of the divine plan, but it also furnishes the basis for a biblical critique of global cultural hegemony."[32]

In retrospect, it was at the Manila Consultation that the line between the two perspectives was drawn. A day before Hanciles' presentation, the organizers asked if I could respond to the "diaspora objection," which had its own merit. I obliged by giving a brief elucidation on diaspora over migration as a trajectory for applying missional initiatives among scattered peoples. Hanciles spoke with humility, clarity, and confidence-- gleaning insights from biblical, historical, and contemporary sources. Apparently, no participant was persuaded despite his "building blocks" that resonate with diaspora missiology: globalization, migration, and

---

[31] For a critique on diaspora missiology, see Mathew Krabill and Allison Norton, "New Wine in Old Wineskins: A Critical Appraisal of Diaspora Missiology," *Missiology 43*, no. 4 (2015): 442-455.

[32] Jehu J. Hanciles, *Beyond Christendom: Globalization, African Migration, and the Transformation of the West* (Maryknoll: Orbis Books, 2008), 4.

mission. I reckoned that day that differences between the two perspectives were reconcilable. As early as 2004, Wan cautioned practitioners and scholars of challenges regarding the application of diaspora to missiology in verifying accurate figures in identifying diaspora groups. Among other reasons were "high mobility, the tendency towards cultural/ethnic hybridity, confused identity (due to cultural assimilation, genetic amalgamation of inter-racial marriages, psychodynamic marginality of the "self" or divided loyalty)."[33]

Creative Tensions

Proponents of viewing human mobility in relation to the spread of the gospel can be categorized into three: generalist, particularist, and integrationist. A *generalist* may use diaspora or migration (either/or) freely, although, in most cases, mostly on the right flank of diaspora. A *particularist* prefers to use migration exclusively (*migration alone*) as a descriptor with no reference to diaspora either in academic conversation or publication. An *integrationist* combines both perspectives (both/and) without sacrificing the peculiarities of each descriptor. Popular among integrationists is the term "people on the move." This section focuses on the three-fold tension that exists between diaspora and migration.

The first tension lies in **concept.** The cognitive aspect of understanding diaspora and migration seems highly technical, but not to the proponents of both conceptual categories. Some view diaspora and migration as conceptually *two-dimensional,* like two sides of a coin in the reality of human movements. Accordingly, one exists for the other to inform, shape, and challenge. Generalists, and to some degree, integrationists, belong to this category. They ask critical questions about the *concept*. Should diaspora restrict its usage and application to the scattering of the Jews during and after the two major exiles in the Old Testament? How do we account for people's mobility from the post-fall stage to the exilic period and to the church's diasporic conditions across the Roman Empire? What about the dispersion of people outside biblical

---

[33] Enoch Wan, "The Phenomenon of Diaspora: Missiological Implications for Christian Missions," in *Scattered: The Filipino Global Presence*, eds. Luis Pantoja, Sadiri Joy Tira, and Enoch Wan (Manila: LifeChange Publishing, Inc., 2004), 117.

history with no missional component or connotation?[34] In contrast, particularists refer to types, forms, and patterns of people's mobility exclusively in terms of "migration" without mentioning diaspora despite the latter's appearance in biblical history.[35]

The second tension involves **semantics**. Proponents of diaspora and migration know how meanings are assigned to terminologies. Meanings are drawn from the existential realities of people's mobility within a particular setting. Probing questions help define categories. What do diaspora and migration exactly mean? Are they one and the same? What is the proper way of defining two realities and processes of people's dispersion? Do both terminologies have common features, characteristics, or traits? These questions are critical to understanding the essence and content of each language. For example, migration may feature economic, cultural, historical, and socio-political, and legal realities, whereas diaspora highlights the missiological framework in which God is sovereign over the processes of people's mobility. Meanings could be subjective and sometimes lost in linguistic jargons.[36] Defining terms could be challenging because new meanings evolve from the fluidity of time or environmental factors. When missiology students at Gardner-Webb University School of Divinity in North Carolina were tasked to research definitions of "diaspora" between 2013 and 2015, they were surprised to identify over a hundred entries.[37]

Other derivatives exist, too: migrant mission, migrant ministry, diaspora missions, diaspora ministry, international ministry, intercultural ministry, multicultural ministry, multicultural missions, refugee and displaced missions, trafficked and smuggled people's ministry, among others. Despite variants in meaning, one fact remains: "If we look at the

---

[34] For types of diaspora, see Robin Cohen, *Global Diasporas: An Introduction*, 3rd ed. (New York, NY: Routledge, 2023), 1-201.
[35] See J. N. Manokaran, *Christ and Migrants: Biblical Understanding of Migration, Missional Response to Migration* (Secunderabad, India: GS Books, 2017).
[36] Sam George et al, *People on the Move*, Lausanne Occasional Paper 70 (Quezon City, Philippines: Global Diaspora Network, 2024), 22-23.
[37] See Sadiri Joy Tira and Tetsunao Yamamori, eds., *Scattered and Gathered: A Global Compendium of Diaspora Missiology*, ed. Sadiri Joy Tira and Tetsunao Yamamori, rev. and updated ed. (Cumbria, UK: Langham Global Library, 2020), 633-634.

foreigners as Diaspora, maybe we can change our views on mission."[38] Specifically, "Diaspora refers to the overarching structure under which all forms of mobility take place; migration serves as a tool to account for diasporic movements."[39] In a word, "Diaspora accentuates a strong, broad missiological perspective over the sociologically-oriented acts of migration."[40] Even conceptual semantics reveal an indissoluble link between diaspora and migration in a book chapter: "We Are All Migrants: The Scope of Diasporas."[41]

The third tension is a matter of **relevance**. Diaspora and migration point to the existential realities and missional opportunities of people's dispersion. *Biblical history shows migration as inherent in human being as diaspora is intrinsic in human becoming.* Both forms of human movements trace back to Genesis 1:28 that frames the universal mandate of creation care and ecological responsibility. Diaspora and migration flow requires physical mobility that could accentuate sparks of human spirituality.[42] In diaspora missiology, opportunities for *missions to*, *missions through*, and *missions beyond* the diasporas abound.[43] Diasporas and migrants face different realities and experience numerous transformational processes either voluntarily or involuntarily. Some moments turn into movements—culturally, religiously, economically, ideologically, and wholistically. Border crossings provide people unique opportunities to learn from other cultures and worldviews; many migrants gradually contribute to current and future stability of host

---

[38] Ki-won Seo, "Case Study: Mongolian Diaspora Ministry," in *21C New Nomad Era and Migrant Mission*, ed. Chan-Sik Park and Noah Jung (Seoul: Christianity and Industrial Society Research Institute, 2010), 291.

[39] Chandler H. Im and Tereso C. Casiño, "Introduction," in *Global Diasporas and Mission*, eds. Chandler H. Im and Amos Young (Eugene, OR: Wipf & Stock, 2014), 3.

[40] Im and Casiño, 3.

[41] David Claydon, ed., *The New People Next Door*, Lausanne Occasional Paper 55 (n.p.: Lausanne Committee for World Evangelization, 2005).

[42] Mark A. Knoll, *The New Shape of World Christianity: How American Experience Reflects Global Faith* (Downers Grove, IL: IVP Academic, 2009), 32.

[43] Lausanne Diaspora Leadership Team, *Scattered to Gather: Embracing the Global Trend of Diaspora* (Manila: LifeChange Publishing Inc., 2010), 24-27. Wan's revision is notable. missions to the diaspora, missions through the diaspora, missions by and beyond the diaspora, and missions with the diaspora (*Diaspora Missiology*, 6.)

societies. In some cases, the settlement of foreigners could address governmental concerns affecting low birth in many countries.[44]

Sensitivity to culture and language is relevant to people's diasporic process. In 2014, a student in Diaspora Missiology class conducted research on the Japanese community in South Carolina. At first, the Japanese pastor refused to accommodate her, explaining that in Japanese context, the word "diaspora" has negative connotations. Migration was acceptable, but certainly not "diaspora." So, I sent a copy of the "Seoul Declaration on Diaspora Missiology."[45] Only then that the Japanese missionary approved the student's research after learning the biblical usage of "diaspora."

People on the Move: An Integrationist Approach

In recent years, an integrationist nomenclature has emerged, namely, "people on the move" (PoM). This "descriptor" seeks to bridge the gap between diaspora and migration.[46] "People on the move" is a valid theological and missiological category because it serves as a functional juxtaposition in differentiating and correlating diaspora and migration. It also reinforces the symbiotic relationship and complementarity between two realities of dispersion. Migration and diaspora intersect in "people on the move," but they are not technically interchangeable.[47] On the one hand, *migrationists* employ an exclusivist trajectory, ignoring the linguistic, conceptual, and hermeneutical validity of diaspora in biblical history, including but not limited to the two Jewish exiles and the scattering of Christians in the first century (Acts 8-28; I Peter 1:1). On the other hand, some *diasporalogists* could identify as *generalists*, especially when they apply loosely the realities of diaspora from Genesis 3 to the Book of Revelation. This approach ignores the peculiarity of the meaning within socio-political, cultural, and historical contexts.[48]

---

[44] Philip Jenkins, *The Next Christendom: The Coming of Global Christianity* (New York: Oxford University Press, 2002), 82.

[45] LDLT, *Scattered to Gather*, 9-10.

[46] George et al., *People on the Move*, 82.

[47] Tereso C. Casiño, "Why People Move: A Prolegomenon to Diaspora Missiology," *Torch Trinity Journal* 13, no. 1 (May 2010): 30.

[48] S. H. Chang, "From Opportunity to Mission: Scattering for the Gospel in the New Testament Story," in *Scattered and Gathered: A Global Compendium of Diaspora Missiology,* eds. Sadiri Joy Tira and Tetsunao Yamamori, rev. and

However, "people on the move" serves as a "strategic middle" that straddles between diaspora and migration in terms of *potential*, *purpose*, and *practice*. It unites two perspectives—a *bridge building* function—without being centrist or eclectic, emphasizing the best of both realities in people's mobility.

A bridge in terms of **potential** is conceivable. "People on the move" allows both perspectives to optimize their potential without erasing their respective peculiarities. It facilitates reciprocity, modesty, and transparency to accomplish what John Corrie calls "genuine interculturality."[49] Hanciles aptly notes, "The religiosity of the new migrants potentially transforms the religious movement into missionary engagement."[50] Diasporic conditions provide migrants opportunities to have transformative social, religious, and cultural encounters.[51] Scattered people cross "cultural frontiers."[52] Their ability to move into various locations could open an opportunity to gather away from their homeland and create indigenous missionary movements outside and within Western hemisphere.[53] As Christian diasporas from the Majority World move within and across continents to engage people groups with the gospel, it is not surprising to hear of a "silent witness of living and working" among several ethnic groups even in creative access regions.[54] A diaspora perspective rejects insularity due to its transnational character and global mindset; it is also "'multidirectional,' and non-spatial, borderless, and not

---

updated ed. (Cumbria, UK: Langham Global Library, 2020), 131-147.

[49] See John Corrie, "Migration as a Theologizing Experience: The Promise of Interculturality for Transforming Mission," *Mission Studies* 31, no. 1 (2014): 9-21.

[50] Hanciles, *Beyond Christendom*, 5.

[51] T. V. Thomas, "Catalyst for Change: The Diaspora Contribution," in *Catalyst for Change: The South Asian Diaspora*, International Network of South Asian Diaspora Leaders (Delhi: South Asian Concern, 2005), 9.

[52] Andrew F. Walls asserts, "Cross-cultural transmission is integral to Christian faith" *(The Missionary Movement in Christian History: Studies in the Transmission of Faith* [Maryknoll, NY: Orbis Books, 2003], 257).

[53] See Timothy K. Park, ed., *Mission History of Asian Churches* (Pasadena, CA: William Carey Library, 2011), 1-223. Hanciles asserts, "Every Christian is a potential missionary" (*Beyond Christendom,* 6).

[54] R. Theodore Srinivasagan, "The Contribution of Indian Churches and Missions in the National/World Scenario," *Indian Missions* (April-June 2006): 7-8.

geographically divided."⁵⁵ J. D. Payne insightfully observes, "Gone are the days when we should think only about sending missionaries *over there*; we must now consider how we can both get to the unreached peoples *over there* while simultaneously working to reach them *over here*."⁵⁶

A bridge in terms of **purpose** is possible. Do diaspora and migration try to accomplish the same missional purpose? Recent literature reveals no disparity in the missional objectives of both paradigms.⁵⁷ Jonathan Bornmann calls for a "fresh missiology" informed by the "realities of a transnational world—a missiology that equips the church to fulfill Jesus's commission to make disciples."⁵⁸ For integrationists, both perspectives address pertinent issues like integration, community, and belonging.⁵⁹ Although Manokaran prefers migration, he echoes the ethos of diaspora missiology: "It is necessary to understand God's purpose in the process of migration and respond knowing the will of God."⁶⁰ Precisely stated, diaspora and migration seek to achieve the same purpose as "tools for mission."⁶¹

A bridge in terms of **practice** is doable. At the Third Lausanne Congress in Cape Town, South Africa in October 2010, diaspora was allotted two multiplex slots. Tira spoke to leaders from 198 nations and territories on the theme, "People on the Move." Fourteen years later, at the Fourth Lausanne Congress in Incheon, South Korea (October 2024), participants held daily discussions on the theme, "People on the Move."

---

[55] Enoch Wan and Sadiri Joy Tira, "Diaspora Missiology and Missions in the Context of the Twenty-First Century," *Torch Trinity Journal* 13, no. 1 (May 2010): 48.

[56] J. D. Payne, *Strangers Next Door: Immigration, Migration and Mission* (Downers Grove, IL: IVP Books, 2012), 151-152.

[57] Jehu J. Hanciles, *Migration and the Making of Global Christianity* (Grand Rapids, MI: William B. Eerdmans Publishing Co., 2023); Manokaran, *Christ and Migrants*.

[58] Jonathan Bornmann, "Toward a Theology of Migration and Transnationality," *Anabaptist Witness* 7, no. 1 (May 2020): 75-93.

[59] Darrell Jackson and Alessia Passarelli, *Mapping Migration: Mapping Churches' Responses in Europe*, rev. and updated ed. (Geneva, Switzerland: WCC Publications, 2016), 39-46.

[60] Manokaran, *Christ and Migrants*, 28.

[61] Samuel Cueva, "Indigenous Churches: Ethnic and Multicultural," in *The Church in Mission: Foundations and Global Case Studies*, ed. Bertil Ekström (Pasadena, CA: William Carey Library, 2016), 170.

Ironically, a program developed by Changsun "Barnabas" Moon in 2007 to equip leaders for missions among the international communities in South Korea prefers "migrant" over "diaspora." The slogan of the Migrant Mission Training School (MMTS) is directional: *For the Migrants, Through the Migrants,* and *Beyond the Migrants.*[62] Sadly, many denominations and missions agencies fail to grasp the "strategic value of reaching the more accessible fragments" of "people on the move."[63] This lack of commitment to missions practice among dispersed people is a grave concern in diaspora missiology.[64] Universality is central to the practice of diaspora missions. Aware of scattering through geographic directions (e.g., South to South, South to North), the scope of Christian witness includes all types of people regardless of ethnicity, class, or cultures.[65] Many of the leading proponents of diaspora missiology are Asians who *practice missions* in non-Western fashion.[66]

Conclusion

Diaspora missiology emerges to complement general missiology, not to supplant it. Proponents acknowledge its *intentionality* (praxis-oriented), *clarity* (research and publications), and *expediency* (relevance). Over the last two decades, a growing number of theological institutions added diaspora missiology to their curriculum; denominations and missions agencies followed suit by embracing the trends in diaspora

---

[62] Changsun "Barnabas" Moon was appointed Vice-Chair of the Lausanne Global Diaspora Network (GDN) in February 2011 at the first Board of Directors' meeting in Paris, France.

[63] Ralph D. Winter and Bruce A. Koch, "Finishing the Task: The Unreached Peoples Challenge," in *Perspectives on the World Christian Movement: A Reader*, 4th ed., eds. Ralph D. Winter and Steven C. Hawthorne (Pasadena, CA: William Carey Library, 2009), 537.

[64] Sadiri Joy Tira, "Preface to the First Edition," in *Scattered and Gathered: A Global Compendium of Diaspora Missiology,* eds. Sadiri Joy Tira and Tetsunao Yamamori, rev. and updated ed. (Cumbria, UK: Langham Global Library, 2020), XXV.

[65] Cf. Steven Sang Hyun Jun, "Weaknesses and Humiliation of the Cross: Theological Reflection on 'Mission beyond the Diaspora" (ThM thesis, Tyndale Seminary, Toronto, 2018).

[66] M. Daniel Carroll R. *The Bible and Borders: Hearing God's Word on Immigration* (Grand Rapids, MI: Brazos Press, 2020),104.

missions. Moving forward, diaspora missiology and "migration missiology" *may* take similar paths; however, both should be considered as *equally* valid *tools* and *strategies* for missions. Diaspora missiology relies on a growing global network for its growth, while "migration missiology" is yet to make an impact as an accessible framework. For migration perspective to thrive, it would require advocates—both practitioners and scholars—to fall in line and create a *parallel* discipline as a movement. Although the impact of "migration missiology" remains sporadic, it may intensify over time. When that happens, diaspora missiology and "migration missiology" would turn into *collaborators* rather than competitors because of their shared potential, purpose, and practice.

Diaspora Missions

"Do not forget to entertain strangers for by doing so,
some people have entertained angels without knowing."
(Hebrews 13:2)

Chapter 3

Chinese Diaspora Mission: A Reflection on Dr. Wan's Kingdom Contributions

Jacky Lau, Ph.D.

Introduction

Dr. Enoch Wan is a prominent leader in the diaspora mission movement. He has played a key role in its growth and has created a strong missiological framework for others to follow. Serving faithfully in churches, seminaries, and mission fields, Dr. Wan has helped Christians become involved in both local and global missions. His work includes extensive research on diaspora missiology, relational paradigm, and new mission ideas, as well as mentoring leaders, teachers, and scholars.

This article aims to honour God, highlight Dr. Enoch Wan's commitment to advancing God's Kingdom, and reflect on his contributions to Chinese diaspora missions. It also shares the personal impact Dr. Wan has had on the author's life - as a student, colleague, and mentee.

Christian and Diaspora Heritage

Dr. Wan was born in Liuzhou, Guangxi, China, as the eldest of seven children. His father came to faith in Jesus through the work of an American missionary. Due to poverty, two of his uncles migrated to Cuba and Myanmar. Later, his cousin and niece moved to eastern Canada and New York City, respectively. Seeking better opportunities, Dr. Wan's father left his village and moved the family to Hong Kong. Enoch's stepmother had a difficult past - she was sold by her father at a young age and worked as a housemaid in Southeast Asia. Many years later, "her elder sister redeemed her and sent her back to their village in China and then another sister took her to Hong Kong."[67]

---

[67] Wan, Enoch. *Diaspora Missiology: Theory, Methodology, and Practice*, second edition, Portland, OR: Institute of Diaspora Studies-USA, Western

Enoch Wan grew up in Hong Kong, where he completed his training in education and earned a teacher's certificate in 1967. In 1970, he moved to New York as an international student far from home. There, he studied diligently in college while supporting himself by working in restaurants in New York's Chinatown. He later shared that he "learnt to trust God for provision and protection and began walking in the Spirit. Those were formative years in lifestyle and academic pursuit."[68] He graduated from Nyack College (B.A. in 1973), Gordon-Conwell (MTS in 1975), and State University of New York - SUNY (M.A. & Ph.D. in 1978). Dr. Wan began his research journey on diaspora mission with his doctoral dissertation in cultural anthropology on Chinese immigrants in New York's Chinatown.[69] He is truly "a product and a participant of the Chinese diaspora."[70]

Professor of Anthropology, Intercultural Ministries and Mission

Dr. Wan is an esteemed educator and researcher in the field of missiological studies, with a focus on mentoring doctoral candidates. He served as a faculty member at Alliance Bible Seminary (Hong Kong, 1978-1981), Canadian Theological Seminary – CTS (Regina, SK, 1981-1992), and Reformed Theological Seminary (Jackson, MS, 1993-1997). Since 2001, Dr. Wan has been a research professor at Western Seminary Portland, OR.

Paving the way for others, Dr. Wan is an insightful researcher, prolific writer and trailblazer. His diaspora roots in Asia and anthropological training in North America prepared him well to bridge the gap between the East and the West. After 20 years of reflections and research, he published a Chinese book in 1998 entitled《破旧与立新－中色基督教神学初探》[7] (*Banishing the old and building the new: An Exploration of Sino-theology*). In this book, Dr. Wan identified the

---

Seminary, 2014, 319.
[68] Wan, Enoch. "A Defining Moment" in https://www.enochwan.com/en/about/ accessed on June 06, 2025.
[69] Wan, Enoch. *The Dynamics of Ethnicity: A Case Study on the Immigrant Community of New York Chinatown*, Unpublished doctoral dissertation, State University of New York at Stony Brook, 1978.
[70] Pocock, Michael. "Forward to the First Edition" in *Diaspora Missiology: Theory, Methodology, and Practice*, second edition, by Enoch Wan, OR: Institute of Diaspora Studies-USA, Western Seminary, 2014.

fragmentation of traditional Western theology and proposed using a holistic perspective and Trinitarian theology to systematically contextualize traditional Chinese theology into what is called Sino-theology (i.e., Contextualized Chinese theology). Since 1998, he published at least seven English papers[72] based on the contents of *Sino-theology*. These papers, together with his arduous quest for new missiological understandings, laid the foundation for the development of the inter-disciplinary and integrative research approach[73], Relational Paradigm[74], Diaspora Missiology[75] and other mission topics.

I have a firsthand experience of Dr. Wan being both a critical thinker and compassionate mentor. As his doctoral student, I greatly benefited from his caring feedback and clear explanations of key theological and missiological concepts and terms, such as:

- Mission is the Mission of God, began in the eternal past by the Father, the Son and the Spirit.
- Mission is "Sending and Witnessing." (this term is better understood as 差傳 in Chinese)
- The difference between what is Biblical and what is Scriptural. (see Mt 4:1-10)
- STARS - "Wan's Way of Integrative Research."[76]

---

[71] 温以诺。《破旧与立新－中色基督教神学初探》基督教与中国文化丛书, 第九册, 主编：温伟耀、陈荣毅, 加拿大恩福协会出版, 1998 年 9 月。(Wan, Enoch. *Banishing the old and building the new: An Exploration of Sino-theology*, Christianity and Chinese Culture Series No. 9, Editors: Wan Wai Yiu and Chan Wing Ngai, Ontario, Canada: Christian Communication Inc. of Canada, September 1998.)

[72] Some of them can be found in *Global Missiology*, October 2003, http://www.globalmissiology.org

[73] Wan, Enoch. "Rethinking Missiological Research Methodology: Exploring a New Direction." in *Global Missiology*, October 2003. http://www.globalmissiology.org

[74] Wan, Enoch. "The Paradigm of Relational Realism" in *Occasional Bulletin of EMS* 19, No. 2, 2006, 1-4.

[75] Wan, Enoch. "Diaspora Missiology" in *Occasional Bulletin of EMS* 20, No. 3, 2006, 3-7.

[76] Wan, Enoch. "Core Values of Mission Organization in the Cultural Context of the 21st Century." in *Global Missiology, January 2009.* http://www.globalmissiology.org
Editorial Notes: Readers may refer to the "Biography of Dr. Wan" section in this book for more details on the STARS integrative research approach.

- Diaspora Missiology Paradigm is an alternative to Managerial Missiology Paradigm.
- Diaspora mission phenomena always happen providentially, not accidentally. (Acts 17:26-27)
- Four types of Diaspora Missions: TO, THROUGH, BY & BEYOND, and WITH the diaspora, "all to be practiced within a relational framework."[77]

Missions TO and THROUGH the Chinese Diaspora

Living in North America for over 50 years, Dr. Wan conveys a deep compassion towards his fellow Chinese and others living in diaspora in his ministries and writings, a compassion similar to that of the apostle Paul. He pastored and helped establish Chinese diaspora churches (CDCs) in Asia and North America. At the CTS in Regina, he served as the founding director of the Centre for Chinese Studies (1982-1988) and the Centre for Intercultural Ministries (1988-1992). Dr. Wan actively encouraged his students and CDCs to engage in Missions TO and THROUGH the diaspora.

Dr. Wan is a respected and highly sought-after preacher and professor. Throughout the 1980s, he frequently ministered to CDCs across Canada, all while teaching at the CTS in Regina and serving as an executive member at the Canadian Chinese Alliance Churches Association (CCACA). My wife and I both came to faith in Christ in 1982. We first met Dr. Wan and his wife Mary at a CDC about three hours from Regina. They often visited our church and encouraged us with God's Word. During the 1980s and 1990s, Canada saw a large increase in Chinese immigrants. Dr. Wan and the CCACA seized this opportunity by mobilizing CTS graduates and existing CDCs to plant over 20 new CDCs nationwide.[78] Many of these CDCs grew to include

---

[77] Wan, Enoch *Diaspora Missiology: Theory, Methodology, and Practice*, second edition, Portland, OR: Institute of Diaspora Studies-USA, Western Seminary, 2014, 127.

[78] 江昭揚, 譚文鈞。《繼往開來－加拿大華人宣道會的歷史與發展》, 香港宣道出版社, 2013。(Chiang, Solomon C.Y., Francis M.K. Tam. *Forging Future with Tradition – The History and Development of Canadian Chinese Alliance Churches*, Hong Kong: China Alliance Press, 2013).

congregations speaking Cantonese, English and Mandarin, helping to expand God's Kingdom both locally and globally.

Dr. Wan has been actively involved in supporting Chinese diaspora missions in Creative Access Countries through short-term mission (STM) trips. In the early 2000s he frequently spoke about reaching thousands of Chinese scholars and workers during Chinese New Year events in Israel. Dr. & Mrs. Wan visited my wife and me during a STM trip in 2003, offering encouragement and guidance as we started Chinese diaspora ministries in the Arabian Peninsula (AP). Many Chinese believers who came to Christ in the AP continue to share their faith and serve faithfully in missions across China and other nations.

Missions BY & BEYOND and WITH the Chinese Diaspora

Dr. Wan's life-long journey and career development is characterized by "the pursuit and practice of relational paradigm (vertical + horizontal relationships, with proper priority and true integrity)."[79] His mission passion is the same as God's – wanting "all people to be saved and to come to a knowledge of the truth" (1Tim 2:4). His profession focuses on multiplying himself by teaching, empowering, networking, and mentoring "reliable people who will also be qualified to teach others" (2 Tim 2:2).

In mid 1980s, Dr. Wan broadened his research from Chinese studies to include intercultural ministries. In 1993, Dr. Wan organized *Missions Within Reach,* "an unprecedented national conference on intercultural ministries" held in Toronto, Canada. This event encouraged churches to seize "the great outreach opportunity" created by the arrival of new immigrants from closed countries.[80] *Missions Within Reach* is recognized as one of the earliest conferences focused on diaspora missions - particularly, Missions BY & BEYOND and WITH the diaspora – well before the formal introduction of Diaspora Missiology by Dr. Wan.

For close to 50 years, Dr. Wan has conducted research in anthropology and missions. In addition to teaching in a seminary, he has served as an adjunct professor at various seminaries worldwide, helping

---

[79] Wan, Enoch. https://www.westernseminary.edu/academics/faculty/enoch-wan accessed on June 14, 2025

[80] Wan, Enoch. *Missions Within Reach*, Intercultural Ministries in Canada. Hong Kong: China Alliance Press, 1995,

to establish centers for diaspora and missiological studies. Dr. Wan has played a vital role in mentoring and influencing hundreds of Chinese diaspora ministry workers and mission leaders. I had the privilege of studying Chinese diaspora missions under his guidance. He served as the primary adviser on my doctoral committee, supported me in completing my dissertation and co-authored a book with me.[81]

God receives the greatest glory when His people work together selflessly to advance His Kingdom. Dr. Wan strongly values networking and sharing insights with fellow Christian workers. He founded *Global Missiology*, an e-journal featuring contributions from mission researchers, practitioners, and scholars with a global perspective. Dr. Wan served two terms as the President of Evangelical Missiological Society and has been involved with various mission boards and mission initiatives. He served as a member of the board of directors and vice president of the Great Commission Center International, an organization founded by Dr. Thomas Wang which focuses on mobilizing hundreds of thousands of Chinese Christians in China and overseas for global mission. Dr. Wan continually encourages his students and mission leaders to extend their missions beyond the Chinese diaspora to the world's least-reached peoples.

In April 2025, Dr. Wan was invited to deliver a keynote address at the First Chinese Diaspora Network Consultation (FCDNC)[82] in Toronto, an event attended by more than 120 Chinese mission and church leaders. Holding back emotion, Dr. Wan reflected, "Praise God, it is finally happening… Over 30 years ago, God led me to challenge His people at the *Missions Within Reach* Conference[83] right here in this city." During the consultation, leaders of CDC and mission organizations shared their insights and convictions on engaging in missions BY & BEYOND and WITH the Chinese diaspora. Key themes included:

---

[81] Wan, Enoch and Jacky Lau. *Chinese Diaspora Kingdom Workers: In Action and with Guidance*, Portland, OR: the Centre of Diaspora and Relational Research, Western Seminary Press, 2019.

[82] The FCDNC was organized by the Chinese Coordination Centre of World Evangelism (CCCOWE) and sponsored by the Global Diaspora Network (GDN) of the Lausanne Movement.

[83] Wan, Enoch (ed). *Missions Within Reach: Intercultural Ministries in Canada*, Hong Kong: China Alliance Press, xi-xiii.

- Exploring effective ways to engage, train, and mobilize locally born Chinese believers to cultivate a passion for God and active involvement in His mission.
- Developing a Chinese Heritage Church network to inspire and empower the next generation of Chinese believers for Kingdom collaboration.
- Challenging CDCs to love their neighbors and to reach out to other ethnic communities, including Indigenous Peoples, new immigrants and international students from Africa, China, India, and the Middle East.
- Encouraging CDCs and mainland Chinese churches to partner with each other for the glory of God.

Concluding Remarks

Dr. Enoch Wan's life and ministry exemplify a faithful response to God's call - rooted in Scripture, shaped by personal experience, and guided by a deep relational commitment to God and others. From his humble beginnings as a member of the Chinese diaspora to becoming a pioneer in diaspora missiology and relational theology, Dr. Wan has influenced generations of mission leaders, scholars, and practitioners worldwide. His integrative approach, tireless mentorship, and visionary leadership continue to shape the way diaspora missions are understood and practiced - Missions TO, THROUGH, BY & BEYOND, and WITH the diaspora.

As we reflect on Dr. Wan's remarkable contributions on Chinese diaspora missions, we are reminded that missions is not a task for a few, but a calling for all who follow Christ. Through his teaching, writing, and example, Dr. Wan has empowered many to see diaspora missions not as a challenge but as a divine opportunity for Gospel advancement. May the legacy of his life and work inspire continued collaboration among Chinese diaspora churches and global mission communities for the glory of God and the fulfillment of His mission.

Chapter 4

The Vietnamese Alliance Church in Edmonton: A Case Study of Diaspora Congregation

Thanh Trung Le, D.Min., D.Miss.

A Tribute to Dr. Enoch Wan: 37 Years of Influence and Partnership

Both directly and indirectly, Dr. Enoch Wan has played a pivotal role in shaping my journey and in advancing the ministries of the Association of Vietnamese Alliance Churches in Canada (AVAC) and the Worldwide Association of Vietnamese Alliance Churches (WAVAC).

I first met Dr. Wan in the summer of 1988 when I began my doctoral studies at Canadian Theological Seminary in Regina, Saskatchewan. He was assigned as my mentor. At that time, I had just moved from Portland, Oregon, to Edmonton to serve as the solo pastor of a newly planted Vietnamese congregation. Filled with hope but burdened with many responsibilities, I was adjusting to a new ministry, a new city, and family life with three small children—ages 4, 1½, and 3 months. The academic pressure was intense, especially studying in English, which was not my first language. I often felt overwhelmed.

Dr. Wan became a wellspring of encouragement and empathy. He assured me of his support and stood by his word. With each trip I made to Regina for intensive courses, our relationship deepened.

At the time, the Center for Intercultural Studies of the Christian and Missionary Alliance in Canada (C&MA Canada) was developing leadership among various ethnic groups—Chinese, Vietnamese, Filipino, and First Nations. Dr. Lightbody, then Vice President of the C&MA, oversaw the initiative. I represented the Vietnamese churches; Dr. Wan, the Chinese; and Dr. Joy Tira, the Filipino. This collaborative context allowed me to work closely with Dr. Wan and observe his wisdom, cultural sensitivity, and servant leadership.

Dr. Wan is both an intellectual and a shepherd. He upholds high standards of academic excellence while showing deep compassion for ethnic pastors and leaders—many of whom, like myself, were still developing English proficiency or lacked formal theological training. He advocated for our development with humility, kindness, and strength.

Outside the academic realm, Dr. Wan and his wife showed genuine care for my ministry at Edmonton Vietnamese Alliance Church (EVAC) and for my family. They frequently checked in by phone, and on several occasions, Dr. Wan made the long eight-hour drive to visit us. Their presence and prayers brought tremendous encouragement not only to my family but to our whole congregation.

During one of those visits, I learned that Dr. Wan prayed with his children before school. Inspired, I adopted this practice. As my children grew older and began driving themselves to school, I witnessed them pause to pray before leaving. This habit left a deep spiritual imprint on our family life. Years later, when one of our sons walked away from the faith, we were devastated. We turned to Dr. Wan, who listened patiently, offered wise counsel, and prayed fervently for us. He and his wife shared vulnerably about their own parenting challenges and how they learned to rely on God. Their transparency gave us strength and renewed our hope.

In 1993, when Dr. Wan later accepted a position as the Founding Director - Ph.D. Intercultural Studies Program of the Reformed Theological Seminary in Jackson, Mississippi, and left Canadian Theological Seminary. I was reassigned to Dr. Jacob Klassen. Yet Dr. Wan remained a consistent source of support from afar. Through prayer, encouragement, and regular communication, he inspired me to persevere. I eventually completed my doctoral program on April 29, 1995—nearly twenty years to the day after I left Vietnam.

Our mentorship only grew stronger over time. We rejoiced when the Wan family moved to Portland, Oregon in 2005, where Dr. Wan became Director of the Doctor of Missiology program at Western Seminary. Portland was especially meaningful to me, as it had been my first home in North America, where I worked as a city bus driver and earned my M.Div. (1983) from Western Seminary.

Despite his demanding responsibilities, Dr. Wan remained a supportive presence in my ministry at EVAC and in my leadership role at AVAC. I frequently sought his counsel and always found in him timely and thoughtful wisdom that shaped my approach to ministry.

At EVAC, Dr. Wan and his wife were regular guests, preaching the Word and leading much-needed workshops on Family Life, Parent-Child Relationships, and Cross-Cultural Ministry. One lasting impact of their ministry was our early decision to launch an English Ministry. Many Vietnamese churches initially sought to preserve the language by teaching Sunday School in Vietnamese. But with Dr. Wan's guidance, we realized that our priority must be biblical instruction in a language our children understood. With less than two hours a week at church, we could not afford to prioritize language learning over discipleship. We invited a Canadian couple to start a small English Bible study for 13 teenagers. From this humble beginning, our English Ministry was born.

At AVAC, Dr. Wan's insights into diaspora missiology had a profound impact on me. Through his lectures and writings, I gained a deeper appreciation for cross-cultural mission and collaboration with other ethnic communities. Although the initial plans for theological education and leadership training within AVAC did not materialize as envisioned, our regular gatherings with other multicultural leaders in the C&MA strengthened our ministry and broadened our missional vision.

At WAVAC, Dr. Wan's influence continued. With a growing desire to unite Vietnamese churches globally, we worked with the C&MA Canada to connect leaders from across the Vietnamese diaspora. WAVAC was formally established in 2006 in Thailand, where I was elected Chairman for a four-year term. At that same gathering, we founded the Alliance Theological College (ATC) under the leadership of Dr. Nha Trong Tran, as the training arm of WAVAC.

This new responsibility led me once again to seek Dr. Wan's guidance, and with his encouragement, I enrolled in the Doctor of Missiology (D.Miss.) program at Western Seminary. Under his mentorship, I completed the program in 2013. I was honoured to co-author with him in the diaspora book series *Mobilizing Vietnamese Diaspora for the Kingdom* (Institute of Diaspora Studies – USA, Western Seminary, 2014).

My growing missional vision led me to join SEND International on a short-term mission to Belarus and Ukraine in 2014. There, we connected with a Vietnamese Bible study group in Odessa under Pastor David Hoang. My wife and I returned each summer to train believers in evangelism and discipleship and to evangelize Vietnamese merchants in local flea markets. We began organizing family camps—starting with 29 attendees in 2015. Over the next three years, attendance grew to over 70. In 2019, Dr. Mary Wan joined us for a summer camp.

Conclusion

The COVID-19 pandemic paused our involvement, but I remained in contact with the believers. When war broke out in Ukraine in February 2022, many of them fled to Germany. I helped connect them with local Vietnamese churches, and despite being scattered across cities, they continued weekly Bible studies. In March 2025, my wife and I visited Stuttgart for a reunion after five years. It was a powerful time of testimony, reflection, and renewed friendship in God's goodness. This testimony only begins to capture the depth of Dr. Enoch Wan's profound and lasting impact over the past 37 years. His intellectual leadership, compassionate spirit, and unwavering commitment to the Gospel have left an indelible mark—not only on my life and family, but also on our church, our ministry networks, and the broader Vietnamese diaspora. In short, I am deeply grateful to Dr. Wan, whose mentorship has extended beyond the academic realm into my personal life and ministries since 1988. It was a profound honor to recognize him as my true "Sifu – 師傅" for life when I received the Presidential Citation Award and served as the Commencement Speaker at the 95th Commencement of Western Seminary on April 23, 2022.

What follows is a brief overview of the ministries of EVAC, AVAC, and WAVAC—each bearing, in some way, the direct or indirect influence of Dr. Wan. I remain deeply grateful to God, and to Dr. Wan, for the invaluable role he has played in shaping our journey and advancing our mission.

A Journey of Faith: Vietnamese Refugees and the Birth of EVAC

The Beginning: 1975 and the Fall of Saigon

The events of April 1975, marked by the Fall of Saigon, triggered a massive exodus of Vietnamese refugees. Canada, among many compassionate nations, responded by opening its doors to resettle these displaced individuals. By May 1975, Canada had begun accepting Vietnamese refugees, and between 1975 and 1978, a total of 9,060 individuals from Indochina were admitted.

Churches across Canada, including many congregations within the Christian and Missionary Alliance (C&MA), responded with open arms. International Workers (IWs) who had previously served in Vietnam played a vital role in bridging cultural and linguistic divides. These missionaries helped resettle refugees, provided pastoral care, and initiated evangelistic efforts at a time when few Vietnamese pastors were available.

Canadian churches offered holistic support, helping refugees find employment, address health needs, and navigate life in a new country. They also hosted English language classes and opened their buildings for Bible studies, many of which eventually developed into fully functioning congregations.

The Birth of Edmonton Vietnamese Alliance Church (EVAC)

One of the earliest Vietnamese congregations in Canada was the Edmonton Vietnamese Alliance Church (EVAC), founded in 1978 under the care of Keith and Maxine Thompson, former missionaries to Vietnam. What began as a house fellowship quickly grew and moved into Beulah Alliance Church, which generously provided space for worship.

By May 1981, the fellowship had grown to over 70 members. In August of that year, it was officially recognized as EVAC, an ethnic congregation under the Western Canadian District of the C&MA.

In June 1982, with support from the District and sacrificial giving from members, many of whom were still refugees, EVAC purchased its church building in southwest Edmonton. That building remains the church's home today, serving as both a spiritual and cultural hub.

Through church sponsorship and Canada's refugee program, EVAC helped resettle over 300 Vietnamese newcomers. As of April 2025, the church has sent out 18 pastors and international workers, a testimony to its missional heartbeat.

Reaching the Next Generations: The English Ministry (EM)

As Vietnamese families established roots in Canada, a new challenge emerged: how to minister to second- and third-generation children more fluent in English than in Vietnamese.

In response, EVAC launched its English Ministry (EM). Pastor Kevin Gartly was the first to lead, followed by Pastor Neil Truong. Although both served part-time, the EM thrived. English-language services began in the church basement, complemented by bilingual communion services on the first Sunday of each month. Over time, EM grew into a distinct congregation, while maintaining unity through shared celebrations like Christmas, Easter, Thanksgiving, and Tết.

Following a period of transition, Pastor Dave Rojas was empowered to revitalize EM as a church-planting initiative called City Light Alliance Church (CLAC). Today, CLAC is a vibrant, multicultural community of over 40 regular attendees—including Vietnamese, Chinese, Japanese, Filipino, Cambodian, Caucasian, Korean, and Ethiopian believers. Together, they worship, engage in small group discipleship, and serve their neighborhoods.

Guided by the mission to love God, learn the ways of Jesus, and serve others, CLAC nurtures emerging leaders and provides age-appropriate ministry environments for all generations. Looking ahead, CLAC is preparing to become an independent, self-governing, and financially sustainable congregation committed to the Great Commission.

A National Movement: The Association of Vietnamese Alliance Churches in Canada (AVAC)

In 1990, only eight Vietnamese Alliance churches existed in Canada. Recognizing the need for coordination and mutual support, the Vietnamese Canadian Alliance Fellowship (VCAF) was established at the General Assembly in Quebec City.

Milestones:
- 1992: First VCAF Conference held in Abbotsford, BC; Rev. Binh Van Nguyen elected Chair (2 terms, 4 years each)
- 2000: VCAF Conference held in Calgary, renamed to AVAC; Rev. Thanh Trung Le elected Director (2 terms)
- 2008: AVAC Conference held in Toronto, ON, Rev. Cuong Thieu Do elected Director (3 terms + 1 year, extended due to COVID)
- 2021: Due to COVID, the AVAC Conference was held via Zoom, Rev. Long Tan Truong completed the term.
- 2024–present: AVAC Conference held in Vancouver, BC, Rev. Binh Van Nguyen re-elected as Director

AVAC supports member churches by:
- Mediating cultural and leadership conflicts
- Assisting Districts with pastoral placements, including translation and credential interviews
- Promoting Vietnamese-language theological education via the TEE (Theological Education by Extension) program
- Hosting Vietnamese pastoral enrichment and fellowship events
- Supporting international missions in Cambodia, Thailand, and Taiwan through short-term teams, leadership training, and financial aid

A Global Vision: The Worldwide Association of Vietnamese Alliance Churches (WAVAC)

Recognizing the global spread of the Vietnamese diaspora, AVAC partnered with the C&MA National Ministry Centre to host the first International Vietnamese Diaspora Conference in September 2000 in

Bolton, Ontario. Vietnamese leaders from around the world, CAMA Vietnam, and international workers serving in Cambodia attended.

The second conference, held in Phnom Penh in March 2006, led to the founding of the Worldwide Association of Vietnamese Alliance Churches (WAVAC) - a network committed to global partnership and resource-sharing to reach Vietnamese communities for Christ.

WAVAC Conference Timeline:
- IV (2010): Vancouver, BC
- V (2012): Toronto, ON – Rev. Binh Nguyen
- VI (2014): Anaheim, California
- VII (2015–16): Sydney, Australia – Rev. Cuong Do
- VIII (2018): Paris – Rev. Chanh Doan
- IX (2022): zoom meeting – Rev. Dr. Thanh Trung Le
- X (2025): Toronto, ON – Rev. Dr. Antoine Hoang

From this network also came Alliance Theological College (ATC), led by Dr. Nha Trong Tran, providing non-formal theological education to equip diaspora leaders globally.

Looking Back and Moving Forward

What began in trauma and displacement has become a vibrant, multi-generational, and multi-ethnic witness to God's faithfulness. From a few refugees in 1975 to over 275,525 Vietnamese Canadians in 2021 (according to the Canadian Census)[84], the journey of faith continues.

Through the ministry of EVAC, AVAC, and WAVAC, God's hand is seen - guiding, restoring, and expanding His Kingdom across continents and generations.

"From one man He made all the nations... and He marked out their appointed times in history and the boundaries of their lands. God did this so that they would seek Him..." (Acts 17:26–27)

---

[84] Statistics Canada. Table 98-10-0355-01 Ethnic or cultural origin by gender and age: Canada, provinces and territories. Retrieved from https://www150.statcan.gc.ca/t1/tbl1/en/tv.action?pid=9810035501

Chapter 5

Engaging the 5th Largest Religious Block: Sikhs and Sikhism[85]

Sadiri Joy Tira, D.Min., D.Miss.

In October 2018, a couple of Punjabi friends invited me for lunch and introduced me to a Christian pastor from a Punjabi Sikh background (Sikh Background Believer – SBB). He shared how he came to faith in Jesus by reading the Bible from cover to cover. He decided to follow Jesus, got baptized, and enrolled in Bible college. Consequently, he was discipled and trained for evangelism and ministry. I was moved to pray intentionally and reach out to the Sikhs in my community, who had been globally dispersed.

My Journey with Sikhs

I first encountered Sikh people as a child in the southern Philippines. Even as a child living in a remote town, I had Sikh classmates whose parents worked in the finance business. In 1970s Manila, I met many Sikhs in my university engineering courses. When my young family arrived in Canada in 1981, the first people we met at the airport were Punjabi Sikhs. Dr. J.D. Payne writes about 'the strangers next door', including my Punjabi Sikh neighbours, whom he lists as a large unreached people group in North America.[86] On reflection, I can see how God, throughout my life, has been shaping my heart for the Sikh people.

In 1988, when the Filipino congregation I first pastored in Edmonton looked to purchase its first property, it chose the property of the *Gurdwara Siri Guru Singh Sabha Society* in west Edmonton. After two years of using the building, when the congregation decided to renovate it,

---

[85] Editorial Notes: this paper was first published in the March issue of Lausanne Global Analysis. Thanks to Lausanne Movement for the permission to re-publish the paper in this book.
[86] See J. D. Payne, *Strangers next Door Immigration, Migration and Mission* (Westmont, IL: IVP Books, 2012).

deacons found, embedded between the dividing walls, the images of the ten 'spiritual masters' who contributed to the establishment of Sikhism.[87] We discovered that the original owners had plans for the property to serve as a *Gurdwara*, and that they had intended those pictures to be a source of teaching and protection for their community. I did not know at the time that God had been providentially orchestrating for me to live and work among the Sikhs, one of the largest unreached and unengaged people groups in diaspora.[88]

These stories of the Sikh as a people and of the SBBs that we have ministered with tie into a larger global reality of Diaspora studies. Just as the Sikh are now found around the world, as those "strangers living next door," so too are people from many other national backgrounds. It is especially appropriate for this Festschrift in honour of Dr. Enoch Wan that we consider the missiological importance of these people groups. As one of the pioneers in the area of Diaspora studies, Dr. Wan has been a key to seeing the importance of ministry in, through, and to the Sikh and other scattered peoples.

Who are they? Where are they?

Sikhs are adherents of Sikhism, a monotheistic religion founded in Punjab, India, in 1469, by Guru Nanak Dev. Today, Sikhism is the world's fifth-largest religion. It is estimated that there are 27 million followers of Sikhism in India, and around the world.[89] While most Sikhs are found in Punjab and other northern states of India, large numbers are in diaspora:

- According to *World Atlas*, Canada, the United Kingdom, then the United States, Australia, and Malaysia have the greatest number of Sikhs outside India.[90]

---

[87] See Sikhism Religion of the Sikh People, accessed December 29, 2019, https://www.sikhs.org/10gurus.htm

[88] Tira, Sadiri. "Global Missions and Local Congregation: A Case Study of the First Filipino Alliance Church in Edmonton, Alberta (Canada)." Unpublished D.Min. Dissertation, Reformed Theological Seminary, 2002.

[89] For more on Sikhism, read Ed Stetzer's post, https://www.christianitytoday.com/edstetzer/2012/august/standing-with-sikh-community-today.html?share=

[90] Pariona, Ameber. 'Countries With The Largest Sikh Populations'. *WorldAtlas*. https://www.worldatlas.com/articles/countries-with-the-largest-

- Sizeable populations are also recorded in Kenya, Uganda, Tanzania, Thailand, Italy, and Mauritius.[91]
- According to M. Sudhir, working in the Philippines, there are currently over 50,000 Sikhs in the Philippines.[92]

The Sikh centre of worship and social life is the *Gurdwara*. Gurdwaras are present in communities where there are large Sikh populations.

Unlike Hindus who are polytheistic, the Sikhs, like Christians, are monotheistic. Furthermore, like Christianity, Sikhism teaches that all humans are created equal, and emphasises a life of worship, discipline, and service. These commonalities provide bridges for discussion and relationship-building.

In recent years, there have been growing reports of Sikhs deciding to follow Jesus in India, and in the diaspora communities. Two Sikhs who decided to follow Jesus Christ and then became prominent ministers of the Gospel are Sahdu Sunder Singh and Bhakt Singh.

Furthermore, Sikhs are influential in every sphere of society. In Canada, for example, we have Sikhs represented at every level of government[93], and in every sector of the marketplace. For kingdom impact, where Sikhs are found, believers must engage them and lead them to the 'ultimate Guru', Jesus Christ. Friendship evangelism is a proven methodology and uses available evangelistic and discipleship tools. However, apologetics is also required to defend the Christian faith.

---

sikh-populations.html (accessed January 1, 2020).
[91] Ibid.
[92] Sudhir, M. 'Research Reports: Philippines'. Global Sikh Consultation. October 24, 2019.
[93] Notably, Jagmeet Singh, party leader of the federal New Democratic Party, a major party in Canada, and Harjit Singh Sajjan, federal Liberal party politician, current Member of Parliament and Minister of National Defence and a Member of Parliament.

Lausanne Movement's Response

As I end my term as the *Lausanne Movement's Catalyst for Diasporas*, I was recently overjoyed to witness the Movement's embrace of the Sikhs, as demonstrated in the support for the first Lausanne Movement-sponsored *Global Sikh Consultation* (GSC).[94]

At least 68 participants from ten countries participated in the consultation, held in Edmonton, Alberta in October 2019. They were welcomed to Edmonton by an organising committee that included two Canadians of Indian heritage, as well as four Filipino-Canadians, and one Chinese-Canadian.

The GSC was convened for two key reasons:

- *Overdue focus* - Although Sikhism is the fifth-largest religion in the world, with adherents widely dispersed globally, there is no Lausanne Movement Catalyst and, before the GSC, no global network among SBBs. In the previous 45 years, Sikhism had only been briefly mentioned twice in Lausanne documents.[95] As far as anyone could tell, there had never been a single Lausanne paper, article, or video focusing on the topic of Sikhism. So, this consultation was long overdue. Anecdotal reports are heard about God's movement among the Punjabi Sikhs at home and abroad. If this report is true, the global church must be summoned to pray and help resource these new believers in Christ.

- *Seeds sown* - Some SBBs say that the Sikh gurus borrowed part of their moral and ethical teaching from the Holy Bible. After over 500 years, the 'seeds' planted in the lives of these people are now germinating and some are bearing fruit. If this observation is correct, the Lausanne Movement needs to accelerate seed sowing, discipleship, planting of local congregations, and developing leadership among SBBs.

These factors alone warranted a special consultation.

---

[94] See www.sikhconsultation.ca and read:
https://www.christianitytoday.com/edstetzer/2019/november/global-sikh-consultation-calling-sikhs-to-christ.html.

[95] See Lausanne Occasional Papers no. 14 and no. 55 at https://www.lausanne.org/category/content/lop.

Concrete outcomes

The tangible results include the adoption of *The Edmonton Appeal*,[96] the formation of the *Lausanne Sikh Working Group* (LSWG), and the designation of every November 12th a *Global Day of Prayer for the Sikhs*. Moreover, a new evangelistic resource, *Have You Heard*, is developing a Sikh version.[97]

Many participants commented enthusiastically about the GSC. Some said they were challenged and moved by seeing the passion and dedication shown by Filipinos and Chinese working so hard to reach Sikh people. They were also encouraged to know that many faithful workers in the vineyard were reaching out to Sikh friends around the globe. As a result, they committed to strategize and implement ministries among Sikhs, mobilizing Christians and local churches to reach out and disciple them.

Others said they valued the connection with like-minded people and the chance to pray together for the Lord to send labourers in the harvest so that the Kingdom of God will grow among the Sikhs. They were blessed to be in a place where there were gathered together so many people reaching out to the Sikhs and to be worshiping Jesus with so many of them from around the globe.

The GSC was an answer to prayer for many, giving them a fresh motivation to stay focused on the Sikhs. One was so encouraged to see God's work among the Sikhs, especially in Africa and Philippines, that they determined to build a network of international ministries working among the Sikhs. Others felt they had learned much from other participants about the challenges and opportunities for engaging with the Sikhs.

---

[96] See *The Edmonton Appeal* in the Appendix of this paper or at https://www.lausanne.org/content/the-edmonton-appeal
[97] View the Jewish version of Have You Heard at https://haveyouheard.ca

One leader said that as a result of the consultation, his ministry had taken six new initiatives: designating Thursday as day of prayer for Sikhs; arranging special prayers on Sikh festival days; developing gospel literature for Sikhs in Punjabi language and in Devnagari (Hindi) script; working on training modules to reach Sikhs; encouraging SBBs; and empowering women of Sikh background.

The GSC was indeed a successful event, but it had faced serious challenges, from which important lessons emerge:

- The vision was launched and implemented without guaranteed funds. Discouragement in the midst of financial uncertainty is real, but God's pocket is deep. Trusting in God is better than trusting in 'horses and chariots'. The fulfilling of the Great Commission should not be slowed because of limited funding.
- Leading up to, and during the event, the organizers experienced a barrage of opposition. The convener experienced a freak car accident that could have been tragic; one committee member was robbed at gun point at her business in suburban Edmonton; and during the last day of the consultation, the committee treasurer and head of logistics experienced a life-threatening massive heart attack. It is interesting to note that these three organizers were ethnically Filipino and Chinese. They were serving the cause of Jesus beyond their own tribes.

I wonder now about the significance of the images of the ten Sikh Gurus, uncovered between the dividing walls of the Filipino church building that they had purchased from the Sikh society? What did the Apostle Paul mean when he wrote to the Ephesians:

'For our struggle is not against flesh and blood, but against the rulers, against the authorities, against the powers of this dark world and against the spiritual forces of evil in the heavenly realms?' (Eph 6.12)

Implications

The consultation's 'invitation to prayer' for the Sikh people would be a good starting point in seeking to engage with Sikhs in friendship evangelism:

- Pray for renewed conviction that every Sikh—man and woman, adult and young person and child—needs to discover Jesus as the way, the truth, and the life.
- Pray for Spirit-led creativity to identify new strategies for reaching Sikhs, and for forming various communities of Jesus' followers that are accessible to different kinds of Sikhs.
- Pray for humility and love towards co-workers in Christ, and for the ability to find new ways to collaborate with one another as servant leaders.
- Pray for a new vision for the workplace, and for Sikh people in the workplace, in order to see kingdom impact in every sphere of society where Sikhs are found.

God has orchestrated the planting of the 'seed' in the hearts of many Sikhs in India and those scattered outside their homeland. We must be courageous and persistent in our ministry to the 27 million Sikhs, adherents of the world's fifth-largest religion. The global church must open its doors, extending hospitality and friendship. The Lausanne Movement is committed to mobilising *'the whole church to take the whole gospel to the whole world'.*[98] Let us support the LSWG in prayers and in practical ways, helping this young movement become a catalyst of ideas, raising influencers for global missions.

---

[98] Read more at https://www.lausanne.org/content/whole-gospel-whole-church-whole-world

Appendix: The Edmonton Appeal

THE EDMONTON APPEAL

Over sixty Kingdom ministry leaders and reflective practitioners from ten nations, gathered at the Lausanne GLOBAL SIKH CONSULTATION in Edmonton, Alberta, Canada on October 22-25, 2019, issue this urgent appeal to the Global Church.

We Acknowledge

1. That Sikhism is the fifth largest organized religion in the world but the Global Church is largely ignorant of its beliefs, culture, and practices.
2. The Global Church has not made reaching the Sikhs with the Good News of Jesus a priority.
3. That God's loving purpose is to see all people including Sikhs experience salvation in Christ and be part of God's forever family.
4. That the Church is God's agent to fulfill the redemptive plan for Kingdom advance.
5. That the Holy Spirit is alive and active today in drawing all sinners to Jesus.
6. That God sovereignly performs miracles, healings and deliverances to demonstrate His Kingdom rule and power.

We Believe

1. That there is only one true and living God, the Almighty Creator and Sustainer of all things existing eternally in three persons—Father, Son, and Holy Spirit—full of love and glory.
2. That all humans are made in the image of God but have been marred by sin since the Fall.
3. That the living God has revealed Himself through the trustworthy Biblical Scriptures and has fully and finally revealed Himself through Jesus Christ, the Son of God when the Word became flesh. Hence, Jesus was fully God and fully man.
4. That through the sacrificial death of Jesus on the cross, He took upon Himself God's judgement due to all sinners by dying in their place and making the way for us to be saved.
5. That the gift of personal salvation and the experience of complete forgiveness of sin are only available by God's grace in Christ through personal repentance of sins and faith in the Lord Jesus Christ.
6. That spiritual life in Christ, of holiness and joyful service, is nurtured by the Word of God and empowered by the indwelling presence and transforming power of the Holy Spirit.
7. That calling of service to others is important but it flows out of one's relationship in Christ and one's love for fellow humans.
8. That fellowship with other followers of Jesus is essential for spiritual growth and balance.

We Appeal

1. That the Global Church seize the opportunities of evangelising and discipling the unreached millions of followers of the Sikh faith everywhere and develop them to be Great Commission disciple makers.
2. That the followers of Jesus and congregations will focus and fervently pray for the salvation of all Sikhs.
3. That relevant demographic research continue to be undertaken to define missiological and evangelistic priorities to reach Sikhs.
4. That the followers of Jesus be encouraged and equipped to contextually share the Good News of Jesus with Sikhs in word and deed.
5. That the followers of Jesus will live as authentic witnesses and personally engage with their Sikh contacts and neighbours, and build meaningful relationships with sincere Christ-like love.
6. That the Good News of Jesus be sensitively communicated in a clear, coherent, consistent, and culturally appropriate manner.
7. That Sikh Background Believers (SBBs) be developed into Christ-like leaders for the Global Church.
8. That local churches and ministry agencies will collaborate to develop resources, strategize effective approaches to reach Sikhs with the Good News of Jesus and plant contextual churches.
9. That those engaged in evangelizing and discipling Sikhs need prayer, patience, and perseverance.

October 25, 2019

Relational Paradigm

"Love the Lord your God
with all your heart and with all your soul and with all your mind.
This is the first and greatest commandment.
And the second is like it: Love your neighbor as yourself.
All the law and the prophets hang on these two commandments."
(Matthew 22:37-40)

Chapter 6

Unmerited Grace in Relationships: A Reflection on the Influence of Enoch Wan on My Life and Ministry

Juno Wang, D.I.S.

"I was locked out of my room after spending hours casting out a demon from a training participant, so I slept in a meeting room with a piece of carpet in the room to keep me warm." This was my first conversation with Dr. Enoch Wan when he came to speak at a training in Dallas, Texas in December of 1995. He has many eye-opening spiritual warfare stories to share with the staff when he was a volunteer Vice President of the Great Commission Center International (GCCI) under the leadership of the late Dr. Thomas Wang. While attending the 20th anniversary banquet of GCCI in 2013, he suddenly felt weak and was rushed to the emergency room (ER) that evening. Within hours, his health deteriorated rapidly, and later the ER doctors even asked his family whether or not to continue treatment. While in the ER in an unstable state of consciousness, he vowed to devote the rest of his life to developing and teaching relational realism and the unmerited grace (in Chinese 恩情 ēn qíng) theology. God heard him and granted him what he asked for. Several years later, I became his doctoral student at Western Seminary, and I was very impressed with his wisdom and very broad knowledge beyond demon-casting stories.

Unmerited Grace in All Relationships

It was a learning buffet to sit in his class; but it was hard to accept relational realism, which is very different from what I knew and practiced. During the break, the class shared our opinions, thinking that Wan was not there, but later he came in and talked with us wholeheartedly. First, he taught us to understand relational realism through his STARS missiological integrative research methodology to be evangelical, doctrinally sound, and theologically grounded (Wan, 2017). Second, he led the class to think more deeply about unmerited grace through our vertical relationship with God. Third, he explained the relational theology of realms for the relationships with God, man, and other spirits (Wan and Hedinger, 2006). Thus, we undertake missions out of gratitude for the unmerited grace we receive from God to people who are spiritually blinded through our horizontal relationships with them. Lastly, he talked about the heavy influence of functionalism, in which all aspects of ministry practically serve as functional acts with a pragmatic and managerial approach. Yet, it is the power of God that brings salvation to everyone who believes (Rom. 1:16); it is definitely not the tactical skills and strategies of the evangelist or missionary that lead to a "paradigm shift."

A Pivotal Moment

Wan grew up in Hong Kong with a family history of generations of diaspora, where competitiveness and efficiency are well known. Through the functionalism learned from Western scholars and missionaries, the concept of missions among most Christians is rooted in the Great Commission, and the mandate is to make disciples, with an emphasis on "doing for God." Later, when he came to America in 1970 as an international student, trusting God for provision and protection and beginning to walk in the Spirit, he was transformed. He realized that functionalism fails to recognize that our being is primary and that God works *in* us first before God works *through* us as His instruments. It is by obeying the two greatest commandments that we would fulfill the Great Commission. During his 2006 sabbatical at Yale Divinity School, he developed the relational realism paradigm and diaspora missiology.

As a Chinese, Wan was born, grew up, and lives in a complex web of relationships. Relationships are not only something to be cared about, but also something to take delight in talking about, "If you have a relationship, nothing matters; if you have no relationship, everything matters." Based on his STARS research methodology, he integrated the traditions of Chinese culture with the structure of relational thinking and developed relational realism. Wan proposed relational realism as an application of relational theology in connection with the practice of

Christian missions. Relational theology refers to the nature of, and relationships between God, humanity and spirit beings. Reality is based on those interactive relationships.

What is Relational Realism

Wan defines the 'relational realism' paradigm as, ontologically, "the systematic understanding that 'reality' is primarily based on the 'vertical relationship' between God and the created order and secondarily 'horizontal relationship' within the created order." Epistemologically, 'relational realism' is to be defined as "the systematic understanding that God is the absolute Truth and the Perfect Knowledge, and only in relationship to HIM is there the possibility of human knowledge and understanding of truth and reality." (Wan, 2006). Hence, our existence, ability to know and undertaking in missions are all dependent on God (Acts 17:28) who is the great I AM (Exd. 3). Our existence and our involvement in missions is God-centered (Wan, 2014).

The relational concept of love firstly towards God and secondly with our neighbor is the essence of the biblical faith Jesus summarized (Matt. 22:37-40). Christian ministry in discipleship, education, and leadership needs to be relational as well (Wan and Hedinger, 2018). The paradigm also nurtures a Kingdom orientation and strategically fulfills the Great Commission through a vertical relationship with the Triune God, and a working relationship with fellow Kingdom workers through a horizontal relationship with one another. It is transculturally relevant because the majority of the world is highly relational. Consequently, the approaches in diaspora missiology and missions are all relational in nature and can be synthesized through the paradigm (Wan, 2014). While the recognition and acceptance of diaspora missiology is relatively easy, the promotion of relational realism has a long way to go. In spite of that, the pursuit, practice, and development of relational realism is his life-long journey.

God's Total Grace

Seeing that traditional Western theology has proven difficult to implement when imposed on non-Western cultural contexts in highly relational societies, in 2016, Wan contextualized relational realism in Chinese culture and called it unmerited grace theology. Historically, "*sola gratia*" (grace alone) refers only to the doctrine of salvation (soteriology). Yet theologically, the "unmerited/graceful relationship" between God and God's people transcends time and space and circumstances. All that the gracious God reveals to His people is a gracious relationship. It is beyond grace alone, but total grace (Wan, 2014).

"恩情 ēn qíng" means "favor and relationship," which is derived from grace, and specifically puts God's grace into the interaction and correlation of persons. The apostle Paul repeatedly mentioned and emphasized the specific unmerited grace given to him in 1 Cor. 15:9-11, Eph. 3:8, and 1 Tim. 1: 15-16. Thus, gratitude in the heart, giving thanks with the mouth, and returning unmerited grace with the hands and feet are examples of grace-oriented ministry. The theological understanding of 恩情 ēn qíng is based on the vertical unmerited gracious relationship shown to us by God as the axis, followed by the horizontal transmission of the graciousness received by the graced person as a continuous extension of the mode of channeling such gracious relationships (徐, 2022). It can be simplified as "a systematic theological conceptualization of the phenomenon and network of first vertical and then horizontal, and also both vertical and horizontal, interactions among God, man and angels, that is, the relational network among God, man and angels" *(my translation)*.

The Continual Developments

In the post-Christian and post-modernist 21st century, the understanding and application of relationality is essential. Wan integrated relational theology, relational realism, unmerited grace theology, along with his experience of exorcism and the interactions among God, man and angels in Job into his recent studies. He developed relational transformation paradigm (Wan, 2021) and relational interactionism (Wan and Raibley, 2022). As a professor and director of three doctoral programs at Western Seminary, I am convinced that Wan will continue to develop more relational paradigms.

His Influence on Me

I really appreciated the devotion led by Wan with the vertical and horizontal relationships in the Scriptures at the beginning of each class. The concept of unmerited grace helps me to understand more about God's love and mission, and especially to evaluate my motive and approach in missions and in every relationship. How I see each lost soul is now different because the unmerited grace given to me is also given to them. Functionalism may produce the desired results, but it loses the genuine love and extension of God's grace. Since then, I have been practicing relational realism in every aspect of how I minister and live. Sadly, when some Christians see or hear my ministry approach, they quickly call the relational approach the social gospel; or become unwilling to wait for the work of the Spirit sent for God's mission. In fact, they may label everything that has to do with the Holy Spirit as Charismatic or Pentecostal. Wan has been an encouragement to me to be a practitioner of relational realism.

In a current trial, I have tried everything for deliverance, including fasting, confessing my sins, forgiving all offenses and so on, but gradually losing hope for deliverance. It is relational realism which helps me to see the trial is only a little taste what Christ experienced and suffered for us, and Satan is waging war to take me and other Kingdom workers down. It is also through interactions with Wan and several mature Christians who recognized this as a spiritual warfare and interceded on my behalf that brought me comfort and helped me to stand firm. Wan shared his testimony to encourage me to persevere, grow, and depend on the Spirit for deliverance and healing. Gradually, I learned to focus on God and worship Him through the trial, and the Spirit gave me peace and joy although I still do not know when He will deliver me. Once I turned my eyes to God's glory, I was transformed. My life is no longer about me, but about taking up the cross, following Him, and extending His unmerited grace in relationships with Christians and with people who have yet to enter His Kingdom.

Conclusion

Dr. Wan, who would have known that you would be my professor 20 years after we met in Dallas? It is a privilege for me to study diaspora missiology and relational realism paradigm from you, the pioneer of these fields. May God's unmerited grace humble us and allow the Holy Spirit to "shift our paradigm" from functionalism to relational realism in all relationships and ministry practices in order to be faithfully evangelical and Scriptural. Thank you very much for your teaching and for your journey with me, Dr. Wan.

Bibliography

Wan, Enoch. "Beyond 'Solar Gratia' (Grace Alone)." *Billy Graham Center for Evangelism* (June 23, 2014). http://www.evangelvision.com/beyond-solar-gratia-grace-alone/

Wan, Enoch. "Inter-Disciplinary and Integrative Missiological Research: The 'What,' 'Why' and 'How.'" *Global Missiology* (July 2017). http://ojs.globalmissiology.org/index.php/english/article/viewFile/2019/4514 (accessed March 8, 2025).

Wan, Enoch. "Relational Paradigm for Practicing Diaspora Missions in the 21st Century." In *Diaspora Missiology: Theory, Methodology, and Practice*, edited by Enoch Wan, 191-203. 2nd ed. Portland, OR: IDS-USA, 2014.

Wan, Enoch. "Relational Transformational Leadership: An Asian Christian Perspective." *Asian Missions Advance* 71, (April 2021): 2-7. https://www.asiamissions.net/wp-content/uploads/2021/04/AMA71_EnochWan.pdf (accessed March 12, 2025).

Wan, Enoch. "The Paradigm of Relational Realism." *Occasional Bulletin of EMS* 19, no. 2 (Spring 2006):1-4.

Wan, Enoch and Jon Raibley. *Transformational Change in Christian Ministry*. Portland: Western Academic Publishers, 2022.

Wan, Enoch and Mark Hedinger. "Transformative Ministry for the Majority World Context: Applying Relational Approaches." *Occasional Bulletin of EMS* 31, no. 2 (Spring 2018): 4-17.

Wan, Enoch and Mark Hedinger. "Understanding 'Relationality' From A Trinitarian Perspective." January 2006.

https://www.enochwan.com/english/articles/pdf/Relationality%20and%20Trinity.pdf (accessed March 8, 2025).

徐濟時。<訪問溫以諾牧師>《中華神學研究中心研究季報》(2022 年 1 月 。) https://ctrcentre.org/wp-content/uploads//2021/12/2.溫以諾.pdf (accessed March 5, 2025).

Chapter 7

The Relational Teacher - The Theory and Practice of Relational Interaction by Educators

Mark R. Hedinger, D.I.S. and Karen R. Hedinger, Ed.D.

Purpose

In honor of Dr. Enoch Wan, we are contributing this short article that advances his contributions to missiology through the application of relational interactionist theory and practice. Our focus is on the educational practitioner in the context of relational interactionism.

Definitions

- *Relational interactionism* - an interdisciplinary narrative framework that develops from practical considerations of dynamic interaction of personal Beings/beings, forming realistic relational networks in multiple contexts (i.e. theo-culture, angel-culture, and human culture) and with various consequences.[99]
- *Relational Educator* - a teacher who understands the theory and practice of relational interactionism, and who applies those principles appropriately in their educational ministry.

Theoretical Background

We build on two theoretical foundations.

First foundational theory: Curriculum development models of process/product. Author Geraldine O'Neill[100] describes "process models" and "product models" of curriculum design. The process model

---

[99] Enoch Wan and Mark Hedinger. *Relational Intercultural Communication for Relational Intercultural Education.* Portland, OR: Western Academic Publishers. 2025. Page 7.

[100] O'Neill, G. (2015). *Curriculum Design in Higher Education: Theory to Practice*, Dublin: UCD Teaching & Learning. ISBN 9781905254989 http://www.ucd.ie/t4cms/UCDTLP0068.pd. Especially chapter 4

emphasizes learning activities that lead to appropriate educational outcomes expecting that good results grow from the right processes, conditions and messages. The product model emphasizes the plans and intentions that an educator seeks to achieve. These are often communicated through Bloom's taxonomy of "cognitive, affective, and psychomotor" objectives[101] or through UNESCO's educational pillars of "learning to know, learning to do, learning to live together and learning to be.[102]" These two models are the extremes of a continuum. The middle ground between them is found in Problem-Based Learning which includes elements of both Process and Product[103]. Rather than focusing on curriculum, we will use the "process" and "product" continuum to consider the educator. Some educators focus on the fulfillment of goals and objectives so intently that they lose personal interaction and curricular flexibility. Other educators can be so involved in their teaching process that they do not lead toward meaningful goals or results.

Second Theoretical Background: the relational interactionist approach. Dr. Wan and his students have developed this approach.[104]
- Reality is based on relationships, first vertically (between Creator Beings and created beings), and secondarily horizontal relationships between created beings.
- Both vertical and horizontal relationships are dynamic: They grow, recede, or change over time.
- Relationships are not universally God-honoring. There are "transformative relationships" which encourage growth in godliness. There are "transgressive relationships" that move people away from God.

---

[101] Benjamin Bloom. *Taxonomy of Educational Objectives*. Boston MA: Allyn and Bacon, 1956. Republished by Pearson Education, 1984.
[102] UNESCO. https://unesdoc.unesco.org/ark:/48223/pf0000109590. Accessed June 8, 2025. *Treasure Within*. Report to UNESCO of the International Commission on Education for the Twenty-first Century. 1996.
[103] O'Neill page 35.
[104] Wan, Raibley *Transformational Change in Christian Ministry*. Chapter 7

Introduction

As a Professor, Dr. Enoch Wan has pioneered the introduction of relational interactionism into the realm of missiological education. This chapter is appropriate for a Festschrift because, besides introducing the concept, Dr. Wan is a prime example of its application. In the interest of brevity, we will only consider a few areas of application, but we hope that this article will spark other publications on relational interactionism and the educational practitioner.

Part One: The Relational Interactionist Educator in Theory

Life experience will confirm that some educators are effective, and other teachers are not so effective. Our life experiences also confirm that often the most successful teachers of content are involved with students in ways that go beyond classroom "knowledge transfer." We maintain that excellent teachers are agile at balancing human interactions (horizontal relationships), God-honoring vertical relationships, and content mastery all together.

We begin by considering the healthy relational interactions that might exist between an educator and his/her students. The lefthand column in Figure 1 includes eleven elements that will be present in a relational educator. These elements grew from inductive Bible study on the topic of "teacher" and from the experiences of the authors.

Figure 1 takes those elements further by including biblical and real-life illustrations. The figure also places the elements into a continuum from "process-oriented education" to "mid-point" and on to "product-oriented."

Both process and product-orientation can be approached in a relational-interactionist way. Yet we also note differences in healthy relational interaction between those two contexts. The relational-interactionist educator, in other words, is aware of situations that call for a product mindset and those that call for a personalized and flexible process-mindset.

Figure 1: Elements that characterize a relational teacher

Element	Placement on process/ product continuum	Biblical example	Description	Examples in a teacher
Empathy	Process	John 16:12 "I have more to say to you, more than you can now hear."	Teacher able to understand student's life and academic realities	A teacher who helps learners be persistent through the ups and downs of academic life.
Trust	Process	2 Tim 2:2 The things you have heard from me, entrust to others who can teach others also	A relational teacher shares freely and encourages their students to also share freely	Sharing unpublished journal submissions as a way to keep student learning up-to-date and relevant yet trusting the students to protect the material.
Care for student as a person	Process	1 Thes 2:7-8 "like a mother cares for her children, we cared for you".	A relational teacher knows the student, and has a relationship of whole-hearted sharing	A relational teacher is involved with students in ways that include content but goes beyond that into other parts of life.
Work ethos	Mid-point	2 Tim 2:15 study to show yourself approved	The relational teacher models and expects good work ethic.	A teacher/student relationship that encourages good work ethic and balance of work with rest.
Patience	Mid-point	2 Tim 4:2 Preach the Word... with great patience.	The relational teacher recognizes that it takes time for new skills, knowledge and ideas to grow	Especially in graduate studies, research and writing need patience.

Element	Placement on process/ product continuum	Biblical example	Description	Examples in a teacher
Encouragement	Mid-point	Heb 10:24 Consider how we may spur one another on toward love and good deeds 1 Thes 2:11-12 We dealt with each of you as a father deals with his children, encouraging. . .	Relational teaching includes ongoing encouragement toward a challenging goal	A relational teacher mixes correction with encouragement toward favorable outcomes. Both are part of spurring students on to growth.
Experience in the field	Mid-point	2 Cor 1:3-11. Paul, writing about compassion and comfort, tells his own stories of God meeting him in times of suffering	A teacher who knows life outside of academic contexts and teaches in light of real-life realities.	Student testimonies reflect the importance of teachers who understand and teach about the realities of their areas of expertise.
Connections with other academics and practitioners	Mid-point	Romans 16	A relational teacher will introduce students to academics and practitioners who can help their growth.	Through conferences, emails, and personal conversations a relational teacher helps to network students with others
Generous with knowledge and resources	Mid-point	2 Tim 4:13 when you come, bring my scrolls	A relational teacher knows the books, websites, interviews etc. to help student progress and make resources available	Suggestions of relevant books, articles, websites, and other resources. The relational teacher freely shares their knowledge.

Element	Placement on process/ product continuum	Biblical example	Description	Examples in a teacher
Skill in posing problems, researching, writing	Product	Acts 15 and Galatians – Peter and Paul identify the problem of Jew/Gentile interaction. They research and communicate to the churches.	Good academic work recognizes specific problems, digs into the relevant research, and communicates what is learned.	A relational teacher is excellent in academics: identifying problems, researching and communicating with clarity.
Subject Matter knowledge	Product	Phil 3:4-6 Paul's credentials as a leader among the Jews	A teacher must be an expert in their content material	A relational teacher is a master of their field of study who uses that expertise for academic and relational benefit.

This section of our paper describes an educator who is a master of their content and also interacts in relationship with the students. This is the teacher who is aware that educational standards are important for both the individual learner and for the institution. This is the teacher who defines and achieves student-learning outcomes in cognitive, affective and psychomotor domains and also creates an interpersonal interactive ethos and context that demonstrates real interest in the student's wellbeing.

This is Paul, who said, "Run the race...." and pointed his disciples toward challenging product-oriented outcomes. This is also Paul who said, "I have you in my heart." There is a desired outcome – a product. The relational interactionist educator knows how to work toward that desired outcome, not by raw force, but by a process including encouragement, coaching, care, empathy, and understanding.

Conclusions: The Relational Interactive Educator in Theory

We have seen how a relational interactionist educator will at times be process-focused and at other times will be product-focused. In either case, there is a balanced view of excellence in achieving student learning outcomes on one hand, and the personal interaction that shows up as encouragement, personal involvement, and availability outside of the classroom. This is the relationship that says, "besides teaching you my subject matter, I want to see you grow in the grace and the knowledge of our Lord and Savior Jesus Christ." (2 Peter 3:18)

Part Two: The Relational Interactive Educator in Practice

The practice of relational interactionism in the life and work of a teacher calls for two key foci: balance and discernment.

The educator who loses balance will find themselves in one of two unhealthy extremes: either being overly concerned with being the "popular teacher" or being mechanistic and formulaic. It is that middle ground between "product" and "process" where relational interactionism has proper influence.

The other focus is the need for discernment. One level of discernment has been introduced: a discerning attitude that finds a healthy balance between personal involvement and achieving educational goals.

Another level of discernment has to do with how process and product are expressed. Imagine a professor who is high on empathy. A learner in his class is struggling. The empathetic educator feels for that student and reduces the learning goals. Another professor, also highly relational, sees the same student in the same predicament. But this second educator, with a higher level of discernment, walks alongside the learner. The goals are not reduced, but personal encouragement and help is offered to meet those goals. This second approach, high in relational interaction and high in educational discernment will achieve the best outcomes for the student.

Conclusion

This chapter has considered teacher interactions with students. The healthy balance is found when the teacher walks in interactive relationship with students to accomplish goals. The relational interactionist educator will seek what is best for the learner. At times, the pathway toward "best outcome" is through a sympathetic, caring human touch. At other times, the best way to facilitate growth is to focus on product outcomes. Seen in this light, the apparent dichotomy between "process" and "product" fades and we see two realities which both need to be addressed: program accomplishment AND healthy, appropriate relational interactions.

Thank you, Dr. Wan, for modeling this balanced approach to excellent education. Your students have heard your exhortations to create clarity through figures and tables (frightening figures and terrifying tables, they have been called!). We have had you return our drafts to us numerous times, each time with new suggestions for improvement. You have shown us how to write and research using the STARS approach. You have taught us, by precept and example, the importance of pursuing high quality academics.

You have done this in a personal, relational way. You model process as you work out each student's individualized learning plan - the merging of product and process. Your students have received an email of encouragement exactly when we were despairing of finishing our programs. We have seen you model both the process and the product of high-quality education; a merging together that we now seek to carry into our own interactive, teaching relationships.

Chapter 8

Missiology for the 21st Century: The Point-Line-Plane Perspective of Relational Interactionism

Elton Siu Lun Law, D.Miss.

Traditional missiology has often regarded the "Great Commission" (Matthew 28:18-20) as its core driving force and paradigm. However, when confronted with the intricate realities of 21st Century missionary work—whether it be the call for Integral Mission advocating holistic gospel and social justice, Workplace Mission, Diaspora Mission seizing opportunities within population movements, Urban Mission addressing the challenges of globalized urban jungles, or the urgency of Unreached People Groups (UPG) Mission[105]—a paradigm relying solely on the "Great Commission" as its engine proves inadequate. Such a narrow focus may even reduce mission to mere "ecclesiastical programs" or "human initiatives."

Missiological thought and practice have often leaned toward a single-focus model. Churches and mission agencies tend to concentrate heavily on specific but limited aspects, such as church planting, short-term missions, spiritual warfare, or cross-cultural adaptation. However, overemphasizing these individual dimensions risks neglecting the inherent wholeness and multidimensionality of mission itself.[106]

This paper critiques reductionist approaches to mission and proposes "Relational Interactionism" as a multidimensional framework for holistic missional engagement.[107] Drawing from biblical theology and intercultural studies, I argue for integrating six core relationships—

---

[105] The themes listed are currently promoted by the Lausanne Movement. Please see https://lausanne.org.

[106] Enoch Wan and Sonia Chan, "Contextualization the Asian Way: Relational Contextualization", *Asian Missions Advance* 78 (2022), accessed June 26, 2025], https://www.asiamissions.net/wp-content/uploads/2022/12/AMA78_EnochWan.pdf.

divine, ecclesial, cultural, spiritual, ecological, and interpersonal—to advance a transformative praxis grounded in God's reconciling mission.[108]

The Limitations of a Single-Focus Approach

Many churches begin engaging in mission work when members commit to serving as missionaries. While this is praiseworthy, the focus often remains on the missionaries' personal updates, ministry progress, or the outcomes of short-term teams. Though these concerns are necessary, they confine the missional vision to a single-focal point, exemplified by questions like:

- "How many missionaries have we sent?"
- "How many short-term trips have we organized?"
- "How many people have professed faith?"

Such a point-centric missiology risks falling into what Enoch Wan has called "Managerial Mission Practice" based on pragmatism and numerical metrics, overlooking the spiritual foundations and cultural depth of mission.[109] This oversimplified approach fails to address the challenges of today's multicultural, complex societies and intense spiritual warfare. It also fails to foster a sustainable and healthy missional ecosystem.

---

[107] Enoch Wan, "Transformational Change in Christian Ministry: Relational," *Relational Realism* (blog), May 25, 2022, accessed June 26, 2025, https://relationalrealism.net/2022/05/25/transformational-change-in-christian-ministry-relational/.

[108] Wan and Ramirez argue that the Triune nature of God should be the starting point when studying Christian Missions. See Enoch Wan and Alonzo Ramirez, "Biblical Theology of Multi-Culturality: Original Research Article" (Enoch Wan Ministries, 2020), accessed June 24, 2025, https://www.enochwan.com/english/articles/pdf/Biblical%20Theology%20of%20Multi-Culturality.pdf.

[109] Enoch Wan, "Relational Theology and Relational Missiology," *Global Missiology* 18, no. 3 (2021): p.5-6, accessed June 24, 2025, http://ojs.globalmissiology.org/index.php/english/article/view/2234/5154.

From Points to Lines, Planes, and Multidimensional Expansion[110]

If mission is viewed as an expanding vision, we can progress from a "point" perspective to "line," "plane," and ultimately "multidimensional" paradigms.[111] For example, when a church not only cares for individual missionaries but also considers the collaboration between mission fields and sending agencies, it moves from a point to a line. Further, when the church connects multiple mission fields, cultural contexts, and strategic reflections, the vision expands into a plane.

Yet, for mission to mature, it must advance to a multidimensional level, integrating spiritual, cultural, ecclesiastical, theological, economic, and ethical factors into a cohesive framework. Only then can we avoid a flattened or fragmented perspective and develop a missional theology more aligned with biblical teaching.

The Cultural Dimension and Its Tensions

A significant shift in modern missiology has been the emphasis on moving from a "church-centered model" to "culture-centered model."[112] This requires missionaries to learn local languages, cultures, and religious contexts to establish indigenous churches through contextualization.

However, this cultural focus introduces tensions. When culture dominates missiology, it can lead to excessive cultural relativism, even displacing commitment to biblical truth. For instance, some missionaries, in their efforts to assimilate, may compromise core doctrines, while some scholars reduce missiology to cultural studies, detaching it from

---

[110] Enoch Wan, "Relational Theology and Relational Missiology: Original Research Article" (Enoch Wan Ministries, 2020), accessed June 24, 2025, https://www.enochwan.com/english/articles/pdf/Relational%20Theology%20And%20Relational%20Missiology%20-%20Orig.pdf.

[111] Enoch Wan, "Biblical Theology of Multi-Culturality,"

[112] Since the 1970s, missiologists such as Charle Kraft, Paul Hiebert, Donald Smith, and many others have written books on "cultural anthropology" and missions. Intercultural studies become the key elements for mission education.

scriptural foundations.[113] This reminds us that while culture is vital, it must not "hijack" missional theology.

The Reality of Spiritual Warfare

On the mission field, missionaries often confront not only linguistic and cultural barriers but also opposition from spiritual forces. Spiritual warfare is not abstract but a daily reality. As the Bible reminds us:

"For our struggle is not against flesh and blood, but against the rulers, against the authorities, against the powers of this dark world and against the spiritual forces of evil in the heavenly realms." (Ephesians 6:12)

Yet, overemphasizing spiritual warfare may neglect other critical dimensions, such as cultural adaptation and church building. A healthy missional theology must integrate spiritual, cultural, strategic, and communal aspects.

Returning to God: The Core Motive of Mission

Every missional act originates from God's sending and calling.[114] Mission reflects God's heart for all nations, not human zeal. To "return to God" is not just theological centering but a return to mission's source—God Himself.

Relational Interactionism: An Integrative Framework for Mission

Relational Interactionism posits that mission is inherently relational—a redemptive, reconciling, and restorative endeavor. It outlines six core

---

[113] The Muslim Idiom Translation of the Bible is one of the examples that has provoked debate in the missiological world.
See also, Timothy Hwang, "A Concern About the Recent Trends in Contextualization Discussions: A Lack or Absence of a Biblical Theological Emphasis (Part 3 of 5: Muslim Idiom Bible Translations)," *Biblical Missiology* (blog), November 19, 2018, accessed June 24, 2025, https://biblicalmissiology.org/blog/2018/11/19/a-concern-about-the-recent-trends-in-contextualization-discussions-a-lack-or-absence-of-a-biblical-theological-emphasis-part-3-of-5-muslim-idiom-bible-translations/.

[114] Christopher J. H. Wright, *The Mission of God: Unlocking the Bible's Grand Narrative* (Downers Grove: IVP Academic, 2006), 62–65.

relationships: divine, ecclesial, cultural, spiritual, ecological, and interpersonal.

1. The divine relationship between humanity and God establishes mission as fundamentally about reconciliation through Christ, the essence of the Gospel.
2. The ecclesial relationships between churches across regions and denominations should be characterized by mutual respect and collaboration rather than competition.
3. The cultural relationship between church and world calls for faithful engagement without compromise, fostering genuine interactions in secular spaces.
4. The spiritual relationship acknowledges our need to resist evil through the Spirit's power while engaging in spiritual warfare.
5. The ecological relationship reminds us of our stewardship over creation, reflecting humanity's original mandate as caretakers of God's world.
6. Interpersonal relationships among believers and across cultural divides manifest Christ's reconciling love in tangible ways.

The six-dimensional relational framework provides a robust theological architecture for 21st-century missiology. By centering mission on God's cosmic work of reconciliation (Colossians 1:20), this paradigm transcends fragmented approaches and anchors specialized fields in the 21st century—Diaspora, Workplace, Urban, UPG, and Creation Care missions—within a cohesive narrative of restoration.

Far from abstract theory, this framework compels the global church toward holistic participation in *Missio Dei*, where every act of justice, every bridge built between cultures, every liberated community, and every healed ecosystem proclaims the advent of God's Kingdom—until the day all relationships are restored under the headship of Christ (Ephesians 1:10), and the earth is "filled with the knowledge of the Lord's glory as the waters cover the sea" (Habakkuk 2:14).

This integrated vision calls the church not merely to *do* mission, but to *embody* God's reconciling love in every fractured relationship—for the glory of the One who makes all things new.

To implement these relationships, the Church should:
1. Prioritize spiritual formation through prayer, meditation, and fellowship.
2. Foster inter-church collaboration based on trust and humility.
3. Engage society authentically, building relationships through service and love.

Mission then becomes not just task completion but participation in God's kingdom.

In this fractured and rapidly changing era, we urge the church to move beyond single-dimensional models and embrace an integrated, multidimensional vision. Only within the framework of relational interactionism can we balance spiritual depth, cultural insight, strategic application, and spiritual warfare, forging a missional practice that aligns with God's heart.

May every believer and every church strive faithfully within these six relationships, fulfilling the Great Commission. Thus, our mission ceases to be a human endeavor and becomes a divine partnership—a glorious testimony to the inbreaking of God's kingdom.

Bibliography

Bauckham, Richard. 2010. *Bible and Ecology: Rediscovering the Community of Creation*. London: DLT.

Bosch, David J. 1991. *Transforming Mission: Paradigm Shifts in Theology of Mission*. Maryknoll: Orbis.

Escobar, Samuel. 2003. *The New Global Mission: The Gospel from Everywhere to Everyone*. Downers Grove: IVP.

Hiebert, Paul G. 1985. *Anthropological Insights for Missionaries*. Grand Rapids: Baker.

Hwang, Timothy. "A Concern About the Recent Trends in Contextualization Discussions: A Lack or Absence of a Biblical Theological Emphasis (Part 3 of 5: Muslim Idiom Bible Translations)." *Biblical Missiology* (blog). November 19, 2018. https://biblicalmissiology.org/blog/2018/11/19/a-concern-about-the-recent-trends-in-contextualization-discussions-a-lack-or-absence-of-a-biblical-theological-emphasis-part-3-of-5-muslim-idiom-bible-translations/. Accessed June 24, 2025.

Kraft, Charles H. 2005. *Anthropology for Christian Witness*. Maryknoll: Orbis.

Lingenfelter, Sherwood. 2008. *Leading Cross-Culturally: Covenant Relationships for Effective Christian Leadership*. Grand Rapids: Baker.

Moreau, A. Scott. 2012. *Contextualizing the Faith: A Holistic Approach*. Grand Rapids: Baker.

Enoch Wan and Alonzo Ramirez, "Biblical Theology of Multi-Culturality: Original Research Article" (Enoch Wan Ministries, 2020), https://www.enochwan.com/english/articles/pdf/Biblical%20Theology%20of%20Multi-Culturality.pdf. Accessed June 24, 2025.

Wan, Enoch. "Biblical Theology of Multi-Culturality: Original Research Article." Enoch Wan Ministries, 2020. https://www.enochwan.com/english/articles/pdf/Biblical%20Theology%20of%20Multi-Culturality.pdf. Accessed June 24, 2025.

Wan, Enoch. "Relational Theology and Relational Missiology: Original Research Article." Enoch Wan Ministries, 2020. Online: https://www.enochwan.com/english/articles/pdf/Relational%20Theology%20And%20Relational%20Missiology%20-%20Orig.pdf

Wan, Enoch, and Sonia Chan. "Contextualization The Asian Way: Relational Contextualization" *Asian Missions Advance* 78 (2022). https://www.asiamissions.net/wp-content/uploads/2022/12/AMA78_EnochWan.pdf. Accessed June 24, 2025.

Wan, Enoch. "Transformational Change in Christian Ministry: Relational." *Relational Realism* (blog). May 25, 2022. https://relationalrealism.net/2022/05/25/transformational-change-in-christian-ministry-relational/. Accessed June 26, 2025.

Wright, Christopher J. H. 2006. *The Mission of God: Unlocking the Bible's Grand Narrative*. Downers Grove: IVP.

Church Planting

"I will build My church"
(Matthew 16:18)

Chapter 9

Cross-Cultural Church Planting in Latin America: Reflections by an American Missionary Fifteen Years Later

Matt Cook, Ph.D.

Introduction

To say that Enoch Wan has been influential in shaping my academic research would be a significant understatement. During my doctoral studies at SBTS, where I focused on the immigrant practice of world religions in the United States in multiple research papers, I quickly encountered Dr. Wan as the leading authority on ministry to global immigrant communities. It was through his work that I was introduced to the term "diaspora missiology," a term he developed in collaboration with Sadiri Joy Tira (the original promoter of this volume).[115] Ultimately, I centered my dissertation research (2018–2019) on diaspora missiology, and Dr. Wan's scholarship proved indispensable. If an award could be given for most references in a bibliography, Dr. Wan would effortlessly win that award for his *seventeen* references in my bibliography (with Dr. Tira easily sliding into second place). Just last year, without having met in person, Dr. Wan assisted me in the publication of my dissertation through Western Seminary. My indebtedness to him is profound.

Ironically, during my tenure as a church planter in Latin America, I was unfamiliar with Dr. Wan's work. When we departed for Peru in 2009, I had completed two graduate programs, but diaspora missiology was still an "emerging discipline,"[116] and my coursework in missiology

---

[115] Sadiri Joy Tira, "Diaspora Missiology and the Lausanne Movement at the Dawn of the Twenty-First Century," in *Global Diasporas and Mission*, Im and Yong, 217. In this chapter, Tira does a favor for those interested in diaspora missiology by describing more fully the development of the field.

[116] Michael Pocock referred to it this way several years later (2015) in his introduction to *Diaspora Missiology: Reflections on Reaching the Scattered Peoples of the World*, eds. Michael Pocock and Enoch Wan, Evangelical

did not address it. Over fifteen years later, I reflect on our experience in Peru as a season marked by both God's provision and our inexperience. Like many cross-cultural missionaries, there are numerous insights I wish we had possessed at the outset. In this chapter, I will examine three themes in Enoch Wan's scholarship that—had we known them—could have enriched and enhanced our ministry as church planters in Latin America.

Contextualization and Enoch Wan

In the first edition of *Diaspora Missiology*, Dr. Wan noted the importance of contextualization as a tool in diaspora missions: "The focus is on holistic missions and contextualization, integrating evangelism and social concern. For example, Christian workers cannot just start a local church among refugees without also addressing their physical needs and becoming their advocate."[117] From the early stages of the diaspora missiology movement, Dr. Wan has called for diaspora missions to focus on holistic ministry.[118] Diaspora people face a myriad of problems. These problems, however, can be seen by Christians as opportunities to demonstrate the love of God. Though we were confident in our church planting strategy in Latin America, confidence does not always equate to effectiveness. Most cross-cultural missionaries likely recall specific moments of confident and zealous proclamation of the gospel or protracted planning for a project and cringe at how they failed in connecting the message or the methods effectively to their host culture. These moments, while they make for humorous stories, represent the source of much consternation not only for cross-cultural missionaries, but also for Christians sharing the message of Jesus in their own culture. When sharing the message in one's own culture to someone who identifies more closely with an immigrant culture, the potential for a lack

---

Missiological Society Series 23 (Pasadena: William Carey Library, 2015), xv.

[117] Enoch Wan, "Diaspora Missiology–A Different Paradigm for the 21st Century," in *Diaspora Missiology: Theory, Methodology, and Practice*, ed. Enoch Wan, (Portland, OR: Institute of Diaspora Studies, 2011), 139, Kindle.

[118] Enoch Wan, "The Phenomenon of Diaspora: Missiological Implications for Christian Missions," in *Scattered: The Filipino Global Presence*, eds. Luis L. Pantoja, Sadiri Joy Tira, and Enoch Wan (Manila, Philippines: LifeChange Publishing, 2004), 112.

of connection increases. This is where Wan's emphasis on holistic ministry as a form of contextualization could have proven very helpful.

Gleaning from multiple sources on contextualization, I define it in this way: Contextualization is the process by which the Word of God is faithfully communicated and obediently put into practice in constantly changing human cultures in ways that are sensitive, understandable, and meaningful to any one culture so that the members of that culture may follow Jesus without leaving their culture.

Upon reflection today, a greater emphasis on Wan's descriptions of holistic ministry would have helped us to share the Gospel in a way that was more sensitive, understandable, and meaningful, especially for members of the diaspora community in Peru. Kim's adaptation of Hiebert's critical contextualization model[119] for the purpose of diaspora missions is helpful here. His four-step process is similar to Hiebert's, and he calls it "the contextual theologizing process." He describes, "It starts with (1) the theologizing subject, the church; (2) the church understanding the context–diaspora in globalization; (3) the church interpreting the Bible and applying it to the context from the interdisciplinary perspectives; and finally (4) we confirm the guidance of the Holy Spirit for the theologizing process."[120] This process could be followed in sticky situations to determine if a contextualized practice is legitimate or syncretistic. Interestingly, after a lengthy discussion of contextualization, Kim describes both hospitality[121] and holistic ministry[122] as effective contextualized practices in diaspora ministry, confirming what Dr. Wan has been communicating for years.

---

[119] Paul G. Hiebert, *Anthropological Insights for Missionaries* (Grand Rapids: Baker Book House, 1985)186–87; see also, Hiebert, *Anthropological Reflections on Missiological Issues* (Grand Rapids: Baker Books, 1994), 88–91.

[120] Luther Jeom O. Kim, *Doing Diaspora Missiology toward "Diaspora Mission Church": The Rediscovery of Diaspora for the Renewal of Church and Mission in a Secular Era* (Eugene, OR: Wipf and Stock Publishers, 2016), 206–7.

[121] Kim, 208.

[122] Kim, 255.

Diaspora Missions and Enoch Wan

Diaspora missiology studies occur at the intersection of missiology and migration theory, with an emphasis on strategies to minister to and through the diaspora populations of the world.[123] As mentioned previously, one could argue that Enoch Wan is the academic father of this discipline. His articles are among the earliest and his seminal *Diaspora Missiology* was one of the first comprehensive works in the field.[124] His definitions of diaspora missiology, ministry, and missions are crucial to the field and are included in glossary form in both the Evangelical Missiological Society's treatment of diaspora missiology[125] and the most comprehensive resource available on diaspora missiology, *Scattered and Gathered: A Global Compendium of Diaspora Missiology*.[126] Upon reflection, our ministry could have been far more effective in Peru had we been influenced by Dr. Wan's work in diaspora missiology.

While immigration in urban Peru is not the phenomenon that it is in the United States, immigrants from Asia, other parts of Latin America, and rural Peru are still an important part of the landscape, especially missiologically. Though we attempted to serve these immigrants, the work by Dr. Wan and other influential diaspora missiologists would have been valuable. Dr. Wan and Dr. Tira were a part of the Lausanne Diasporas Leadership Team that produced, in my opinion, a most useful framework for the practice of diaspora missions in their booklet *Scattered to Gather: Embracing the Global Trend of Diaspora* (released in 2010, revised in 2017). Church leaders or missionaries in any culture (including Peruvian culture) could adopt the seven steps the team suggests: 1) Embrace the vision for diaspora peoples. 2) Ensure the right

---

[123] For an extended list of definitions of diaspora missiology, see Tira and Yamamori, *Scattered and Gathered*, 538–43.

[124] Enoch Wan, introduction to *Diaspora Missiology: Theory, Methodology, and Practice*, ed. Enoch Wan, 2nd ed. (Portland, OR: Institute of Diaspora Studies, 2014).

[125] Michael Pocock and Enoch Wan, eds., *Diaspora Missiology: Reflections on Reaching the Scattered Peoples of the World*, Evangelical Missiological Society Series 23 (Pasadena: William Carey Library, 2015) 215.

[126] Sadiri Joy Tira and Tetsunao Yamamori, eds., *Scattered and Gathered: A Global Compendium of Diaspora Missiology*, Regnum Studies in Mission (Eugene, OR: Wipf and Stock Publishers, 2016), 636-37.

attitudes. 3) Explore your neighborhood. 4) Engage in holistic ministry. 5) Equip for effective ministry. 6) Encourage building genuine relationships. 7) Empower the diaspora Christians or churches for ministry.[127] Powerful, yet simple and achievable, these steps could be used as an evangelistic strategy by any church, especially ethnic majority churches that want to minister to the immigrant minorities in their neighborhoods.

The Relational Paradigm and Enoch Wan

Dr. Wan also has emphasized the importance of building relationships as the most important strategy in diaspora missions. In response to the lack of relational skills of Westerners, Wan argues that "the rediscovery of *'relationalship'* in Christian faith and practice is desperately needed."[128] He argues that Westerners lack "relational reality" and that diaspora missions will only be effective if Westerners rediscover the ability to have healthy relationships both in ministry to diaspora people and partnership with diaspora Christians.[129] He provides nine reasons why "the relational paradigm is deemed the most appropriate choice in the practice of diaspora missions in the 21st century."[130]

> "Firstly, the rediscovery of *"relationalship"* in Christian faith and practice is desperately needed… Secondly, it is an excellent Christian response to the cry for relationship from people of the twenty-first century. Thirdly, it is a practical way to rediscover 'relationship' which is the essence of Christian faith and practice. Fourthly, it has been proven to be effective in ministering to diaspora communities and individuals in need of Christian charity….. Fifthly, it is a paradigm that enables the synthesizing of diaspora missiology and diaspora missions. Sixthly, it is transculturally relevant to societies in the majority world which are highly relational. Seventhly, it nurtures a Kingdom orientation and strategically fulfills the Great Commission (a vertical relationship with the Sovereign

---

[127] Lausanne Diasporas Leadership Team, *Scattered to Gather*, 31–36.
[128] Enoch Wan, "Relational Paradigm for Practicing Diaspora Missions in the 21st Century," in *Diaspora Missiology*, 192.
[129] ibid
[130] ibid

Lord), and a working relationship with fellow "Kingdom Workers" (horizontally with one and other). Eighthly, it enables the practice of "strategic stewardship" and "relational accountability." Ninthly, in light of the various approaches in diaspora missions, (e.g. to, through, by/beyond, and with) which are all "relational" in nature.... Lastly, in light of the shift of Christendom's center from the West to the majority world, strategic partnership and synergy require the practice of relational paradigm; instead of the popular managerial tendency and entrepreneurship of the West."[131]

Upon reflection on our time as church planters in Peru, while we were committed to being relational, earlier exposure to Wan's work would have enhanced our effectiveness in cross-cultural ministry.

Conclusion
Our time as fulltime cross-cultural missionaries came to an abrupt end because of a family health crisis. At the time, I wrestled with the question: How could God still use me if I was no longer on the mission field—the very place I believed He had called me to serve? Had I known of Dr. Enoch Wan's work earlier, I might have recognized sooner that faithful kingdom service can take many forms. Dr. Wan's example illustrates that God uses academic scholar-practitioners to make significant kingdom contributions. While I may never have the reach or impact that Dr. Wan has achieved, his life and work have taught me that meaningful ministry can occur both in the classroom and through the written word, just as surely as it can on the mission field.

---

[131] ibid

Bibliography

Hiebert, Paul G. *Anthropological Insights for Missionaries*. Grand Rapids: Baker Books, 1985.

———. *Anthropological Reflections on Missiological Issues*. Grand Rapids: Baker Books, 1994.

Im, Chandler H., and Amos Yong, eds. *Global Diasporas and Mission*. Regnum Edinburgh Centenary Series 23. Oxford: Regnum Books International, 2014.

Kim, Luther Jeom O. *Doing Diaspora Missiology toward "Diaspora Mission Church": The Rediscovery of Diaspora for the Renewal of Church and Mission in a Secular Era*. Eugene, OR: Wipf and Stock Publishers, 2016.

Lausanne Diaspora Leadership Team. *Scattered to Gather: Embracing the Global Trend of Diaspora*. Rev. Ed. Lausanne Movement and Global Diaspora Network, 2017. Kindle.

Pantoja, Luis L., Sadiri Joy Tira, and Enoch Wan, eds. *Scattered: The Filipino Global Presence*. Manila, Philippines: LifeChange Publishing, 2004.

Pocock, Michael. Introduction to *Diaspora Missiology: Reflections on Reaching the Scattered Peoples of the World*, edited by Michael Pocock and Enoch Wan, xv–xviii. Evangelical Missiological Society Series 23. Pasadena: William Carey Library, 2015.

Pocock, Michael and Enoch Wan, eds. *Diaspora Missiology: Reflections on Reaching the Scattered Peoples of the World*. Evangelical Missiological Society Series 23. Pasadena: William Carey Library, 2015.

Tira, Sadiri Joy. "Diaspora Missiology and the Lausanne Movement at the Dawn of the Twenty-First Century." In *Global Diasporas and Mission*, edited by Chandler H. Im and Amos Yong, 214–27. Regnum Edinburgh Centenary Series 23. Oxford: Regnum Books International, 2014.

Tira, Sadiri Joy, and Tetsunao Yamamori, eds. *Scattered and Gathered: A Global Compendium of Diaspora Missiology*. Regnum Studies in Mission. Eugene, OR: Wipf and Stock Publishers, 2016.

Wan, Enoch. "Diaspora Missiology–A Different Paradigm for the 21st Century." In *Diaspora Missiology: Theory, Methodology, and*

Practice, edited by Enoch Wan, chap. 7. 1st ed. Portland, OR: Institute of Diaspora Studies, 2011. Kindle.

᠆᠆᠆᠆᠆᠆᠆᠆, ed. *Diaspora Missiology: Theory, Methodology, and Practice*. 1st ed. Portland, OR: Institute of Diaspora Studies, 2011. Kindle.

᠆᠆᠆᠆᠆᠆᠆᠆, ed. *Diaspora Missiology: Theory, Methodology, and Practice*. 2nd ed. Portland, OR: Institute of Diaspora Studies, 2014.

᠆᠆᠆᠆᠆᠆᠆᠆. Introduction to *Diaspora Missiology: Theory, Methodology, and Practice*, edited by Enoch Wan, 3–12. 2nd ed. Portland, OR: Institute of Diaspora Studies, 2014.

᠆᠆᠆᠆᠆᠆᠆᠆. "The Phenomenon of Diaspora: Missiological Implications for Christian Missions." In *Scattered: The Filipino Global Presence*, edited by Luis L. Pantoja, Sadiri Joy Tira, and Enoch Wan, 103–21. Manila, Philippines: LifeChange Publishing, 2004.

᠆᠆᠆᠆᠆᠆᠆᠆. "Relational Paradigm for Practicing Diaspora Missions in the 21st Century." In *Diaspora Missiology: Theory, Methodology, and Practice*, edited by Enoch Wan, 191–98. 2nd ed. Portland, OR: Institute of Diaspora Studies, 2014.

Chapter 10

Diaspora Missions and Church Planting: Three Lasting Lessons Learned by Greenhills Christian Fellowship Canada

Narry Santos, Ph.D.

Introduction

The influence of Enoch Wan as missionary, anthropologist, and professor extends significantly to me. I met Enoch through Sadiri Joy Tira and Luis Pantoja, Jr. (two other influential pastors and academics in my life) when I was resident pastor in the first church plant of Greenhills Christian Fellowship[132] (GCF) in the Philippines and when I participated in the first two Filipino International Network[133] Theological Consultations in Seoul, Korea in 2004[134] and in Edmonton, Canada in 2006.[135] My exposure to Enoch and his diaspora missiology shaped the

---

[132] The first GCF church plant, where I served for ten years (1997-2007), is called GCF South Metro (located south of Manila). The main GCF was started in 1978 by David Yount, a Baptist missionary who sought to reach the prime movers in Philippine society. After 15 years, Pastor Dave passed the senior pastoral baton to Luis Pantoja, Jr., who served for 18 years, leaving behind 23 GCF churches after his untimely passing. Pastor Luis was the one who asked me to lead GCF South Metro.

[133] Led by Saditi Joy Tira, the Filipino International Network (FIN) was a catalytic movement to motivate and mobilize Filipinos globally to partner for worldwide mission. For more details about FIN, see Sadiri Joy Tira, "Filipino International Network: A Strategic Model for Filipino Diaspora Glocal Missions," in *Scattered: The Filipino Global Presence*, edited by Luis Pantoja, Jr., Sadiri Joy Tira, and Enoch Wan, 151-172 (Manila: LifeChange, 2004).

[134] The proceedings of this first theological consultation (including my paper "Survey of the Diaspora Occurrences in the Bible and of Their Contexts in Christian Missions") were put together as an edited book entitled *Scattered: The Filipino Global Presence*.

[135] My paper in this second theological consultation ("Exploring the Major Dispersion Terms and Realities in the Bible") became part of Enoch Wan's book *Diaspora Missiology: Theory, Methodology, and Practice* (Portland, OR: Institute of Diaspora Studies Western Seminary, 2011).

trajectory of my diaspora church planting in Canada in 2007–2013. Such exposure also opened opportunities for me to write about diaspora missions in edited books [36] and academic journals,[137] in light of our church planting story through GCF Canada.[138]

I remember three occasions when God used Enoch to bless me in my academic journey. First, when I was already a church planter and pastor in Toronto, Enoch asked me to write a journal article with him on the Gospel of Mark (which is my primary research interest) using his missio-relational approach of reading the Bible. I count it a privilege to have co-authored this article with Enoch.[139] Second, when I asked him for advice on my Ph.D. dissertation on Philippine Studies, he (as a wise anthropologist) counseled me to write it in Pilipino (the national language in the Philippines) since I was researching on an indigenous religious group at that time.[140] Had I written the dissertation in English,

---

[136] As a result of our initial diaspora church planting in six Canadian cities (2007-2013), we were able to share these experiences in various publications: Narry F. Santos, "What's a Missionary Doing in Canada?" in *Green Shoots out of Dry Ground: Growing a New Future for the Church in Canada*, edited by John Bowen, 95-108 (Eugene, OR: Wipf & Stock, 2013); Narry F. Santos, "'Diaspora Missions': Contemporary Missiological Significance of the People on the Move," in *Rejection: God's Refugees in Biblical and Contemporary Perspective*, edited by Stanley E. Porter, 191-208, McMaster Divinity College Press New Testament Series (Eugene, OR: Pickwick, 2014); Sadiri Joy Tira, and Narry F. Santos. "Diaspora Church-Planting in a Multicultural City: A Case Study of Greenhills Christian Fellowship," in *Reflecting God's Glory Together: Diversity in Evangelical Mission*, edited by Scott Moreau and Beth Snodderly, 63-90, Evangelical Missiological Society Series 19 (Pasadena, CA: William Carey, 2011); Narry F. Santos, and Eunice L. Irwin. "A Filipino Congregation in Diaspora as Church-Planting Revitalization Movement," in *Revitalization amid Diaspora (Consultation Three: Explorations in the World Christian Revitalization Movements)*, edited by J. Steven O'Malley, 37-57 (Lexington, KY: Emeth, 2013).

[137] Here is my journal article on diaspora and Christian mission: Narry F. Santos, "Diaspora in the New Testament and its Impact on Christian Mission." *Torch Trinity Journal* 13, no. 1 (2010): 3-18.

[138] After ten years of planting and pastoring GCF South Metro and after helping to give birth to three other church plants farther south of Manila (GCF Batangas; GCF Parañaque; GCF Santa Rosa), I (along with my family) was sent by GCF Philippines in April 2007 to do more church planting in Canada.

[139] This is the co-authored article: Enoch Wan, and Narry F. Santos, "A Missio-Relational Reading of Mark," *Occasional Bulletin* 24, no. 2 (2011): 1-17.

[140] This is the title of my dissertation written in Pilipino: "*Tagapamagitan: Ilaw sa Landas ng Pagiging Makadiyos, Makatao, at Makabayan ng Pilipino*

many of the local terms of the religious group could have been lost in translation. Third, Enoch was the one who recommended me to the board of the Evangelical Missiological Society (EMS) to serve as VP of EMS Canada beginning 2017. This role has allowed me to engage missiologists, pastors, and reflective practitioners in the Canadian context in order to reflect collaboratively and write on relevant missiological issues.[141] Thus, through these three occasions, Enoch has extended his influence in shaping and expanding my ministry in North America and the Philippines.

Diaspora Missions and GCF Canada Church Planting Lessons

Diaspora missions has been a strategic approach in our Filipino-Canadian church planting story through GCF Canada. In this paper, I will highlight three lasting lessons we learned in our diaspora missions journey in the first seven years (2007-2013). Before going to these diaspora church planting lessons, it is important to first understand why diaspora missions is a strategic and relevant approach of reaching the diaspora in Canada.

(Ayon sa Pananampalataya ng Kapatirang ang Litaw na Katalinuhan)" ("Mediator: Light in the Way Toward the Filipino's Love for God, People, and Country [According to the Faith of the Brilliant Knowledge Brotherhood]." Unpublished Ph.D. dissertation, Philippines Studies, University of the Philippines, 2006.

[141] Enoch's recommendation has allowed me to be part of putting together EMS compendiums, which are as follows: Narry F. Santos, and Xenia Ling-Yee Chan (eds.), *The Past and Future of Evangelical Mission: Academy, Agency, Assembly, and Agora Perspectives from Canada*, Evangelical Missiological Society Monograph Series 15 (Eugene, OR: Pickwick, 2022); Kenneth Nehrbass, Aminta Arrington, and Narry F. Santos (eds.), *Advancing Models of Missions: Evaluating the Past and Looking to the Future*, Evangelical Missiological Society Series 29 (Pasadena, CA: William Carey, 2021); Narry F. Santos, and Mark Naylor (eds.), *Mission Amid Global Crises: Academy, Agency, and Assembly Perspectives from Canada* (Toronto, ON: Tyndale Academic Press, 2020); Narry F. Santos, and Mark Naylor (eds.), *Mission and Evangelism in a Secularizing World: Academy, Agency, and Assembly Perspectives from Canada*, Evangelical Missiological Society Monograph Series 2 (Eugene, OR: Pickwick Publications, 2019). Enoch Wan gave the foreword in the last compendium from this list.

Diaspora Realities in Canada

Unrelenting migration is a global reality for the 21st century, despite the recent disruptive realities of the COVID-19 pandemic. According to the World Migration Report 2022 of the International Organization for Migration, "The current global estimate is that there were around 281 million international migrants in the world in 2020, which equates to 3.6 per cent of the global population."[142] Overall, the estimated number of international migrants has increased over the past five decades. The total estimated 281 million people living in a country other than their countries of birth in 2020 was 128 million more than in 1990 (120% increase in 30 years) and over three times the estimated number in 1970.[143]

Canada is also experiencing immigration influx. According to Statistics Canada's 2021 Census, there are 36,991,981 people who reported living in Canada. From 2016 to 2021, the population increased by 1.84 million (or 5.2%).[144] Just over 1.3 million new immigrants settled permanently in Canada from 2016 to 2021, the highest number of recent immigrants recorded in a Canadian census.[145] Among the 10 places of birth reported by new immigrants in 2021, the top three are India (though it was number two in 2016), the Philippines (though it was number one in 2016), and China.

The Filipinos are a growing number of immigrants in Canada. According to the 2021 National Household Survey, there are 957,000 people of Filipino descent living in Canada (or 2.6% of the country's

---

[142] International Organization for Migration (IOM), "World Migration Report 2022 (Migration and Migrants: A Global Overview)," Geneva, IOM. Accessed June 17, 2025. https://publications.iom.int/books/world-migration-report-2022-chapter-2.

[143] Ibid. the International Organization for Migration called 2015 as "The Year of the Migrant."

[144] Statistics Canada, "Key Indicators: Census of Population 2021 Census Data," modified May 7, 2025 https://www12.statcan.gc.ca/census-recensement/index-eng.cfm, accessed June 17, 2025.

[145] Statistics Canada, "Canada Welcomes Historic Number of Newcomers in 2022," modified January 3, 2023 (https://www.canada.ca/en/immigration-refugees-citizenship/news/2022/12/canada-welcomes-historic-number-of-newcomers-in-2022.html), accessed June 17, 2025.

total population).¹⁴⁶ Moreover, during the 2021 census, 757,410 reported they were born in the Philippines and had migrated to Canada, making the Philippines is the third largest source country for immigration to Canada, following India and China.¹⁴⁷ They are also the largest Southeast-Asian ethnic group in Canada.¹⁴⁸ Just over seven in ten Filipinos (72.6%) immigrated to Canada in the previous 20 years; nearly three-quarters were born in the Philippines (73.9%), while others were born in Canada (24.7%). More than half (58.4%) reported Tagalog as their mother tongue, alone or with other languages, and 44.1% reported English.¹⁴⁹

Given these multicultural and Filipino-Canadian diaspora realities, such trend is attracting more Filipinos and other ethnic groups to consider multicultural Canada as their new homeland. Thus, there is a need to understand how to creatively engage various ethnicities in God's diaspora missions. It is in this context that our GCF Canada church planting story is set. In the next section, I will share GCF Canada's three life-changing church planting lessons that relate directly to diaspora missions.¹⁵⁰

---

[146] Statistics Canada. "The Canadian Census: A Rich Portrait of the Country's Religious and Ethnocultural Diversity," modified October 26, 2022 (https://www150.statcan.gc.ca/n1/daily-quotidien/221026/dq221026b-eng.htm), accessed June 17, 2025.

[147] Statistics Canada, "Filipino Canadians Proud with a Strong Sense of Belonging," modified June 19, 2023 (https://www.statcan.gc.ca/o1/en/plus/3883-filipino-canadian-proud-strong-sense-belonging), accessed June 17, 2025.

[148] Statistics Canada, *National Household Survey (NHS) Profile, Canada, 2011*, modified May 24, 2018 (https://www12.statcan.gc.ca/nhs-enm/2011/dp-pd/prof/index.cfm?Lang=E), accessed June 17, 2025.

[149] Statistics Canada, "The Canadian Census."

[150] For an expanded version of these three lasting lessons and for more details on the GCF Canada story, see Narry F. Santos, "A Mission, Migration, and Multiplying Movement," in *From the Margins to the Centre: The Diaspora Effect*, edited by Michael Krause with Narry Santos and Robert Cousins, 110-122 (Toronto, ON: Tyndale Academic Press, 2018).

Three Lasting Lessons on Diaspora Missions

In presenting these lessons, I will use the diaspora missions framework developed by Enoch Wan.[151] His framework was adopted by the Lausanne Diasporas Leadership Team of the Lausanne Movement and was presented at the third Lausanne Congress on World Evangelization in Cape Town, South Africa on October 16-24, 2010, as a booklet entitled *Scattered to Gather: Embracing the Global Trend of Diaspora*.[152]

The diaspora missions framework has three components; namely: (1) mission **to** the diaspora (i.e., mission by the host countries to reach the diaspora); (2) mission **through** the diaspora (i.e., mission by the diaspora to reach the same diaspora group); and (3) mission **beyond** the diaspora (i.e., mission by the diaspora cross-culturally and inter-culturally, reaching members of the host country and other ethnic groups in their context).[153]

Lesson #1 (Mission to the Diaspora): Seeking Intentional Partnerships

Under the mission-to-the diaspora component of the diaspora missions framework, we learned this major lesson: the value of intentional partnerships. We discovered that effective mission to the diaspora happens when there is collaboration among the 3A's (i.e., **A**ssembly [local church]; **A**gency [denomination/missions group]; **A**cademy [seminary/Bible college]).

When we started GCF Toronto in 2007, we realized that we needed to be part of a bigger family in Canada—a family that knows who we are, our dreams and needs. So, we affiliated with the Canadian Baptists of Ontario and Quebec (CBOQ), which also later became the family for our churches in Peel and York regions. After three years, GCF was introduced to the Canadian Baptists of Western Canada (CBWC), which served as the bigger family for our churches in Vancouver, Calgary, and

---

[151] Wan defines diaspora missions this way: "Christians' participation in God's redemptive mission to evangelize their kinsmen on the move, and through them to reach out to natives in their homelands and beyond" (Wan, *Diaspora Missiology*, 5).

[152] Lausanne Diasporas Leadership Team (LDLT), *Scattered to Gather: Embracing the Global Trend of Diaspora* (Manila, Philippines: LifeChange, 2010).

[153] LDLT, *Scattered to Gather*, 27-29.

Winnipeg. We saw how the Assembly (GCF) and the Agency (CBOQ and CBWC) developed a relationship of trust.

When our GCF Toronto leaders saw the need to become missional and multicultural in doing diaspora missions, God opened up training and coaching relationships with the Tyndale Intercultural Ministries (TIM) Centre, through the leadership of Robert Cousins. The TIM Centre creatively offered the two-year certificate and diploma program called "Missional Ministry and Church Leadership" for our 20 GCF leaders. Robert also journeyed with me as pastor and with our church leaders by coaching us and by serving in GCF Toronto for eight years. Such partnership forged the Assembly (GCF) and Academy (TIM Centre) collaboration. What even solidified the training experiment was the involvement of CBOQ in providing financial support for the GCF leaders throughout the program. Thus, the three-part partnership of the Assembly (GCF), Agency (CBOQ), and Academy (TIM Centre) was born. This certificate/diploma program, which has now served more than 400 students, continues to be a model of the mission-to-the-diaspora component of diaspora missions.

The impact of intentional partnerships to diaspora missions is that it opens more doors of opportunity in serving the diaspora together. The Academy can interface better with the Assembly by listening to the joys, struggles, and needs of diaspora church planters, pastors, and leaders, and can collaborate more with the Agency, by convening relevant dialogue with mission groups and denominations. Such renewed efforts to work together can help us fulfill more meaningfully and strategically God's mission to the diaspora in Canada.

Lesson #2 (Mission through the Diaspora): Showing Missional Ministry through Hospitality

Aside from learning the value of intentional partnerships in the mission-to-the-diaspora component of the diaspora missions framework, I also appreciate this second lesson that we learned from the mission-through-the-diaspora segment: the value of missional ministry through hospitality. Amos Yong argues that the study of a missional hermeneutic should also include a theology of hospitality (welcoming the stranger).[154] He writes, "Christian hospitality is grounded in the hospitable God who through the Incarnation has received creation to himself and through Pentecost has given himself to creation."[155]

Just as there is a need to develop a missional theology of hospitality, there also needs to be a missional practice of hospitality. Christine Pohl emphasizes that as a way of life, act of life, and expression of faith, our hospitality reflects and anticipates God's welcome. She also contends that the practice of hospitality often involves small deaths and little resurrections. She states, "When we offer hospitality to strangers, we welcome them.... Such welcome involves attentive listening and mutual sharing of lives and life stories. It requires an openness of heart, a willingness to make one's life visible to others, and a generosity of time and resources."[156]

To apply the practice of hospitality in our GCF Toronto context, we sought to connect with and engage the international students in our community. At that time, we were meeting on Sundays at the Centennial College Residence and Conference Centre in Scarborough. I asked the director of the centre how we could help the more than 200 international students there. She willingly opened doors for us to help the students feel at home. She asked our church to help carry the luggage of the new students from the parking lot to their dorm rooms. Later she gave us permission to host a thanksgiving dinner for them at the main hall, a luncheon for them on the Family Day weekend and a Good Friday event at the reception area. She also welcomed our effort to invite a Christian immigration barrister, in order to talk with the graduating international students and to answer their questions on immigration.

What I find encouraging in this ministry of hospitality is that the director, after seeing our efforts to serve the international students, told me, "Your church has been doing these things for the students and you

---

[154] For more details about this, see Amos Yong, *Hospitality and the Other: Pentecost, Christian Practices, and the Neighbor* (Maryknoll, NY: Orbis, 2008).

[155] Amos Yong, "The Spirit of Hospitality: Pentecostal Perspectives toward a Performative Theology of Interreligious Encounter" *Missiology* 35 (January 2007): 62.

[156] Christine Pohl, *Making Room: Recovering Hospitality as a Christian Tradition* (Grand Rapids, MI: Eerdmans, 1999), 13.

have not asked us for anything back." Then she offered us free use of one room weekly, in order to continue meeting with interested students. So, we accepted her offer and conducted weekly Tuesday night gatherings called "Chips and Chow." This fun and relaxed time with the international students provided free pizza, hotdogs, and chips, offered English practice time and short videos on topics that are relevant to them. We also partnered with a couple of staff from the International Student Ministries Canada to coach us how to serve the students well.

Missional ministry through hospitality allows us to get to know our neighbours, to be aware of their needs and interests, and to add value to our community. It opens more doors to engage our neighbourhood in loving deeds of kindness through the diaspora. Thus, the good news becomes adorned with good works that can attract the diaspora to the Jesus whom we know, love, and serve.

Lesson #3 (Mission Beyond the Diaspora): Starting Multicultural Ministry

The third lesson that we learned under the mission-beyond-the-diaspora component is this: the value of multicultural ministry. In GCF Canada's case, we needed to learn how to reach beyond the Filipino diaspora.

I learned this lesson the hard way. Right after my family and I were picked up at the Pearson International Airport in April 2007, the church leader who picked us up told me point-blank, "Pastor, you cannot start a Filipino church in Toronto." I was taken aback, but I managed to ask, "Why not?" At the back of my mind, I knew I was in trouble, because that was all I knew—planting a Filipino church. I was being told this, after I left a thriving ten-year church ministry in the Philippines, after I uprooted my family from the comfort and safety of a Christian church, school, and friends, and after we travelled halfway around the globe.

When he replied, "It does not make sense to plant a Filipino church in one of the most multicultural cities of the world," I knew I was in trouble. After being a full-time pastor for 13 years at that time, I had to unlearn what I knew and then be willing to learn how to be a new church planter in Canada. But that reality check challenged me, along with the initial core leaders of GCF Toronto, to enter into a period and process of discernment. We basically asked God, "What kind of church do you want us to be in Canada?"

After this season of discernment, we landed on our 3M ethos: (1) **M**issional; and (2) **M**etropolitan; and (3) **M**ulticultural. By "missional," we mean that we commit to be on mission with God by intentionally multiplying churches and incarnationally adding value to the community where we belong by serving the people there. By "metropolitan," we mean that we commit to intentionally go where the people are flocking and to strategically minister in the urban centres (i.e., targeting the cities). By "multicultural," we mean that we commit to intentionally reach out to the different diaspora groups and those from our host country of Canada.

To help fulfill our multicultural mandate, the TIM Centre again came alongside GCF through training and coaching in multicultural ministry. I remember the two words that Robert told me to describe this kind of ministry: "difficult" and "slow." Those two words went against my preferred style of ministry. I wanted an easy and fast multicultural ministry. Robert assured me, though, that he would journey with the church leaders and me in this difficult and slow journey. Looking at where we are now and where we need to be, we still have a long, long way to go in this journey, but it is worth the trip. A key step to this trip is taking the Intercultural Development Inventory (IDI), an assessment tool that measures orientation to cultural differences. The IDI has helped me and our leaders to move toward an intentional journey toward intercultural competence or fluency.

Conclusion

In the first seven years of GCF Canada (2007-2013), we have discovered three church planting lessons—seeking intentional partnerships; showing missional ministry through hospitality; and starting multicultural ministry—as foundational in pursuing diaspora missions in Canada. Looking back, after 17 years of church planting through our nine GCF churches in Canada (five in the east [Toronto; Mississauga; Vaughan; Ajax; and Oakville] and four in the west [Vancouver; Calgary; two in Winnipeg]), we still see the value of these lessons. Our prayer is that our younger leaders will keep seeing and living out these lessons for their own generation and the succeeding ones, not just for Filipino-Canadians but for other ethnic and cultural groups as well. Thank you, Enoch, for influencing us to go beyond ourselves through diaspora missions.

Bibliography

Bowen, John, ed. *Green Shoots out of Dry Ground: Growing a New Future for the Church in Canada*. Eugene, OR: Wipf & Stock, 2013.

International Organization for Migration (IOM). "World Migration Report 2022 (Migration and Migrants: A Global Overview." Geneva, IOM. https://publications.iom.int/books/world-migration-report-2022-chapter-2.

Krause, Michael, with Narry Santos and Robert Cousins, eds. *From the Margins to the Centre: The Diaspora Effect*. Toronto, ON: Tyndale Academic Press, 2018.

Lausanne Diasporas Leadership Team, *Scattered to Gather: Embracing the Global Trend of Diaspora*. Manila, Philippines: LifeChange, 2010.

Moreau, Scott, and Beth Snodderly, eds. *Reflecting God's Glory Together: Diversity in Evangelical Mission*. Evangelical Missiological Society Series 19. Pasadena, CA: William Carey, 2011.

Nehrbass, Kenneth, Aminta Arrington, and Narry F. Santos, eds. *Advancing Models of Missions: Evaluating the Past and Looking to the Future*. Evangelical Missiological Society Series 29. Pasadena, CA: William Carey, 2021.

O'Malley, J. Steven, ed. *Revitalization amid Diaspora (Consultation Three: Explorations in the World Christian Revitalization Movements)*. Lexington, KY: Emeth, 2013.

Pantoja, Luis, Jr., Sadiri Joy Tira, and Enoch Wan, eds. *Scattered: The Filipino Global Presence*. Manila: LifeChange, 2004.

Pohl, Christine. *Making Room: Recovering Hospitality as a Christian Tradition*. Grand Rapids, M: Eerdmans, 1999.

Porter, Stanley E., ed. *Rejection: God's Refugees in Biblical and Contemporary Perspective*. McMaster Divinity College Press New Testament Series. Eugene, OR: Pickwick, 2014.

Santos, Narry F. "'Diaspora Missions': Contemporary Missiological Significance of the People on the Move." In *Rejection: God's Refugees in Biblical and Contemporary Perspective*, edited by Stanley E. Porter, 191-208. McMaster Divinity College Press New Testament Series. Eugene, OR: Pickwick, 2014.

―――――. "Diaspora in the New Testament and its Impact on Christian Mission." *Torch Trinity Journal* 13, no. 1 (2010): 3-18.

―――――. "Exploring the Major Dispersion Terms and Realities in the Bible." In *Diaspora Missiology: Theory, Methodology, and Practice*, edited by Enoch Wan, 21-38. Portland, OR: Institute of Diaspora Studies Western Seminary, 2011.

―――――. "A Mission, Migration, and Multiplying Movement." In *From the Margins to the Centre: The Diaspora Effect*, edited by Michael Krause with Narry Santos and Robert Cousins, 110-122. Toronto, ON: Tyndale Academic Press, 2018.

―――――. "Survey of the Diaspora Occurrences in the Bible and of Their Contexts in Christian Missions." In *Scattered: The Filipino Global Presence*, edited by Luis Pantoja, Jr., Sadiri Joy Tira, and Enoch Wan, 53-66. Manila: LifeChange, 2004.

―――――. "*Tagapamagitan: Ilaw sa Landas ng Pagiging Makadiyos, Makatao, at Makabayan ng Pilipino (Ayon sa Pananampalataya ng Kapatirang ang Lita~ na Katalinuhan)*" ("Mediator: Light in the Way Toward the Filipino's Love for God, People, and Country [According to the Faith of the Brilliant Knowledge Brotherhood]." Unpublished Ph.D. dissertation, Philippines Studies, University of the Philippines, 2006.

―――――. "What's a Missionary Doing in Canada?" In *Green Shoots out of Dry Ground: Growing a New Future for the Church in Canada*, edited by John Bowen, 95-108. Eugene, OR: Wipf & Stock, 2013.

Santos, Narry F., and Eunice L. Irwin. "A Filipino Congregation in Diaspora as Church-Planting Revitalization Movement." In *Revitalization amid Diaspora (Consultation Three: Explorations in the World Christian Revitalization Movements)*, edited by J. Steven O'Malley, 37-57. Lexington, KY: Emeth, 2013.

Santos, Narry F., and Mark Naylor, eds. *Mission Amid Global Crises: Academy, Agency, and Assembly Perspectives from Canada*. Toronto, ON: Tyndale Academic Press, 2020.

⎯⎯⎯⎯. *Mission and Evangelism in a Secularizing World: Academy, Agency, and Assembly Perspectives from Canada*. Evangelical Missiological Society Monograph Series 2. Eugene, OR: Pickwick, 2019.

Santos, Narry F., and Xenia Ling-Yee Chan, eds. *The Past and Future of Evangelical Mission: Academy, Agency, Assembly, and Agora Perspectives from Canada*. Evangelical Missiological Society Monograph Series 15. Eugene, OR: Pickwick, 2022.

Statistics Canada. "The Canadian Census: A Rich Portrait of the Country's Religious and Ethnocultural Diversity," modified October 26, 2022. https://www150.statcan.gc.ca/n1/daily-quotidien/221026/dq221026b-eng.htm.

⎯⎯⎯⎯. "Canada Welcomes Historic Number of Newcomers in 2022." Modified January 3, 2023. https://www.canada.ca/en/immigration-refugees-citizenship/news/2022/12/canada-welcomes-historic-number-of-newcomers-in-2022.html.

⎯⎯⎯⎯. "Filipino Canadians Proud with a Strong Sense of Belonging." Modified June 19, 2023. https://www.statcan.gc.ca/o1/en/plus/3883-filipino-canadian-proud-strong-sense-belonging.

⎯⎯⎯⎯. "Key Indicators: Census of Population 2021 Census Data." Modified May 7, 2025. https://www12.statcan.gc.ca/census-recensement/index-eng.cfm.

⎯⎯⎯⎯. "*National Household Survey (NHS) Profile, Canada, 2011*, modified May 24, 2018 (https://www12.statcan.gc.ca/nhs-enm/2011/dp-pd/prof/index.cfm?Lang=E.

Tira, Sadiri Joy, and Narry F. Santos. "Diaspora Church-Planting in a Multicultural City: A Case Study of Greenhills Christian Fellowship." In *Reflecting God's Glory Together: Diversity in Evangelical Mission*, edited by Scott Moreau and Beth Snodderly,

63-90. Evangelical Missiological Society Series 19. Pasadena, CA: William Carey, 2011.

Wan, Enoch, ed. *Diaspora Missiology: Theory, Methodology, and Practice*. Portland, OR: Institute of Diaspora Studies Western Seminary, 2011.

Wan, Enoch, and Narry F. Santos. "A Missio-Relational Reading of Mark." *Occasional Bulletin* 24, no. 2 (2011): 1-17.

Yong, Amos. *Hospitality and the Other: Pentecost, Christian Practices, and the Neighbor*. Maryknoll, NY: Orbis, 2008.

————. "The Spirit of Hospitality: Pentecostal Perspectives toward a Performative Theology of Interreligious Encounter." *Missiology* 35 (January 2007): 55-73.

Chapter 11

One Meal, One Prayer, One Neighborhood at a Time. A Case Study of Relational Mission

Sadiri Tonyvic Tira

Dedication

To Dr. Enoch Wan,

A family friend, and guide who first introduced me to the relational paradigm over coffee just before the pandemic, and whose scholarship and life have deeply shaped both my theology and practice.

This case study is offered in gratitude for your enduring influence and the legacy of a truly incarnational witness.

Abstract

This case study explores Supper Club—a polymorphic congregation in Edmonton formed during the COVID-19 pandemic through relational presence, hospitality, and prayer. Rather than being planted, it was birthed—emerging from everyday mission around the table. Informed by Dr. Enoch Wan's Relational Missionary Training, Supper Club reflects how Millennials and Gen Z are forming self-governing, Spirit-led communities in a post-Christendom context. Through shared meals, discernment, and discipleship, Supper Club offers a practical, incarnational model of church for today.

Definition of Terms

- *Table Group* - A recurring, meal-based gathering that integrates prayer, Scripture, friendship, and open conversation. At Supper Club, table groups are disciple-forming communities that serve as formative spaces for leadership, discernment, and mission.

- *Polymorphic Church* - A theologically unified church that takes diverse forms—meeting in homes, campuses, parks, or online—adapted to cultural and contextual needs. Supper Club reflects this non-institutional model, prioritizing relational presence over programmatic uniformity.
- *Incarnational Presence* - A missional posture modeled after Jesus' ministry, emphasizing humility, proximity, and relational commitment. Supper Club embodies this by prioritizing "being with" over "doing for" others, embedding gospel witness in everyday relationships.
- *Post-Christendom* - A sociocultural context where Christianity no longer holds dominant cultural influence. In post-Christendom cities like Edmonton, Supper Club responds by fostering trust through story, hospitality, and relational engagement rather than institutional authority.
- *Relational Missionary Training* - A paradigm for local and cross-cultural mission formation, developed by Dr. Enoch Wan, which emphasizes embedded presence, cultural fluency, and long-term discipleship. Supper Club builds on this by equipping laypeople to engage missionally within their own neighborhoods and networks.

Where Mission Begins: Stories from the Table

Supper Club wasn't built around a program—it was built around a table. Most key moments happened in living rooms and parks, not on stages. These aren't stories of big campaigns, but of everyday people living as relational missionaries.

Keith didn't plan to stand up. At a regular Supper Club potluck, I invited anyone needing prayer to stand—with eyes closed. Keith thought, *"Why not?"* Then came the curveball: *"Open your eyes."* He was the only one standing. That moment became a turning point. "Church isn't a stage," he later said. *"It's a table."*

That table kept showing up. As students at the University of Alberta, Keith and Kessiah began attending Thankful Thursdays—a weekly meal marked by gratitude and open fellowship across cultures and faiths. About 15 students came each week, many from Muslim backgrounds. It started with pizza and conversation but became a place to be real.

Eventually, they began leading—offering halal and gluten-free meals, and creating space where people felt safe to share. During Ramadan, they over-ordered halal food. Students took it home to break their fast, and one returned just to say thank you. *"The table might've looked like just a meal,"* Kessiah said, *"but it became a space where people shared their struggles and gratitude."*

Stories like these aren't exceptions—they're examples of how the Spirit uses availability over ability. Weekly faithfulness becomes witness. Hospitality becomes mission.

Joey and Steph are another example. In 2022, they faced the heartbreak of an infertility journey and a devastating miscarriage diagnosis. But their Supper Club community—a relational network of gatherings centered on meals, prayer, and mission didn't just pray once. They persisted—laying hands on them and checking in often. When a follow-up scan revealed their baby was alive, it wasn't just a medical miracle. It was a shared testimony of God's presence. Their daughter was born that December, a tangible reminder of what happens when community doesn't look away from suffering but instead invites Jesus into it.

While some stories begin in crisis, others start with a simple yes—where obedience meets opportunity in the ordinary. Eleesha—a young dentist who grew up in the church but began to see incarnational presence differently through Supper Club. What struck her was how simple evangelism and mission could be—hospitality instead of a script. She started by joining prayer walks and serving meals to international students with her husband. Over time, she began taking initiative: inviting students to eat meals in a home and eventually responding to a need for free dental services among refugee families—complete with a meal from Supper Club. Her story shows how mission grows through availability, not expertise.

Supper Club also sends. Joshua and Susan, supported spiritually and financially, now serve students at UBC—leading groups, discipling others, and baptizing new believers. Our prayer coach, Dr. David Chotka, recently partnered with us to distribute 5,000 prayer books in Vietnamese to networks across Vietnam and Cambodia. Whether across the street or overseas, the DNA remains: presence, prayer, and faithful friendship.

Barriers to Belonging: What We Encountered

Each story began with a challenge. Students faced loneliness. Young professionals lacked models of lived mission. Couples needed more than sympathy. Our neighbourhoods, reeling from pandemic disconnection, longed for community.

In more traditional church expressions, challenges like these are often addressed through structured programs—sermons, events, and institutional models of care. There's value in those systems. But Supper Club was born from a conviction that the church can also be lived differently: not from a stage, but from a table. This is what we call *a table-shaped way of being the church*—where people are not passive attendees but active participants in prayer, presence, and shared life. Instead of waiting for the perfect plan or position, Supper Club affirms a context where everyday believers can act on mission now. Through simple rhythms like shared meals, honest conversation, prayer walks, and consistent hospitality, people begin to practice the way of Jesus with others—right where they are.

Practicing Presence: What We Did

Rather than launch another church service or curriculum, Supper Club invites and equips people to start meals where they are—with what they have. Some were students on campus, others were families in townhouse or new developments. Some happened in homes, others in university lounges or public parks. A core rhythm emerged: eat together, share honestly, listen for God's voice, pray simply, stay curious. We call this table groups (our term for intentional, recurring meal-based gatherings that nurture faith and friendship)—a simple framework for gathering that involves sharing a meal, engaging in open conversation, praying together, and remaining curious about each other's stories and journeys. It was designed to be flexible enough for newcomers to faith, deep enough for mature believers, and safe enough for those with questions or doubts. Far more than the name of a church, it is a method of evangelism, a discipleship pathway, and missional expression.

In 2024 alone, Thankful Thursdays continued weekly. City-wide prayer walks covered 13 Edmonton neighbourhoods. Bible studies took root not because of pressure but because of prayerful discernment. People began leading their own Bible studies, without waiting for permission.

Our approach isn't perfect. But it's personal. And that's the point. Each small act—bringing soup, asking a good question, inviting someone back next week—became part of a larger organic story. These rhythms of hospitality weren't just activities—they became the training ground for transformation.

From Belonging to Sending: Transformation Through Community

Discipleship, in our experience, doesn't start at belief—it starts with belonging. People often begin by bringing food to a meal, joining a prayer walk, or simply showing up. Through these relational rhythms, transformation unfolds.

We describe this as a discipleship pathway—a relational journey that begins with presence, grows through participation, and leads toward leadership and, eventually, sending. But that pathway isn't taught in a classroom—it's formed around the table. Table Groups became more than gathering points; they became training grounds where people practiced presence, led with care, and discerned Spirit-led action in their own contexts.

While regular Bible engagement remains low among younger generations, openness is growing. According to the American Bible Society, *81% of Gen Z youth and 74% of Gen Z adults express curiosity about Scripture, even if they don't read it regularly* (American Bible Society 2021). Supper Club provides a natural setting for that curiosity—through shared meals, peer dialogue, prayer, and spiritual inquiry. Rather than handing out leadership manuals, we invite people to listen—practically to one another, spiritually to God. In this environment, discernment isn't top-down; it's formed through Spirit-led community.

Recent studies affirm what we've seen: *57% of Millennials and Gen Z Christians say they value strong relationships in church more than traditional sermons* (Barna Group 2024). This deeply aligns with Supper

Club's approach. Table Groups aren't just gatherings—they are relational hubs where faith, service, and discipleship unfold naturally.

Eleesha's story reflects this well. Without seeing herself as a leader, she showed up—serving meals, walking and praying, and welcoming others. Over time, her eyes opened to how God was using her availability. When she saw a gap in dental care for refugee families, she didn't just notice the need—she responded. In this way, Supper Club isn't just growing church membership; it's forming everyday missionaries—long before people might call themselves that.

This mirrors broader generational values. According to the Millennial Impact Report, *53% of Millennials want their passions and talents recognized and engaged* (Achieve and The Case Foundation 2014). Supper Club taps into that impulse—not through complex programs but by inviting people to serve and lead right where they are. As Steph reflected, *"[This way of church] has really affirmed mine and [my husband's] calling to use our house as a refuge for His people."*

These small acts add up. In 2024, over 50 international students joined meals and spiritual conversations. One student said, *"This is the first time I've felt like I belonged in Canada."* Others began asking about Jesus, reading Scripture, and sharing with friends.

At one end-of-summer celebration, three spontaneous baptisms took place—unplanned but embraced with joy and tears. Young adults stepped into incarnational mission, often without titles or formal training. Prayer became less programmed and more present—emerging through Spirit-led conversations and shared moments. In August, prayer walks spanned 13 Edmonton neighborhoods, involving over 60 participants praying for peace and healing in their communities.

Joey and Steph's daughter is a clear sign of transformation. But so is Eleesha organizing dental care. So is a new believer now leading a Bible study. So is a child in Central McDougall receiving a backpack and hot meal.

During our second summer in Central McDougall—a diverse, low-income neighborhood—Supper Club hosted weekly meals in a public park and distributed school supplies to over 40 children. A volunteer recalled, *"One mom said this was the first time her kids were excited to go back to school, wondering when we would return. That meant everything."*

These aren't flashy numbers. They're personal markers of transformation. They reflect what Lesslie Newbigin called a *"hermeneutic of the gospel"*—a lived witness that makes the good news visible. Supper Club contributes to community resilience: restoring trust, deepening relationships, and offering stability through hospitality. These aren't metrics. They're people. And their lives and communities are being reshaped. This is the slow, faithful work of the gospel lived out: a theology practiced around tables, rooted in presence, and open to the Spirit.

In Step with Wan: A Shared Heart for Mission

Wan's paradigm equips missionaries for long-term cultural immersion. Supper Club offers a local complement: near-term spiritual hospitality that empowers people to live missionally in their own neighborhoods. You don't need a visa—just a table. No program—just a meal.

Through our *Vision 2030* framework, Supper Club equips people with simple tools, coaching, and encouragement to start Table Groups in their homes, dorms, or neighborhoods—reflecting a *"table-shaped way of being the church"* (Supper Club 2025). Whether through starter kits, prayer guides, or one-on-one mentoring, Supper Club helps people practice presence, listen well, and follow the Spirit's leading in everyday life.

If Wan's model is long-term cultural embedding, Supper Club's is accessible, relational witness—rooted in meals, prayer, and friendship. While his framework prepares people to cross cultural and linguistic boundaries for sustained discipleship, Supper Club invites people to begin right where they are. We're cultivating the same soil—just starting with what's already in our hands. Both are slow. Both require presence. Wan equips people to cross cultures. Supper Club invites them to cross the street.

Theological Foundations: Scripture at the Table

Underpinning all of this is a scriptural vision of missional discipleship and hospitality rooted in the life and teachings of Jesus. In Luke 14, Jesus tells a parable about a great banquet where the invited guests fail to come, so the host sends his servant to invite *"the poor, the crippled, the blind and the lame"* and compels people from the streets and alleys to fill the table (Luke 14:15-24). This picture of mission is radically inclusive, persistent, and generous—a banquet where everyone is welcome and no seat stays empty for long. Supper Club lives this out around real tables in real neighborhoods, where invitation is a spiritual act and meals become moments of grace.

Romans 12:13 urges believers to *"practice hospitality,"* while Hebrews 13:2 reminds us that by doing so, *"some have entertained angels without knowing it."* The early church in Acts 2:46-47 *"broke bread in their homes and ate together with glad and sincere hearts,"* and it was in these everyday rhythms of worship, fellowship, and meals that *"the Lord added to their number daily."*

This isn't a new strategy. It's a return to the table, to shared lives, to the very places where Jesus so often ministered. And it's here that we've seen the Spirit move—quietly, faithfully, powerfully.

What we've seen is this: mission doesn't require extraordinary people. It requires ordinary people willing to open their lives. You don't need to be trained to be kind. You don't need a platform to be present.

Our meals are more than nourishment. They're both evangelism and discipleship. Our prayers are not just strategic programs—they are our dependence. Our neighborhoods aren't projects—they're our calling.

A Growing Table: The Ongoing Invitation

Supper Club isn't a launchpad—it's a long table. What begins with a simple meal gradually cultivates deep trust, spiritual formation, and multiplying relationships. Through this slow, faithful presence, we've seen neighbours become friends, friends become family, and guests become hosts.

This is the power of a relational missiology lived out in local contexts:

- Mission begins with meals, not membership.

- Availability often outweighs expertise.
- Ordinary rhythms—shared meals, simple prayers, listening presence—become the very grounds where discipleship is forged.
- The table becomes not just a setting, but a formational space—shaping identity, inviting vulnerability, and fostering discernment.

This approach reflects a theological conviction that the Spirit of God often works profoundly in the margins—through presence more than programs, through hospitality more than hierarchy. In this way, Supper Club contributes not just to community development but to ecclesial imagination: rethinking what it means to be the Church in a pluralistic, post-Christendom context.

Discipleship doesn't multiply through formulas. It multiplies through faithfulness - one meal, one prayer, one neighbourhood at a time.

Bibliography:

Barna Group. 2024. "Building Authentic Community Among Gen Z." Barna.com. https://www.barna.com/research/authentic-community-gen-z/ (accessed July 2025).

Achieve and The Case Foundation. 2014. *The 2014 Millennial Impact Report*. Indianapolis: Achieve. https://www.themillennialimpact.com/research/millennial-impact-report-2014/ (accessed July 2025).

American Bible Society. 2021. *State of the Bible: USA 2021*. American Bible Society. https://1s712.americanbible.org/state-of-the-bible/stateofthebible/State_of_the_bible-2021.pdf (accessed July 2025).

Supper Club. 2025. *Vision 2030: A Table-Shaped Way of Being the Church*. Edmonton: Supper Club. https://tithely-media-prod.s3.us-west-1.wasabisys.com/894898/Vision-2030.pdf (accessed July 2025).

Hybridity and Home

"Lord, You have been our dwelling place throughout all generations."
(Psalm 90:1)

Chapter 12

Jewish-Gentile Intermarriage and Family: A Perfect Missiological Opportunity

Tuvya Zaretsky, D.I.S.

Introduction: An Unexpected Mission Field and Approach

The story of Micah* and Alice* is real, though their names have been changed. Their relationship, like many others today, is a complex meeting of cultures and spiritual heritages. Micah, raised in a secular Jewish Los Angeles family, described himself as "spiritual but not religious." Alice came from a Midwest evangelical background. After dating and living together, they married—only then realizing how different their images were for raising children, honoring religious identity, and spiritual life. The tension escalated when his parents turned to Orthodox Judaism and Alice rediscovered her relationship with Jesus.

Reaching a cultural and spiritual impasse, they found www.jewishgentilecouples.com and reached out for guidance. That began a journey of honest questions and relational discipleship—one that has become increasingly common. Over the past 25 years, I've had the privilege of walking alongside hundreds of such couples. And what I have discovered is this:

Jewish-Gentile intermarriage is not merely a sociological trend—it is a Spirit-prepared cross-cultural mission field. While many see these marriages as a threat to Jewish continuity, I see in them a profound opportunity: a safe relational space where gospel witness can flourish, where identity and grace meet and where Jesus-centered discipleship can bring deep reconciliation. For this perspective I want to acknowledge the influence of my mentor, Enoch Wan, who introduced me to this **relational approach to discipleship.**

This essay argues that Jewish-Gentile intermarriage, far from being a threat to Jewish continuity, presents an urgent and strategic opportunity for relational discipleship, incarnational witness, and gospel engagement within the Jewish Diaspora. Drawing from relational theology, diaspora missiology, and real ministry experiences, I hope to mobilize and equip mission-minded Christians to actively respond to what God is doing in this quiet, growing, and gospel-hungry field.

The Biblical Foundations for This Missional Frontier
God's Heart for the Nations Through Israel

Enoch Wan's argument for Relational Theology is helpful for understanding the salvation plan of God. He depicted the *Missio Dei* as "the Triune God pressing Himself out thus showing forth His nature of love, communion, commission (sending) and glory."[157] At its root, the intent of God's creation activity took a relational aim. God in his holiness created humanity for the purpose of engaging with his perfect love and grace. From the very beginning, in Genesis, sin, salvation and the Savior were essential to his salvation plan.

Traumatic tension entered the Biblical narrative when Adam and Eve broke their relationship with the Lord in the Garden of Eden. Their failure to reciprocate God's love was an offence to his glory. He is worthy of perfect trust. In that moment, God demonstrated His grace with the promise of "the Seed of a woman" by whom all could be restored in relationship with Him.[158] That is the seminal description of His intent to provide salvation, sufficient for all, in Jesus on the cross of Calvary.

In the patriarch Abram, the LORD introduces the biblical reader to the line of people through which God would enter human history, divine and human, to accomplish His redemption. He said to Abram, "And in you all the families of the earth shall be blessed".[159]

The people of Israel were sanctified to accomplish God's salvation plan. However, individual Israelites do not participate in that salvation apart from personal faith in the God who extends grace. Nevertheless, the Israelite nation had a two-fold role in the LORD's salvation plan. 1) The nation is the conduit for the blessing of God's personal intervention

---

[157] Enoch Wan. "Relational Theology and Relational Missiology", *Occasional Bulletin* of the Evangelical Missiology Society, Vol 21 #1.
[158] Genesis 3:15
[159] Genesis 12:3

in salvation history through Jesus; 2) The people of Israel are a continual testimony of God's covenant with Abraham before all nations.

Isaiah spoke about God's servant, his chosen Messiah, saying,

> "I, the Lord, have called you in righteousness, and will hold your hand; I will keep you and give you as a covenant to the people, as a light to the Gentiles." [160]

Messiah Yeshua, Jesus, read the same passage to announce his Messianic call at his home synagogue.[161]

Wise and faithful Simeon was waiting for the Messiah when Joseph and Mary brought the baby Jesus into the Jerusalem Temple. He recognized Jesus as the fulfillment of God's salvation plan saying,

> "For my eyes have seen your salvation which you have prepared before the face of all peoples, a light to bring revelation to the Gentiles, and the glory of your people Israel." [162]

The Mystery of the Gospel Revealed Now to All the Nations

New Testament writers speak of the blessing that has come to all the nations including Israel. The Apostle Paul addressed Gentiles who were once *uncircumcised* and "strangers from the covenants of promise" and who have now been "brought near by the blood of Christ (Messiah)."[163] Like a mystery revealed, the good news of salvation in Jesus was first revealed among the Jewish people and now has come to all the nations.[164]

In the *Tanakh*, God spoke of a remnant, *she'arit*, of people who, by faith, were loyal to love God and reciprocate his lovingkindness.[165] In the New Testament, the concept of *remnant* is referred to as "the *elect*," or *elektos* in Greek.

The Apostle Paul highlights the faith that has dawned within a remnant among Israel and the nations through Messiah Jesus. Paul wrote of the LORD'S remnant, in Romans 9-11 saying, "At this present time

---

[160] Isaiah 42:6
[161] Luke 4:18-21
[162] Luke 2:29-32
[163] Ephesians 2:11-13
[164] Ephesians 3:1-7
[165] See for example II Kings 19: 30-31, Ezra 9:8, 14-15; Isaiah 1:9, 10:20-22

there is a remnant according to the election of grace."[166] Throughout those three chapters, Paul remarked on the incredible news that God, at that time, was fulfilling His promise to bring blessing to the Gentiles by faith in Messiah. Just as significant, Paul emphasized God did not reject Israel, which He sanctified by which to deliver His salvation blessing. Today, Gentile believers have a role and an opportunity to bring that salvation message back to a modern remnant among Jewry.[167] For that very reason, we should take note of the current opportunity observed today in the increasing number of Jewish-Gentile intermarriages.

The Rise of Jewish-Gentile Marriages:
The Fields are White Sociological Trends

I became aware of the dramatic demographic changes happening in the Jewish community in 1990. That was the year the Combined Jewish Philanthropies *National Jewish Population Survey* reported an intermarriage rate of 52%.[168] From 1946 - 1990, American Jewish focus was to rebuild Jewish population after the Holocaust. Sociologists hypothesized that acceptance and assimilation into American life changed that priority.

Traditional Jewish community emphasis was on reattaching American Jewry to religious cultural practices and expressions. That was how the *Brandeis University Series on American Jewish History, Culture and Life* measured Jewish identity in 2004.[169]

In contrast, my doctoral work with Drs. Donald K. Smith and Enoch Wan at Western Seminary was to discover the challenges being reported by couples in mixed marriages where only one partner was Jewish.[170] The 2020 Pew Research of American Jewry reported a Jewish intermarriage rate of 72% among non-orthodox Jews between 2010 and 2020.[171] And the Jewish children of those couples are reportedly

---

[166] Romans 11:4-6
[167] Romans 11:11-25
[168] https://www.bjpa.org/content/upload/bjpa/c_c/NJPS%201990%20Highlights.pdf
[169] Fishman, Sylvia Barack. *Double or Nothing? Jewish Families and Mixed Marriage.* (Lebanon, NH: Brandeis University Press) 2004.
[170] Zaretsky, Tuvya with Enoch Wan. *Jewish-Gentile Couples: Trends, Challenges and Hopes.* (Pasadena, CA: Willaim Carey Library) 2004.
[171] https://www.pewresearch.org/religion/2021/05/11/jewish-americans-in-2020/

marrying Gentiles at a rate of 82%.[172] Pew Research estimated that nearly half (47%) of all American Jews in 2020 were intermarried. In America, Jewish intermarriage has become the norm and is no longer an exception. The missiological implications are pointing to an incredible opportunity for ministry.

Cultural Realities and a Missiological Opportunity

My work at Western Seminary sought to understand the challenges reported by Jewish-Gentile Couples. Two significant challenges JGCs reported were, 1) Difficulty for finding a mutually satisfying spiritual harmony between partners and 2) Creating a family experience that equally honored Jewish identity and the religious culture of a non-Jewish partner.[173] These revealed two clear, need based entry points for missional engagement. Here, Wan's *Relational Theology* is helpful to understand how the salvation plan of God is for all nations—Jews and Gentiles.[174] Relationship with the God who is, as opposed to a religious ideology, is the LORD'S unique and sufficient intent.

Pew and Barna research studies highlight interest among American Jewish millennials related to faith and Jesus. Pew Research in 2013 reported "34% said belief in Jesus as Messiah is compatible with being Jewish." The Barna Group study of American Jewish millennials in 2017 found that "58% of respondents are children of interfaith marriages…". And "21% of Jewish millennials believe Jesus was God in human form who lived among people in the 1st Century." It also found that 66% of Jewish millennials are "very open" to exploring other faiths including Christianity.[175] In response to the Barna study, Jewish demographer Alan Cooperman observed, "The rate of intermarriage for non-Orthodox Jews

---

[172] Ibid.
[173] Zaretsky, Tuvya. *The Challenges of Jewish-Gentile Couples: A Pre-evangelistic Ethnographic Study* (Doctoral Dissertation in partial fulfillment of the Doctorate of Intercultural Studies at Western Seminary 2004).
[174] Enoch Wan. "Relational Theology and Relational Missiology, *Occasional Bulletin* of the Evangelical Missiology Society, Vol 21 #1.
[175] "The Evolving Spiritual Identity of Jewish Millennials" in *The Barna Group Study*, October 10, 2017. https://www.barna.com/research/beliefs-behaviors-shaping-jewish-millennials/

is 72%. And for the rapidly growing group who identify themselves as Jews of no religion, that rate is 79%."[176]

So, what does this mean for missionaries, pastors and church outreach leaders? All the research indicates a significant portion of the American Jewish population is now spiritually accessible through relational engagement within mixed families. This is a population of younger couples that need ministry which is conversational, relational and non-judgmental. We must train and mobilize more workers for this group who can minister with humility, cultural intelligence, and theological clarity. That's our opportunity.

Forming Missional Communities Among Hybrid Families
Missional Presence Within the Jewish People

Intermarried American Jewry is now the majority experience of Jewish life. Seen from the perspective of traditional Judaism, that is considered a threat to Jewish survival. Have you ever heard someone say, "Hey, I'm Jewish and we don't believe in Jesus"? Biblically informed Christians should recognize two biblical apologetics against that fearful assertion.

1. The continuing presence of the Jewish people is established by and dependent on God's faithful covenant with Abraham.[177]
2. Jews and Gentiles are reconciled to God in Messiah Jesus (Yeshua) through the one, same and unique salvation plan for all humanity. Reconciliation with God, as the priority, is on the vertical plane. That then makes possible a spiritual harmony between marriage partners on the horizontal plane.[178]

Today, Gentile Christian spouses have a unique and intimate door into Jewish family networks. However, the effectiveness of that opportunity depends on the virtue of the Jesus-follower to insist that their first love in life is the LORD their God. The minister's dilemma is to remain accessible to people who are making sinful choices, while

---

[176] Alan Cooperman, "Barna Group Jewish Millennials: Moment Magazine" 2017.
[177] Genesis 15:4-5; Jeremiah 31:35-36
[178] Enoch Wan, "The Paradigm of 'Relational Realism'" *Occasional Bulletin* of the Evangelical Missiological Society, Vol. 19 #2

suffering the consequences, yet seeking wisdom and hope through spiritual alternatives. Maintaining a non-judgmental heart for the sake of engagement doesn't mean the minister must withhold biblical truth when it is solicited and an appropriate application for the situation.

Jewish-Gentile marriages are incarnational spaces. Non-believing partners have opportunities to witness the impact of a believing partner's intimate relationship with God, not their religion, as they experience horizontal relationships with their loved one. Cobi, a Jewish guy once described the prayers of his Christian girlfriend with words like *intimate, authentic* and *informal*. I asked, "How do you feel about her relationship in that kind of conversational prayer with someone you don't know?" He said, it made him curiously "open." Jesus' followers should realize they bear cross-cultural witness to the presence and activity of God in Jewish-Gentile, mixed couples and to their family members.

Congregational Responsibility: Relational Discipleship of Mixed Culture Families

American evangelical churches and Messianic congregations can make an intentional commitment to offer relational discipleship for mixed-culture families. Of course, that extends beyond Jewish and Gentile partners. The intermarriage rate of Jewish millennials is 61% and much higher for Gen Z. There is significant challenge to raising children with dual-culture heritage. Churches and Messianic congregations must recognize and welcome Jewish-Gentile couples and hybrid families as an important and contemporary ministry opportunity.

Christians can keep their antenna up for these Jewish visitors. It is important to extend an intentional welcome to culturally mixed couples including where one partner is Jewish.

Relational Discipleship (Evangelism): Honoring Identity

One of Donald K. Smith's propositions of missiological anthropology is that "all communication is cross-cultural."[179] All people have a tendency to assume that we all share the same cultural software.

---

[179] Smith, Donald K. *Creating Understanding: A Handbook for Christian Communication Across Cultural Landscapes,* Grand Rapids, MI: Zondervan Publishing House, 1992.

In conversations among American Jews, the terms "Christian" and "Gentile" are often used as synonyms. Yet it is important to recognize that some have negative sensitivities to bad things done by alleged "Christian" nations like the Germans of WWII. Consider the importance of understanding what calling yourself a Christian might mean to the hearer. Patiently investigate the receiver's culture as you grow your understanding for them.

One difficult challenge in this process is to address the Jewish notion that salvation in Jesus is incompatible with Jewish identity. Today, research through Barna and Pew show that younger Jewish people are more open to exploring other faiths. We can show them that not only were the first followers of Jesus mostly from His own people, but that a faithful remnant from all the nations, including Israel, is what God's salvation plan was meant to accomplish. So, faith in Jesus doesn't negate Jewish identity. Some will say it fulfills it.

Communal Opportunities Through Existing Social Structures

The Jewish-Gentile family is a primary opportunity for missional parenting. We believe the most successful approach is where both parents can share their faith in Jesus. A J-C couple once told me that they didn't want to confuse their daughter with their different religions, so they chose not to teach her either one. I met their daughter, who was left spiritually on her own, dressed in Gothic black and professing Wiccan beliefs. A unified faith conviction from both parents can preserve a rich Jewish heritage for the children and a faith in God that is consistent with both testaments. Jews for Jesus offers specialized help from its Youth and Family Ministry: Helping children, youth and parents navigate Jewish identity and faith in Jesus.[180]

Messianic congregations can serve as cross-cultural bridges for the partners. They can be natural settings to bring faith in Yeshua together with participation in contemporary Jewish life. This bridge can extend to campus fellowships, family camps and retreats that minister to Jewish-Gentile children and their families.

It's also fruitful when Jewish-Gentile families get involved in their urban communities. Participating in activities like the lighting of Hanukkah candles, Christmas trees or in Jewish community center

---

[180] https://jewsforjesus.org/youth-family

activities are examples of community involvement. Public, social or life cycle events are another example as are public gatherings to show support for Israel or to stand in solidarity against anti-Semitism as Jews and Christians.

A Missional Frontier Worth Pursuing

Jewish-Gentile intermarriage is more than a demographic trend—It is a lived expression of God's power to reconcile and redeem people to himself. I'm grateful to Enoch Wan for his influence and assistance to think of discipleship as a relational paradigm.

The subject of Jewish intermarriage is a subject of missional opportunity when viewed in the frame of Diaspora Missiology. In that perspective Enoch Wan said, "It is holistic, transnational, accessible, breaking down old traditional borders and boundaries."[181]

Evangelical churches and Messianic congregations can do the following:
- Recognize and welcome Jewish-Gentile couples in your congregation.
- Start learning the basics of Jewish culture and history.
- Practice relational discipleship to engage with unbelievers.
- Partner with ministries like Jews for Jesus—use their resources.
- Develop your resources to address JGC and family questions.

This subject is not simply a sociological concern—it is a kingdom priority. The Jewish-Gentile couple and family represent a missiological frontier in our generation. Will more of Jesus' followers recognize this need and opportunity? Will we respond now with relational courage, passion for the gospel, and hope for the future?

Let us pray and get involved to disciple and walk alongside these families—because through them, the nations are still being blessed.

---

[181] Wan, Enoch. *Diaspora Missiology: Theory, Methodology and Practice* (Institute of Diaspora Studies, Portland, Oregon: 2011), 134.

Chapter 13

On Hospice, Home, & Host

Lorajcy Tira-Dimangondayao

Introduction

As multiculturalism largely shaped by patterns of migration, reveals its challenges and limitations, churches are recognizing the mere gestures of "hospitality "are no longer sufficient. In this context, hospitality as a short term, transitional welcome is inadequate for cultivating lasting belonging. What is needed is a deeper theological and relational vision—one that moves beyond surface-level inclusion toward a reimagined community of faith capable of flourishing life together—a home.

I am thankful to the editors of this volume who have given me the space to write this theme and time to develop thoughts in honour of Drs. Enoch and Mary Wan who were some of my early mentors and exemplary role models. They have demonstrated a "home" to us—the Tiras family. I first met them when I was in my preschool year. I would play with their two sons as my mom Lulu would babysit the students' kids of Canadian Theological Seminary where my father Joy was studying. When my dad was pastoring in a church after graduation, Dr. Wan arranged scholarships for him. Dr. Wan became my dad's mentor, hosted him in their home while studying for his two doctorates. They travelled and ministered together internationally and Dr. Wan continued to mentor my father. When my parents were in their low times, both Dr. Enoch and Dr. Mary encouraged them to move on and provided ways to help them. My parents call Dr. Enoch Wan, *Kuya* (big helping brother). Auntie Mary Wan recruited my sister-in-law and mentored her in a short-term mission trip in Thailand. Auntie Mary is like a "big sister" to my mom. Drs. Enoch and Mary Wan have showed me that ministry was for making a home with God and for actively participating in the family life of the Church.

In the course, *The Home of God*, Professor Miroslav Volf hits the nail on the head: what we long for as individuals and as a community of believers is beyond a state of hospice—what is longed for is actually "home"[182] in its fullest sense—more than "a concrete site of our living and belonging…[h]ome is also a powerful image of wholeness and fulfilment."[183] To be precise, it is a home with God, and it is a home that Christ-followers work together, with God, to build. Volf and McAnnally-Linz expound the concept of God's home "among humans,"[184] particularly God's home in human flesh.

This brief chapter will attempt to articulate my developing thoughts on "the home of God" as it relates to the local church and its multicultural reality. Drawing upon the aforementioned course and my reading of Miroslav Volf co-authored Fribourg Lectures and volume, *The Home of God: A Brief Story of Everything*, I will also interact with the Orthodox East's Alexander Schmemann, *Celebration of Faith, volume 3, The Virgin Mary*. In discussing the Virgin Mary, I will pay less attention to the Western church's preoccupation posed by Mary's theological complexities, and more attention to the Eastern church's focus on Mary's role as the Mother of God, or *Theotokos, the bearer of God*.

Advising my deliberations on the local congregation's manifestation of the Universal Church as family, and more recently, Mary's role in this family, my professor, David Goa, explained: "Mary is the icon of the Church's vocation. She was willing to say, 'yes,' to God." If Miroslav Volf suggests that Christians partner with Jesus—God Incarnate, in the business of "home-making," then, Mary, Jesus's mother, would be an apt guide.

This chapter will be structured around three themes: hospice, home, and host. It is my prayer that the thoughts developed here will assist in a fuller understanding of God's home-making mission through the Church for the flourishing of life, and in a ministry practice that is as profound as it is simple.

---

[182] Miroslav Volf with Ryan McAnnally-Linz, "Modern Homelessness," *Fribourg lectures*.

[183] Ibid., 1.

[184] Miroslav Volf and Ryan McAnnally-Linz, "Overture: A Story of Home," in *The Home of God: A Brief Story of Everything*.

Hospice

My Evangelical denomination, at least in its local forms, is doggedly committed to the term "reaching out." In my own church we say, BLESS. The acronym stands for: (B)egin with prayer; (L)isten; (E)at; (S)erve; (S)tory (i.e., "share the story of Jesus").[185] While BLESS is a trademark saying, other congregations design similar sayings to describe the "reaching out" process. The rhetoric is focused on getting people to enter the church building and to participate in church activities. It is expected that somehow inclusion in church life will lead to the Evangelical notion of "coming to faith in Jesus," and being "saved" from one's sins so that they could go to Heaven.

Raised by theologically educated parents who valued theological discussions with their children, I was disillusioned by the "flat" Gospel that I was often taught in Sunday School. While "Jesus saved," there was less teaching on how Jesus transforms *all things and all relationships*; there was certainly less teaching on how Jesus was on the mission of making an eternal home for God to live with his beloved creation. This want for more has bloomed into a full questioning of the limitations of my tradition's choice of wording. "Reaching out," understood and acted upon as it is, falls short of the transformative profundity of the Gospel of Jesus—one in which God indwells human flesh and from it shines forth divine glory. "Reaching out," a revered teacher commented to me, "is what we do from boats when people are sinking." I wonder if our understanding of the Church simply as life-raft perpetuates the idea that the local church is meant solely for hospice. Do we pride ourselves on our full hospices where the dying are fed a reduced nourishment of "basic instructions before leaving earth?"

In terms of Canadian diversity, if Canadian society is sensing cultural rifts and church leaders are desperate to repair them in congregations, then employing strategies of modern society to solder together a people culled from the people of the earth is an insufficient approach. A fuller understanding of the Church's mission is required and a new imagery must be employed. Volf expressed in a lecture, "we long for what we have already known."[186] In "Modern Homelessness," he suggests that what is longed for is actually *home*. *Gessellschaft* alone,

---

[185] Beulah Alliance Church, https://beulah.ca/bless/

working towards a reification of diversity and multiculturalism, sees people's physical needs met, but fails to provide *belonging*. While "rescue" is a valuable image, hospice alone is on a trajectory to departure and cushions people for death. In contrast, home—that is, the home we long for—is a dimension that nurtures belonging and flourishes life.

Home

What then is "home"? In the documents Professor Volf shared with the class, he employs multiple pages to establish a description of "home." I suggest that, the local church would benefit from his descriptions,[187] but specifically from the foremost theme of the course and the material Volf provided: the aim of creating the world is both simply and profoundly to create a home for humanity to live with God.[188] As microcosms of this world, the Christian home and the Christian congregation are in the business of making a home for the indwelling of God. In a Matryoshka doll effect, the world, the congregation, and the home are in the process of "home-making" a dwelling for God to live with humanity. Thus, the whole of Christian life, individual and corporate, relates to the hope of the indwelling of God.

What does this idea of home have to do with the local church and its activity with new Canadians? There seems to be, at least in my circles, a genuine concern for assisting migrants (i.e., New Canadians, temporary foreign workers, asylum seekers, etc.) in resettlement, but what is taught in the congregation's programs is that assistance is given in order to "reach out." As expressed earlier in this essay, "reaching out," though noble and good, is simplistic[189] and reduced, falling short of the glorious point of it all: the home-making project of God. In contrast to hospice, the revolutionary idea of the "home of God" points to a flourishing life! While the distinction of "home" over "hospice" may seem minuscule, a shift in vocabulary and in teaching may revitalize the simplistic (and I

---

[186] This is my paraphrase from a lecture of Miroslav Volf, "The Home of God: A Brief Story of Everything TH5/734," Vancouver School of Theology, class lecture, July 5, 2021.

[187] Miroslav Volf and Ryan McAnnally-Linz, "Modern Homelessness" in Fribourg lecture series, p. 4 & 5.

[188] Miroslav Volf, "The Home of God: A Brief Story of Everything TH5/734," Vancouver School of Theology, class lecture, July 5, 2021.

[189] "Simplistic" should not be confused with "simple."

would suggest, often "empty") attempts to "temporarily assist" for "opportunities to make a difference," and "opportunities to evangelise"—neither for the goal of nurturing mutually beneficial life-changing relationships. The goal of Christian charity is the meeting with God, and evangelism refers to the sharing of the Good News. Volf has convinced me that this good news is glorious—the making of God's home with creation is here to stay.

Host

The bay window by the main entrance at the seniors' residence, facing the parking lot, frames my petite mother's silhouette. Her right palm is raised, pressed to the glass. I have seen it a million times. She used to do this same thing in the house I grew up in, framed by the kitchen window, facing the road. Mom would go through this routine every time my brother and I left the house. I learned when I was expecting my first child, that what my mother was doing was standing vigilant in prayer. She would stand at the window until our figures disappeared from sight, praying that my brother and I would sense God's presence and in Him find our home. She said that though we were beyond her sight and control, she could always follow us in prayer. I have often thought on this in the endless hours of mothering, and lately, as adolescence pulls my children into further walks from home, I am finding myself positioned at the window, in the model of my mother.

This is my own primordial symbol of home—my mother, the keeper of the dwelling and all who lived in it. She nurtured everything found within—her goal was the flourishing of life in everything that was contained and encountered inside her house. The plants grew limbs, the visitors left full, her children grew tall, and her husband (my father) grew a waistline; relationships were deepened. In all the nurturing, however, the outstanding picture of her in my mind is that of her standing in the window, hand raised—vigilant in prayer.

In recent months, I have encountered a similar symbol of home in the Virgin Mary, the Mother of Jesus, revered by the Orthodox and Roman Catholic churches (as well as by the Muslims[190]). Called the *Theotokos*,

---

[190] Mary is the only woman who is mentioned in the Quran by name. Qur'an 3:42, *Tafheem-ul-Quran* - Abul Ala Maududi: "Then came the time when the

"bearer of God," by the Eastern Church, Mary stands like my mother, framed by human-built structures, but symbolising the indwelling of God. For me, two images stand out of her role as the Mother of God: first, Mary gives us the image of a woman dedicated to the teachings of the Kingdom of God; and second, she gives us the image of the protection of a mother in prayer.

Schmemann writes:

Christ's first gift to us, the first and most profound revelation of His teachings and call is given in the image of a woman. Why is this so important, so comforting and so redeeming? Precisely because our world has become so completely and hopelessly male, governed by pride and aggression, where all has been reduced to power and weapons of power, to production and weapons of production, to violence, to the refusal to willingly back down or make peace in anything or to keep one's mouth shut and plunge into the silent depths of life… In the image of the Virgin Mary we find what has almost completely been lost in our proud, aggressive, male world: compassion, tender-heartedness, care, trust, humility.[191]

Thus, in Mary, we find an image that is not dedicated to the pursuit of superiority, and to reified production, but to the seeking of the Kingdom, to finding it, and living by it.[192]

Schmemann goes on to describe Mary as an image of "a Mother protecting, covering and comforting her afflicted children."[193] He refers to John 19:26-27 in which it is recorded that at the Cross, Jesus charges the care of his mother to his beloved disciple: "When Jesus saw his mother there, and the disciple whom he loved standing nearby, he said to her, 'Woman, here is your son,' and to the disciple, 'Here is your mother.' From that time on, this disciple took her into his home."[194] Though not widely acknowledged in Evangelical traditions, for many

---

angels said: 'O Mary! Behold, Allah has chosen you, and made you pure, and exalted you above all the women in the world."
https://quran.com/3/42?translations=17,18,19,20,22,85,95,101

[191] Alexander Schmemann, *Celebration of Faith Volume 3 The Virgin Mary*, (Crestwood, NY: St. Vladimir's Seminary Press) 1995, 21-22.

[192] Ibid., 22.

[193] Ibid., 36.

[194] John 19:26-27, NIV

Christians globally, and through history, Mary the mother of Jesus, continues to be sensed through the eyes of faith, praying and weeping for all humanity.

My home church is mostly reticent about Jesus' mother—little exposition of Mary takes place in the congregational learning of the church outside a Christmas-season sermon focused on her obedience to God. In response to what can be a negligent view of Jesus' human family and a resulting imbalanced view of Jesus' humanity, I would suggest that while we are careful not to elevate mother to the level of her son, we ought to revisit Mary, appreciating how she lived her human life, her place in church history, and her current place as one in the great cloud of witnesses.[195] I wonder if a fuller image of her—a human devoted to God and indwelt by God, in whom the Son first made his human home—would point to Jesus and lend a more developed Christology, giving rise to wider implications for spiritual and congregational life. In the way that humans celebrate the mothers who raised celebrated heroes, would it not be relevant to come to know and celebrate the human with whom God Incarnate first dwelt and who shaped his human embodied experience?

In the desire to move beyond government-sanctioned multiculturalism, towards the deep relationships of the family home, Mary provides an icon of homemaker and host. Like my mother who formed my earliest memory of flourishing at home, in her vocation to God, Mary serves as nurturer of life with God. Also, like my mother, Mary continues to be an image of protection and intercession. On the topic of Mary and the home, Professor Goa wrote to me, "It is often so with mothers and those that make a home so we may serve God's world and welcome the stranger." In her vocation, the local church may pattern herself after Mary's devotion and vocation.

---

[195] Hebrews 12

Conclusion

The Government of Canada's most recent plan now targets 395,000 new permanent residents in 2025, 380,000 in 2026, and 365,000 in 2027.[196] This announcement made at a time when many citizens are increasingly and vocally wary of outsiders, and even of each other, presents the local Christian church with a challenge to rethink the practice of hospitality in its modern form that more resembles a temporary hospice based on reified ideals. Volf's work suggests that what people really long for goes beyond a commodified concept of meeting the modern ideal of multiculturalism, and even, a reified idea of "reaching out" for number's or cause's sake. What people actually long for is something that they have already, somehow, known: home and the deep life-giving relationships of a flourishing family.

Mary, the Mother of God provides two integral images for the local congregation to emulate in the process of home-making with God: a devotion to Kingdom values and a commitment to pray and to protect. When indwelt by God, the local church, shed of the trappings of commodified things and reified ideas, becomes a home with unimaginable glory shining forth, as imagined by poet Lawrence Ferlinghetti, into which

> Christ climbs down / from His bare Tree / this year / and softly stole away into / some anonymous Mary's / womb again / where in the darkest night / of everybody's anonymous soul / He awaits again / an unimaginable / and impossibly / Immaculate Reconception / the very craziest of / Second Comings.[197]

---

[196] Government of Canada, "Notice – Supplementary Information for the 2025-2027 Immigration Levels Plan," https://www.canada.ca/en/immigration-refugees-citizenship/news/notices/supplementary-immigration-levels-2025-2027.html.

[197] "Christ Climbed Down," a poem by Lawrence Ferlinghetti. https://www.encyclopedia.com/arts/educational-magazines/christ-climbed-down.

Bibliography

Canada.ca. "Notice – Supplementary Information for the 2025-2027 Immigration Levels Plan," https://www.canada.ca/en/immigration-refugees-citizenship/news/notices/supplementary-immigration-levels-2025-2027.html, accessed July 1, 2025.

Ferlinghetti, Lawrence. "Christ Climbed Down." 1958. https://www.encyclopedia.com/arts/educational-magazines/christ-climbed-down, accessed July 1, 2025.

Rietz, Jeffrey G. and Rupa Banerjee, "Racial Inequality, Social Cohesion and Policy Issues in Canada," https://irpp.org/wp-content/uploads/2014/08/reitz.pdf, accessed July 1, 2025.

Schmemann, Alexander, *Celebration of Faith, Volume 3: The Virgin Mary*. Crestwood, NY: St. Vladimir's Seminary Press. 1995.

Miroslav with Ryan McAnnally-Linz, "Modern Homelessness," Fribourg lectures. n.d.

Volf, Miroslav and Ryan McAnnally-Linz, "Overture: A Story of Home." In *The Home of God: A Brief Story of Everything*. Grand Rapids, MI: Brazos Press, 2022.

Volf, Miroslav. "The Home of God: A Brief Story of Everything." Course lecture for TH5/734, Vancouver School of Theology, Vancouver, BC, July 5, 2021.

Orality in Global Mission

"These commandments that I give you today are to be upon your hearts.
Impress them on your children.
Talk about them when you sit at home and
when you walk along the road,
when you lie down and
when you get up."
(Deuteronomy 6:6-7)

Chapter 14

Will the Three Orality Movements Intersect?

Tom Steffen, D.Miss.

"Have our 'text-bound mind' blinded us to other possibilities?"
(Walter Ong)
"The oral medium... handles information differently from the written medium." (Werner Kelber)
"My greatest fear for you is not that you will fail but that you will succeed in doing the wrong thing." (Leighton Ford)

It was a graduate class on oral hermeneutics. Like many classes, a major paper is required. A student responded: "I'm wondering if I can use a story to introduce my paper? Rather than plainly stating the problem and the background of the paper, is it okay if I tell my story and put a personal touch to the paper? But it doesn't look academic (starting with a story). I was just thinking that it might not 'sound' or 'look' too academic."

I wondered—what have we in the academy done to our students to make them think of story as blue-collar, factory-working communication? What "educational" experience(s) drove this student to such conclusions? Here's my response: *Keep it academic*; this *is* a graduate course. So, I expect to see story not only in the introduction, but throughout. There's nothing more powerful than human experience to make it academic.

It was Easter Sunday, 2025. I wondered how the pastor would handle the sermon with many attendees darkening the door of the church for the first time since Christmas. Luke 24:1-6 was read. The megachurch pastor began his sermon: "Four Characteristics of New Life." Sounds a little propositional.

I waited to hear the ancient story unpacked. There was *no story*! Does he assume everyone knows the story? we can't grasp any new insights from the ancient story? story is secondary to propositions? Had professors infected him like the graduate student?

Sadly, the packed audience didn't get to feel the sting of mocking passer-byers and soldiers, contemplate why a cruel centurion changed his mind or why a mocking thief asked to be remembered on the other side, or Jesus' response, "Today you will be with me in paradise."

We didn't get to experience the agony of abandonment when Jesus cried out, "My God, my God, why have You forsaken Me?" nor consider how the disciples felt that first lonely leaderless night. We missed Mary Magdalene's confusion when seeing an empty tomb and when Jesus reminded her, "Don't you remember . . ." We didn't get to feel Peter and John's wonder as they raced to the tomb nor responses to Jesus' multiple post-resurrection appearances.

On the way home I asked my wife if she remembered the four points. She could not, nor could I. Hermeneutics and homiletics hijacked the story. Sadly, this is the reality for many attendees, and not just on Easter Sunday.

Some years ago, I met Dr. Enoch Wan at an Evangelical Missiological Society (EMS) meeting. I had previously read some of his publications and viewed his presentations, so he was not a total stranger. One thing I had noticed, whether print or presentations, propositions gleaned from linear, cause-and-effect reasoning reigned, illustrated by numerous diagramed categories. That will help explain my surprise when I received a phone call about an opportunity to participate in a new EMS track—orality.

Being involved in orality for four decades I jumped at the chance. We could expose EMS participants to the history and potential of orality in Scripture and communication, and beyond that book publications of presented papers would document ongoing scholarship. Cameron Armstrong and I edited the first orality track's volume published by Pickwick in 2022, titled *New and Old Horizons in the Orality Movement: Expanding the Firm Foundations*.

Dr. Wan is proof positive one does not have to park only on the propositional side of the street. He, like myself through interaction with the Ifugao of the Philippines, learned there is actually another side of the street, and both sides must be connected if robust communication and long-term memory are to materialize. While looking closely, the distance from one side of street to the other can seem distant and dangerous for those enmeshed in print culture.[198] But we learn and change. And so do those God gave us to serve! We all receive a *new* Bible!

As the modern-day Evangelical Strategic Orality Movement marches towards its 45th birthday,[199] much has been learned beyond the use of story. Like most new endeavors it is not without critics—some legitimate, some through misunderstandings. In this chapter I will identify three orality movements, note their interaction or lack thereof, and call for closer interaction between the three which will strengthen the Strategic Orality Movement. Should such happen, Scripture will be communicated with stronger impact and long-term memory will increase because of orality's strong ties to human experience. I begin with a definition of orality.

Setting the Stage

Defining orality is a little like trying to pick up mercury. When you think you have it, it slips through your fingers. But we keep trying. Simply stated, "Orality is holistic, communal communication embodied in relationships that create social identities."[200]

Nothing happens in a vacuum. The same is true of the Strategic Orality Movement. Late to the party, two other movements preceded it. I call the oldest, which began in the mid-1920s, the Secular Orality Movement. This was followed by the Sacred Orality Movement in the 1960s which comprises a broad ecumenical base. The biblical theological world (narrative criticism) entered with some advocates borrowing insights from the Secular Orality Movement. By the early 1980s, the Sacred Orality Movement began (see figure 1).

---

[198] See: Steffen, "Pedagogical Conversions," 141-159.
[199] See: Steffen, *Worldview-based Storying*, chapters 1-3.
[200] Adapted from Steffen and Neu, *Character Theology*, 125.

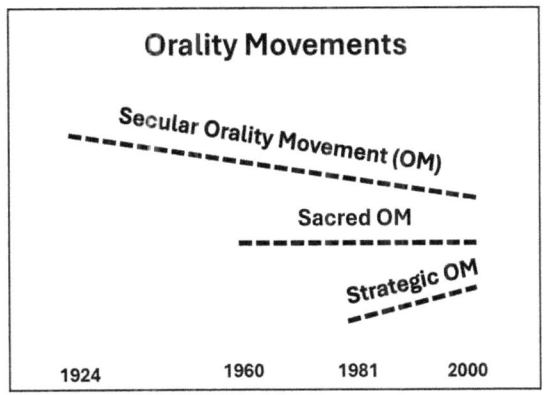

Figure 1. Three Orality Movements

Most participating in the Sacred Orality Movement had little if any knowledge about what was happening in the other two. Jim Slack, of the International Mission Board in the Philippines, introduced Walter Ong's classic *Orality and Literacy* (1982) which created more hunger for orality; researchers went to work. Here's just a handful of authors in each of the movements we met over the years.

The Secular Orality Movement

Marcel Jousse claims to have coined the term "orality" in his *The Oral Style* (1924). Milman Parry (1902-1935),[201] who studied under Jousse, taught epic poetry at Harvard. His research focused on Homeric poems (*Iliad* and the *Odyssey*). How could oral bards tell these long poems verbatim before being written? He developed the "Oral-Formulaic theory"—metrical patterns, structure, and key character repetition made word-for-word memorization possible.

One of his students, Albert Lord, picked up his work and found there was no word-for-word memorization of oral tradition. Rather, in *The Singer of Tales* (1960/2000) and *Epic Singers and Oral Tradition* (1991), Lord notes how tellers memorized thematically. Lord concludes, "In a sense each performance is 'an' original, if not 'the' original."[202]

---

[201] Parry died of an accidental?? self-inflicted gunshot wound.
[202] Lord, *The Singer of Tales*, 100-101.

In 1970, Ruth Finnegan published her classic, *Oral Literature in Africa*. She documents how oral tradition is passed from one generation to the next through stories, song, and performance rather than writing.

A prolific writer, Professor John Miles Foley focused on comparative oral tradition, extending the research of Parry and Lord. But he went beyond the oldest form of communication—speech—to address the internet. Foley founded the open-access *Oral Traditions Journal*.

Another major contributor, introduced above, was the Jesuit priest Walter Ong who was mentored by Marshall McLuhan, author of *The Medium is the Message*. As Ong's title suggests, *Orality and Literacy*, his interests laid the social effects when orality transitions to literacy. He, like his predecessors, separated the two fields which became known as the "Great Divide."

Jack Goody's *The Interface Between the Written and the Oral* (1987) challenged the Great Divide theory. Many others would argue for interconnectedness rather the bifurcation.

The Sacred Orality Movement

Before exploring the Sacred Orality Movement (narrative criticism) something was lurking in the background that was about to explode. In *The Christian View of Science and Scripture* (1954), Bernard Ramm offered two axioms which still influences some today. These stated: "Training in logic and science forms excellent background for exegesis. . . . Systematic teaching of Scripture is the Scriptures final intention."[203] This countered what Richard Niebuhr wrote in *The Meaning of Revelation* (1941), arguing that narrative is irreplaceable and untranslatable. Propositions *distort* the power of story.

Enter Birger Gerhardsson. In *Memory & Manuscript* (1961), he notes how first-centuries rabbis maintained and passed on sacred oral tradition. He argues understanding Rabbinic Judaism will provide interpreters a clearer understanding of Scripture. His book provided credibility for many to step into the ambiguous oral world because it showed content stability throughout the Gospels.

Yale made its contribution, particularly through Hans Frei's *The Eclipse of Biblical Narrative* (1974). He argues we've missed so much in

---

[203] Ramm, *The Christian View of Science and Scripture*, 155.

Bible interpretation because we have bypassed narrative by focusing on the history (historical-critical) and symbols (collective memory anchors). The story itself, he argues, provides the meaning of the story. Is it time to return narrative to its rightful role in Bible interpretation?

In 1981, Robert Alter published his seminal *The Art of Biblical Narrative*. He asks us to expand our view of the Hebrew Bible as theology to its literary composition. If done, we'll be introduced to much more than previously grasped. Come and enjoy the Old Testament authors as they make their stories and characters come alive.

Then an earthquake struck the theological world with Werner Kelber's groundbreaking[204] *The Oral and the Written Gospel* (1983). Influenced by Parry, Lord, Ong and others, Kelber notes our print orientation causes us to search for the "original" words of Jesus. But Jesus' original words, of course, were spoken (oral performances), therefore having an "immediacy" quality (impact on a specific audience). Interpretation and memory, therefore, requires an "oral hermeneutic" rather than a "print-oriented hermeneutic."

Oral tradition preserved Jesus' living words (Mark's version) with some fluidity for 50 years. Kelber asks us to "sense" the original words of Jesus' rather than his "precise" words. He wisely observes—hearing, reading, and interpretation should be done in community, not isolation or silence.[205]

---

[204] Twenty-five years after the publication of *The Oral and Written Gospel*, Tom Thatcher gathered a group of scholars to reflect on Kelber's influence. This resulted in *Jesus the Voice and the Text*, 2008, which addresses his contributions and critics. Kelber responds in the last chapter. This orality pioneer never stops learning.

[205] Many others made contributions to the Sacred Orality Movement. For example, Sternberg, *The Poetics of Biblical Narrative*, 1985; Fokkelman, *Reading Biblical Narrative*, 1991; Ryken, *Words of Delight: A Literary Introduction to the Bible*, 1993; Harvey, *Listening to the Text: Oral Patterning in Paul's Letters*, 1998; Bar-Efrat, *Narrative Art in the Bible*, 2004; Ryken and Longman, eds. *A Complete Literary Guide to the Bible*, 2010; Ryken, *How to Read the Bible as Literature . . . and Get More Out of It*, 2016; Ryken, *How Bible Stories Work: A Guided Study of Biblical Narrative*, 2019; Sandy, *Hear Ye the Word of the Lord: What We Miss if We Only Read the Bible*, 2024; Acker, *Exegeting Orality: Interpreting the Inspired Words of Scripture in Light of Their Oral Traditional Origins*, 2024. See also the Biblical Performance Criticism book series.

Kelber asks, can interpreters wean themselves from the "world of paper communication" so that the contrasts between oral and print become evident? Hints to the Great Divide emerge.

A third orality movement was happening in the missions world during the same timeframe as Alter and Kelber, but neither movement was aware of the other.

The Strategic Orality Movement

The Strategic Orality Movement was birthed in the Philippines under New Tribes Mission (now Ethnos 360). A people movement had begun among the Palawano people on the island of Palawan. It began with an independent missionary who arrived carrying a large black book and presented the gospel using a few words of Tagalog (national language) and English. An immediate response resulted. He instructed them to throw their amulets into the river. They did. He told them to be baptized. They did. Some ran to different villages to baptize others. Unknown to the missionary was the Palawano myth that said if someone shows up carrying something black, do whatever he says. They did.

In the mid-1970s, the Trevor MᶜIlwain family (New Tribes missionaries) was sent to ground the new believers. As he began teaching, MᶜIlwain realized they were not understanding. He wondered if they had really understood the gospel, so he backtracked. They had not! An obvious question arose, "Now what do I do?"

Starting in Genesis, MᶜIlwain highlighted key stories that demonstrated lostness and grace. Sixty-eight lessons later he reached the ascension. Three more story series followed for believers thereby providing a 30,000-foot overview of Genesis to Revelation in a relatively short period of time. Chronological Bible Teaching was born.[206]

Chronological Bible Teaching splashed beyond Philippine shores in 1981 at the Southeast Asian Leadership Conference in Thailand before spreading globally throughout the agency. Having around 3000

---

[206] Movements often have forerunners. In relation to the use of Bible stories in missions, here's a few: Warneck, *The Living Christ and Dying Heathenism*, 1954; Weber, *The Communication of the Gospel to Illiterates*, 1957; Loewen, "Bible Stories: Message and Matix. *Practical Anthropology* (1964) 11(2) 49-54. It was reprinted in Loewen, *Culture and Human Values*, 1975, 370-375; Vicedom, *Church and People in New Guinea*, 1961.

missionaries, many who periodically returned to their home countries, introduced Chronological Bible Teaching (CBT) in Bible studies and Vacation Bible Schools to their supporting churches. CBT moved from tribal people to the West. This required different curricula.[207]

Around a year later, Jim Slack embraced CBT, and along with others modified and advanced it globally, e.g., Wycliff and Campus Crusade. J.O. Terry designed worldview charts of major world religions to aid storytellers, wrote numerous Bible Storying curricula and books, and founded the *Journal of Bible Storying*.[208]

Avery Willis, Grand Lovejoy, and Mark Snowden[209] were instrumental in fanning the oralities flames in the USA. Networks such as the International Orality Movement, Lausanne Orality Movement, and Institutes for Orality Strategies[210] (GOMAP, OralityTalks, OralityResources.International) fan its flames globally. The *Orality Journal* debuted.[211]

In the academy, Daniel Sanchez, of Southwestern Seminary, teamed up with J.O. Terry and taught the Bible Storying course[212] for over ten years beginning in 2007. Two initial institutions offering accredited

---

[207] See: Trevor McIlwain with Nancy Everson, *Firm Foundations: Creation to Christ*, 1991; John Cross, *The Stranger on the Road to Emmaus*, 1996.

[208] Join free at: journalstorying@sbcglobal.net.

[209] See: Willis and Snowden, *Truth that Sticks: How to Communicate Velcro Truth in a Teflon World*, 2010; Barger and Lovejoy, *Unreadable: Another Book You Probably Won't Read*, 2024.

[210] Institutes for Orality Strategies is the legal name but they go by Orality Collaborators (https://orality.co) which better reflects their mission.

[211] Other books that have made a contribution include Klem, *Oral Communication of the Scripture: Insights from African Oral Art*, 1982. Steffen, *Cross-cultural Storytelling at Home and Abroad: Reconnecting God's Story to Ministry*, 1996/2005; Chiang, et al. *Orality Breakouts: Using Heart Language to Transform Hearts*, 2010; Koehler, *Telling God's Stories with Power: Biblical Storytelling in Oral Cultures*, 2010. Steffen and Bjoraker, *The Return of Oral Hermeneutics: As Good Today as It Was for the Hebrew Bible and First-Century Christianity*, 2020; Steffen and Neu, *Character Theology: Engaging God through His Cast of Characters*, 2024. As the Strategic Orality Movement matured, it expanded beyond evangelism and discipleship to include such topics as hermeneutics, health, community development, trauma, business, Bible translation, academic curricula.

[212] The course was initially titled Chronological Bible Storying but was soon changed to Bible Storying to emphasize there are multiple ways beyond chronological to present Bible Storying.

degrees in orality include Asia Graduate School of Theology (Th.M./Ph.D.) and Kairos University (M.A./Ph.D.). Numerous unaccredited Oral Bible Schools were also birthed globally.

Today, a growing number within the Strategic Orality Movement are familiar with the other two movements. Sadly, most in the Sacred Orality Movement are unfamiliar with the Strategic Orality Movement but the boundaries are beginning to blur. May the three vectors continue to intersect.

Tightening the Threads

While Dr. Wan promotes propositions he did not abandon them with the addition of orality. Rather, he integrated aspects of orality to give propositions life and retention. Can we get beyond comfortable reasoned categories to comfortable interactive relationships with biblical characters? Can we relearn what was "second nature to the original audience?"[213] Does a new Bible await us?

The lifeblood of orality is *story*; the lifeblood of story is *characters*; the lifeblood of characters is *relationships*; the lifeblood of relationships is the *Trinity*. Orality has Trinitarian roots. "The long trail of orality, which for any of us has mostly been hidden from sight, is now difficult not to see."[214] I close with a common Ifugao ending to a speech, "Hedin kayyaggud, abulut yu. Hedin lewah, ibeng yu." ["If it's good, accept it. If it's bad, throw it out.]

---

[213] Alter, *The Art of Biblical Narrative*, 62.
[214] Sandy, *Hear Ye the Word of the Lord*, 184.

Bibliography

Barger, Dan and Grant Lovejoy, *Unreadable*: *Another Book You Probably Won't Read.* Richmond, International Mission Board, SBC, 2024.

Cross, John R. *The Stranger on the Road to Emmaus*. Sandford, FL: Good Seed International, Inc., 1996.

Frei, Hans W. *The Eclipse of Biblical Narrative: A Study in Eighteenth and Nineteenth Century Hermeneutics.* New Haven: Yale University Press, 1974.

Gerhardsson, Birger. *Memory & Manuscript: Oral Tradition and Written Transmission in Rabbinic Judaism and Early Christianity with Tradition and Transmission in Early Christianity*. Grand Rapids, MI: Wm. B. Eerdmans Publishing Company, 1961/1998.

Kelber, Werner, H. *The Oral and the Written Gospel: The Hermeneutics of Speaking and Writing in the Synoptic Tradition, Mark, Paul, and Q*. Philadelphia: Fortress Press, 1983.

Lord, Albert B. *The Singer of Tales*. Cambridge, MA: Harvard University Press, 2000.

McIlwain with Nancy Everson, *Firm Foundations: Creation to Christ*. Sandford, FL: New Tribes Mission, 1991.

Niebuhr, H. Richard. *The Meaning of Revelation*. New York City: The MacMillan Company, 1941.

Ramm, Bernard. *The Christian View of Science and Scripture*. Grand Rapids, MI: Eerdmans, 1954.

Sandy, D. Brent. *Hear Ye the Word of the Lord: What We Miss if We Only Read the Bible*. Downers Grove, IL: InterVarsity Press, 2024.

Steffen, Tom A. *Cross-cultural Storytelling at Home and Abroad: Reconnecting God's Story to Ministry*. Waynesboro, GA: Authentic Media/InterVarsity Press, 1996/2005.

_____. "Pedagogical Conversions: From Propositions to Story and Symbol." *Missiology: An International Review* (2010) 38(2) 141-159.

Steffen, Tom and Cameron D. Armstrong, eds. *New and Old Horizons in the Orality Movement: Expanding the Firm Foundations*. Eugene, OR: Pickwick Publications, 2022.

Steffen, Tom and Ray Neu. *Character Theology: Engaging God through His Cast of Characters*. Eugene, OR: Pickwick Publications, 2024.

Steffen, Tom and William Bjoraker. *The Return of Oral Hermeneutic: As Good Today as It Was for the Hebrew Bible and First-Century Christianity*. Eugene, OR: Wipf & Stock, 2020.

Thatcher, Tom, ed. *Jesus the Voice and the Text: Beyond the Oral and the Written Gospel*. Waco, TX: Baylor University Press, 2008.

Willis, Avery T. and Mark Snowden, *Truth that Sticks: How to Communicate Velcro Truth in a Teflon World*. Colorado Springs, CO: NavPress, 2010.

Chapter 15

The Journey from Concept to Story: Orality Comes Full Circle

Danyal Qalb, Ph.D.

After traveling 150 Km on smooth highways with gentle curves through Central Luzon, the "Rice Granary of the Philippines," we took the exit. The road narrowed, and the curves became hairpins as the road started to wind up through the Cordillera mountains. There was hardly a straight road for the next four hours as it let into the clouds with a steep rock wall on one and a deep cliff on the other side of the winding road.

We were still in the same country, but the culture, houses, and people seemed to be from a different world. Here also, the main crop is rice. However, the rice paddies were not just nice squares as if drawn with a ruler like in the plains of Central Luzon. Here, the Ifugao carved rice paddies up the steep slopes of the mountains. Rocks are used to create retaining walls, making the paddies appear like "stairsteps to the sky." Unlike in the rice flats, no machines or engines could be heard. Everything was done by hand, just like it had been done for centuries.

These rice terraces are found in many gorges deep in the Cordillera Mountains in Ifugao Province as different clans tamed the rugged terrain for themselves. Remote and inaccessible, the Spanish colonialization of the Philippines had little impact, and they are today a UNESCO World Heritage site.

After a hike through the rice terraces, my wife and I sat down to rest at the small restaurant of our inn overlooking the majestic rice terraces. Our Ifugao host joined us. As he shared stories about his people, culture, and history, he mentioned that an American family stayed at his guesthouse for one month to experience this simple traditional lifestyle. My wife said that we know someone who lived in these mountains for eight years, about 50 years ago. "They are religious," was the reaction of our host, who did not know that we were talking about Tom Steffen. His arrival and that of other missionaries who worked in the various Ifugao dialects are evidently part of Ifugao's memory.

It is hard to imagine that even as recently as 50 years ago, church planters and Bible translators would need to be flown into the areas as they were inaccessible by road. It was in a similar setting that Tom Steffen tried to teach biblical concepts systematically. He became one of the early forerunners of the orality movement. In his desperation, he discovered that the Ifugao could easily grasp spiritual truths if they were packaged in stories, just as Jesus did, rather than propositions.

Today, despite still hanging onto many of their traditions, the Ifugao have access to the Philippines' educational system, electricity and internet. Right there on that platform overlooking the rice terraces, I took out my smartphone and sent Tom Steffen a message with a picture of me in the province where his role in the orality movement began 50 years ago. At that moment, we realized that orality had come full circle.

The Path Towards Becoming an Academic Discipline

Who am I to come to this conclusion? Just the evening before visiting the place that profoundly influenced the orality movement, my wife and I were in Manila attending my graduation as the first PhD in Orality Strategies. I am new to the orality movement and am not trying to highlight my achievements. Rather, I am the "academic first fruit" representing the efforts of orality pioneers like Tom Steffen, Trevor McIlwain (Steffen, 2014), J.O. Terry, my mentor Charles Madinger, who was the president of the International Orality Network (ION), the orality issue network of the Lausanne Movement, Romer Macalinao who fought to make this an Asia Graduate School of Theology – Philippines (AGST) program, and many others who preceded me.

I met Enoch Wan for the first time at the Evangelical Missiological Society (EMS) 2022 annual conference, where he led the orality paper presentation sessions in which I was scheduled to present a paper that I wrote for one of the subjects at AGST. It was my first time delivering a conference paper, and I was extremely nervous in front of a room full of scholars and academics. I felt I had completely fumbled my presentation. To my surprise, Dr. Wan asked me to assist him with the remaining presenters. Because of that, I ended up spending two days closely involved with the orality track as I sat beside him, listening to papers from various disciplines of orality, including storytelling, frontier missions, Bible translation, and church planting movements (CPM).

Orality made its way into formal theological and missiological training. It is not always named as such, but it is taught in the disciplines of education, anthropology, contextualization, and communication, among others. Leading up to the Fourth Lausanne Congress, Billy Coppedge (2024) wrote an article highlighting the need to integrate orality across all issue networks by demonstrating it as essential for effective communication.

Although not exhaustive, I compiled the following list of areas in formal education and the academy where orality has its foot in the door.

Cross-disciplinary

- Most Church Planting Movements (CPMs) in one way or another, have **Discovery Bible Studies** (DBS) at their core. BDS are usually conducted in group settings and deploy a variety of orality principles and methods.
- Orality is finding its way back to the pulpit through the growing practice of **narrative preaching**. Notable instructors championing this approach include Anne Zaki at the Evangelical Theological Seminary in Cairo (ETSC), Havilah Dharamraj at the South Asia Institute of Advanced Christian Studies (SAIACS), Ezekiel Ajibade at the Nigerian Baptist Theological Seminary (NBTS), and Larry Dinkins at Chiang Mai Theological Seminary (CTS).
- Laurence Gatawa (2017), Nick Acker (2024), Tom Steffen and Ray Neu (2024), Joshua Frost (2023), and Larry Caldwell (2025) - to name just a few - published books on **hermeneutics** with orality at its core. These orality-based approaches complement the traditional grammatical-historical method of Bible interpretation.
- Through **Oral Bible Translations** (OBT), an orality course is taught at Dallas International University (DIU). Wycliffe, the Summer Institutes of Linguistics (SIL), and Spoken Worldwide, among others, are increasingly emphasizing the role of orality in the Bible translation process.

- **Anthropologists** like Paul Hiebert, Darrell Whiteman, Daniel Shaw, Sherwood Lingenfelter, Michael Rynkiewich, and Enoch Wan wrote about the connection between orality and contextualization, and some are advising dissertations in the field of orality.

Global Networks
- Orality is an issue network of the **Lausanne Movement**, known as ION, that was formed in 2005 (Steffen, 2014). In 2010, the **Cape Town Commitment** (2011) declared orality as one crucial aspect of world evangelism.
- For the 2025 gathering in Albania, the **International Council for Evangelical Theological Education** (ICETE) established impact teams[215] to address key issues in theological education. One of the most active is orality. Recognizing its potential, regional theological associations such as ACTEA (Africa), ATA (Asia), ECTE (Europe), and AETAL (Latin America) have begun to encourage the integration of orality into theological education.

Journals & Publications
- During their conferences, EMS and the Asia Missions Association (AMA) feature **orality tracks and breakout sessions**.
- Numerous **journals** regularly publish articles on orality. ION published the now discontinued Orality Journal and other materials on Orality.
- More recently, the interactive OralityTalks Journal (OTJ)[216] and the OralityResources.International (ORI)[217] **publication** regularly release written and recorded materials on orality by experts in the field.

---

[215] https://icete.info/resources/impact-teams.
[216] https://journal.oralitytalks.net.
[217] https://oralityresources.international.

Research

- Today, orality is not just storytelling. It matured far beyond kids' Sunday school and something for remote, unreached people groups, long established and proven effective in frontier mission. Numerous **studies, concepts, and theories**, including but not limited to liminality (Turner, 2008), transportation theory (Green & Brock, 2000), elaboration likelihood model (Slater & Rouner, 2002), story listening pyramid (Savage, 1996), and para-social relationships (Singhal & Rogers, 1999) help us understand "the magical science of storytelling."[218]
- Initiated by ION, the **Global Orality Mapping Project** (GOMAP)[219] aims to analyze and understand the orality reliance of the world's UPGs. This tool provides a report that can be used to develop better communication strategies to reach them.
- An increasing number of **theses and dissertations** have been and are being produced, showing the relevance of orality and communications strategies, especially in education. Some recent examples are Cameron Armstrong (2020), Lynn Thigpen (2020), Charles Madinger (2024), and Daniel Görzen (2025).

Seminaries & Formal Education

- In the academy, Daniel Sanchez of Southwestern Seminary teamed up with J.O. Terry and taught the Bible Storying course for over ten years beginning in 2007.
- Tara Rye was one of the first to offer a full semester course on orality at a university. 2014-18 and 2019-20, she taught two courses at Grace University and Nebraska Christian College (NCC), respectively.
- In 2020, Ray Neu led the development of an orality curriculum for the Nazarene Theological Institute in Africa. Since then, they have completed 10 courses, and the program's impact has extended across eight generations, reaching over 26,000 people in 13 countries.

---

[218] https://youtu.be/Nj-hdQMa3uA.
[219] https:///gomap.pro.

- Tom Steffen taught orality as a missions professor at the Cook School of Intercultural Studies (BIOLA), and Larry Dinkins teaches an orality course at Dallas Theological Seminary (DTS).
- Lynn Thigpen teaches orality as it relates to pedagogies at Liberty University, and Jay Moon teaches orality as key in intercultural discipleship at Asbury Theological Seminary.
- Dallas International University (DIU) also offers subjects in orality related to Bible translation.
- Since 2022, AGST has been offering a Th.M./Ph.D. in Orality Studies as the first theological seminary in the world, where I graduated in 2025 as the first student.
- Beginning in 2025, Kairos University offers M.A. and Ph.D. courses focusing on orality as Larry Caldwell is promoting orality as an integral part of competency-based theological education (CBTE).
- As Orality Collaborators, we are in conversations with several seminaries which are planning to implement orality either as part of their program or as an entire degree in Asia, Africa, and Latin America.

The Road from Storytelling to the Academy

What began as storytelling in the jungle and frontier mission strategy developed into global networks and advanced degrees as the academy realized the effectiveness of orality to reach the world's Unreached People Groups (UPGs), be it in remote corners of the world or megacities flooded with social media and AI-generated content.

As my wife and I were talking with the Ifugao, I began to imagine how Tom Steffen was struggling to teach them theology five decades ago. Today, most Ifugao can read and write and send their children to school. Still, they prefer to learn from people they trust through avenues like music, arts (evident in their weavings and carvings), symbols, drama and stories.

When I met Dr. Wan at EMS 2022 and listened to his presentation, I encountered a true academic, someone marked by deep thought and profound conceptual insight. At the same time, his students admire how he weaves oral pedagogies into his lectures. He not only recognizes the significance of orality but, as director of the program, also includes multiple courses on the subject in the Ph.D. program in Intercultural Education at Western Seminary.[220]

Most readers still prefer, or better yet, rely on, high orality-reliant communication as orality is deeply integrated into their being (Görzen, 2025, p. 216). How their logic works and how they learn and process information remains oral. It is their heart language and communal identity. It is how they best receive, process, remember, and pass on information and truth (Madinger et al., 2024, p. 19).

Through people like Enoch Wan and others mentioned and unnamed in this chapter, orality is increasingly gaining momentum, not just at the grassroots level but in the academy. I believe the inexhaustive list of how orality is now integrated into global networks, research, and theological education hints at a new movement—the **academic orality movement**.

Bibliography

Acker, N. (2024). *Exegeting orality: Interpreting the inspired words of scripture in light of their oral traditional origins*. Wipf & Stock.

Armstrong, C. D. (2020). *Finding yourself in stories: Romanian theology students' experience of oral-based teaching methods* [Doctoral dissertation, Biola University].

Caldwell, L. W. (2025). *The Bible in culture: Reading the Bible with all the world using ethnohermeneutics*. William Carey Publishing.

Coppedge, B. (2024, May 15). *Integrated Orality*. Lausanne Movement. https://lausanne.org/about/blog/integrated-orality

Frost, J. (2023). A method for exegeting emotions in the Bible for higher quality translation. In S. Watters & R. de Blois (Eds.), *Quality in translation: A multi-threaded fabric* (pp. 171–215). Pike Center for Integrative Scholarship.

---

[220] https://www.westernseminary.edu/academics/advanced-degrees/doctor-of-philosophy-in-intercultural-education-phd.

Gatawa, L. B. (2017). *Comparative characterisations of Jesus and the disciples in the Gospel of Mark, with special reference to ancient oral narration* (Publication No. 10245810) [Doctoral dissertation, Middlesex University / Oxford Centre for Mission Studies, Middlesex University Research Repository].

Görzen, D. (2025). *Orality reliance of the Maguindanao of the Soccsksargen region in the Philippines: Balancing identity and education in a changing world* [Doctoral dissertation, Asia Graduate School of Theology – Philippines].

Green, M. C., & Brock, T. C. (2000). The role of transportation in the persuasiveness of public narrative. *Journal of Personality and Social Psychology, 79*(5), 701–721.

Madinger, C. (2024). *Transformative learning: A case study using oral narrative and participatory communication: an inquiry into radio drama-based training among Zambian caregivers of abused and exploited children.* Orality Resources International. https://oralityresources.international/wp-content/uploads/2024/07/Transformative-Learning.pdf

Madinger, C., Madinger, R., & Ponraj, D. (2024). Unleashing the power of orality. *OralityTalks Journal, 1*(1), 19–27. https://oralitytalks.net/wp-content/uploads/2024/03/OralityTalks-Journal-Vol-1-No-1-2024.pdf#page=22

Savage, J. (1996). *Listening & caring skills: A guide for groups and leaders.* Abingdon Press.

Singhal, A., & Rogers, E. M. (1999). *Entertainment-education: A communication strategy for social change.* L. Erlbaum Associates.

Slater, M., & Rouner, D. (2002). Entertainment-education and elaboration likelihood: Understanding the processing of narrative persuasion. *International Communication Association, 12*(2), 173–191.

Steffen, T. A. (2014). Tracking the orality movement: Some implications for the 21st century missions. *Lausanne Global Analysis, 3*(2). https://lausanne.org/content/lga/2014-03/tracking-the-orality-movement-some-implications-for-21st-century-missions

Steffen, T. A., & Neu, R. (2024). *Character theology: Engaging God through his cast of characters*. Pickwick Publications.

The Cape Town Commitment. (2011). Lausanne Movement. https://www.lausanne.org/content/ctcommitment

Thigpen, L. L. (with Steffen, T. A.). (2020). *Connected learning: How adults with limited formal education learn* (American Society of Missiology Monograph Book 44). Pickwick Publications.

Turner, V. (2008). Betwixt and between: The liminal period on rites de passage. In A. C. Lehmann, J. E. Myers, & P. A. Moro (Eds.), *Magic, witchcraft, and religion: An anthropological study of the supernatural* (7th ed, pp. 91–100). McGraw-Hill.

Biography of Dr. Enoch Wan

as related to Karen Hedinger, Ed.D.

Growing Up

Enoch Wan was born in China and moved to Hong Kong with his family when he was young as his mother was sick and needed medical care there. She did not survive, and Enoch's father was not able to take care of Enoch, his sister, and brother due to medical expenses incurred from his wife's illness. He placed the three siblings in an orphanage run by British missionaries. There was abuse that greatly affected Enoch for a time.

By God's grace, Enoch's father married a woman who, though illiterate and redeemed out of slavery, was a godly woman who raised Enoch, his siblings, and four other children born into the family in a loving environment. Enoch says this helped him overcome the negative effects from the orphanage.

Enoch's adoptive mother, from now on referred to as his mother, worked as a cook at the Alliance Bible Seminary that was located on a small island where the only transportation allowed was by foot. There were no motor vehicles on the island. This is where Enoch went to school and church which was the seminary chapel. This is also where he met his wife, Mary.

There were a lot of American missionaries at the Alliance school and Enoch had a conversion experience while in high school. He and Mary became deacons in the church.

Educational Experience

Both Enoch and Mary went on to teacher's college in Hong Kong and from there they attended Nyack College in New York. Enoch was one year ahead of Mary. As they finished, they both felt a call to the mission field, Enoch to Vietnam and Mary to Thailand. He was invited to join the faculty at Alliance Bible School in Indonesia and later a mission team in Thailand. Each time Enoch pursued going to a field, the Lord closed the door. Once it was because of no passport issued. Another time the field misplaced his application.

When doors to the field did not open, Enoch enrolled at Gordon-Conwell and was a double major degree student (Pastoral Counseling and New Testament) with a grade point average of 3.8.

Enoch then went on to study at State University of New York, eventually earning his M.A. and Ph.D. in Anthropology. His dissertation title was, "The Dynamics of Ethnicity: A Case Study on the Immigrant Community of N.Y. Chinatown." To do his research, he had to learn the trade language, "Toi-sang" dialect (台山話 the *lingua franca* of US Chinatowns in the mid-1970s). During his studies, he realized that residents of Chinatown were one of many different ethnic sub-groups – diaspora people-groups in the USA. In addition, his mother had lived as a slave-girl in SE Asia, and two uncles moved to new countries, Burma and Cuba, living as diaspora. These insights would eventually lead him to develop his paradigm of diaspora missiology.

Still with no field experience in missions, Dr. Wan was chosen by Rev. Philip Tang, a family friend and president of the Alliance Bible Seminary in Hong Kong (ABS-HK), to be in charge the missions department which was the first mission degree program among the Chinese globally. That degree program was initially planned by Dr. Jack Shepherd from the New York headquarters but he got sick and had to return to the US for medical treatment. Reluctantly, Dr. Wan accepted the director's position, mostly because at that time in the Alliance, denominational policy was "submit to the spiritual leader." The original plan had been for him to be ordained and be sent to Hawaii as a church planter.

A few years later, Rev. Philip Teng invited the theology professor (at Canadian Theological Seminary - CTS) Dr. M.O. Cheung to succeed him as the president of ABS-HK. Dr. Wan was swapped to teach CTS's students because about 1/3 of them were Cantonese speakers from Hong Kong. While at CTS in Canada, Dr. Wan founded the "Centre for Intercultural Studies" (consisting of five ethnic groups: South Asian, Vietnamese, Filipino, Chinese, First Nations) and later, the "Centre for

Chinese Studies" – the first such program in North America. Over the years, Dr. Wan also taught at many schools aboard such as:
- Alliance Theological College, Canberra, Australia
- Sichuan Theol. Seminary, Chengdu, China
- Yanjing Theol. Seminary, Beijing, China
- PSTI-International Center for Theological Studies, Indonesia
- Alliance Biblical Seminary, Manila, Philippines
- Institute of Chinese Studies, Billy Graham Center & Wheaton Graduate School & Missions, IL, USA
- Tyndale University & Seminary, Toronto, Canada
- Singapore Bible College & Seminary, Singapore
- Ambrose University & Seminary, Calgary, Alberta, Canada
- Southeast Asia Bible Seminary, (SEABS) Malang, Indonesia
- Christian Witness Theological Seminary, CA, USA
- International Theological Seminary, CA, USA
- Logos Evangelical Seminary, CA, USA

In 1993, Dr. Wan was invited to launch a Ph.D. in Intercultural Studies program at the Reform Theological Seminary in Mississippi, USA. Then in 2000, he moved to Western Seminary in Portland, Oregon, to assume directorship of the Doctor of Missiology, later Doctor of Intercultural Studies program. Over the years, he developed a Doctor of Education in Intercultural Education program and a Ph.D. in Intercultural Education at Western Seminary.

To trace Dr. Wan's biography we need to understand the timeline mentioned above. We also need to follow the development of several key ideas. We now turn our attention to three key ideas at the heart of his work: the STARS approach to research, the ministry implications of diaspora study, and his focus on relational interactionism as a lens for correct understanding of human change and transformation.

Development of the STARS Approach

During the 1970s as Dr. Wan was working at the Alliance Bible Seminary in Hong Kong, he tried to integrate his Eastern upbringing with his Western training. He states:

> The development of "STARS" approach for interdisciplinary and integrative study is a personal journey in conducting research. After completion of my doctoral studies, I returned to Hong Kong for teaching ministry for three years when I tried to integrate my Chinese upbringing with western academic training, my Asian cultural orientation with American scholarly orientation. The result is the development of my "STARS approach" as shown in the figure below with five-step systematically and sequentially with priority.[221]

CRITERIA	*	EXPLANATION
1. Scripturally sound	S	Not proof-text; but the "whole counsel of God" (Acts 20:26-27)
2. Theologically Supported	T	Not just pragmatism/expedience; but sound theology
3. Analytically Coherent	A	Not to be self-contradictory; but to be coherent
4. Relevantly contextual	R	Not to be out of place; but fitting for the context
5. Strategically practical	S	Not only good in theory; but can be strategically put into practice

Figure 1. Integrative Research of the "STARS approach" [222]

Listed below are simple explanations of each of the five points in the figure above.

---

[221] Enoch Wan, "Retrospection: My Research and Teaching Career in Missiological Studies of Four Decades," EMS National Conference, Dallas, TX, October 13, 2023.
[222] Enoch Wan, "Core Values of Mission Organization in the Cultural Context of the 21st Century," *Global Missiology*, "Featured Article" January 2009, www.GlobalMissiology.org

- **S**cripturally Sound - As evangelicals, Scripture is to be the basis and guide of Christian faith and practice. It is axiomatic for evangelical Protestants based on the conviction of *"sola scriptura."*.
- **T**heologically Supported - Just based on pragmatism/expedience is insufficient; but sound theology is essential and required.
- **A**nalytically Coherent - Not to be self-contradictory; but to be both consistent and coherent
- **R**elevantly Contextual - Not to be out of place; but it is to be required to be fitting for the context.
- **S**trategically Practical - It is good to have scriptural/theological support with coherent theory and cultural relevance; but can be strategically put into practice. [223]

Wan goes on to say:
The "STARS approach" was originally developed when formulating contextual theology for the Chinese context in the book published in Chinese in 1999.[224] The process and procedures of the "STARS approach" are vigorous and demanding but the outcome is excellent and enduring, i.e., never retracted any published material since first publication in Chinese in 1979 and in English 1982. I also promoted "STARS approach" by publishing several articles on research methodology both in English and Chinese, and inspired many doctoral students to employ it for their dissertation research.[225]

Diaspora Missiology

As mentioned above, Dr. Wan's Ph.D. research and his own family dynamics led him to develop a paradigm termed "Diaspora Missiology." This paradigm initially was not well-received but gained international

---

[223] Ibid.
[224] Enoch Wan, *Sino-theology: A survey study.* Ontario, Canada: Christian Communication Inc. of Canada. "Christianity in the eye of traditional Chinese." *Chinese Around the World* July 1999:17-23.
[225] Wan, "Retrospection: My Research and Teaching Career in Missiological Studies of Four Decades," EMS National Conference, Dallas, TX, October 13, 2023. 6.

recognition when presented at the Lausanne III Congress, also known as Cape Town 2010.

In his presentation at the EMS National Conference in 2023, Dr. Wan said the following:

Diaspora missiology is a newly emerged missiological paradigm which includes and integrates multiple disciplines such as biblical and demographic studies, theology, evangelism, social sciences, arts and technology.[226] It is a contextual response to two global trends that had changed the landscape of Christian ministry/missions:[227]

Trend 1 - the shifting of Christendom's center of gravity from the west to the rest and from the northern hemisphere to the southern hemisphere.

Trend 2 - the phenomena of large scale and increased intensity of movement of people moving (internal migration: urbanization; and international immigration: globalization).[228]

"When people are in transition, they are receptive to change both culturally and spiritually. God has moved many newcomers to Canada and the US spatially to our neighborhood and spiritually to God Himself. Whereas newcomers among diaspora groups are receptive to the gospel, Protestant churches and Christians are to practice the "Great Commandment" and **minister to the diaspora** via "missions at our doorstep" through charitable act and Christ-like love."[229]

---

[226] Enoch Wan and Joy Tira, "Diaspora Missiology and Mission in the Context of the 21st Century." *Torch Trinity Journal*, May 30, 2010, Volume 13, No.1:5

[227] For extensive study on the subject, see Enoch Wan, *Diaspora Missiology: Theory, Methodology and Practice*. IDS 2014:13-33.

[228] Enoch Wan, *Diaspora Missiology: Theory, Methodology, and Practice*, 2nd ed., (Portland, OR.: Institute of Diaspora Studies : Western Seminary, 2014: chapter 1).

[229] Enoch Wan, "Three steps engaging the diaspora in Canada in Christian missions," *Global Missiology,* www.globalmissiology.org July 2010.

Dr. Wan published two books titled, "*Diaspora Missiology*" (one was his own book[230] and the other was co-edited with Michael Pocock and published by William Carey Publishers)[231] and a dozen titles in the same category.

Relational Realism/Interactionism Paradigm

Dr. Wan's Ph.D. research demonstrated "ethnic identity" as being fluid and situational with the ethnic Chinese in New York Chinatown. He said, "Later it led to the definition and concept of "culture" as follows:

Culture: The context/consequence of patterned interaction of personal Beings/beings, in contrast to popular usage of culture applying to the presumed closed system of homo sapiens. This definition of culture can freely be applied or referred to angelic (fallen or good) beings of the angel-culture and the dynamic interaction of the Three Persons of the Triune God in theo-culture."[232]

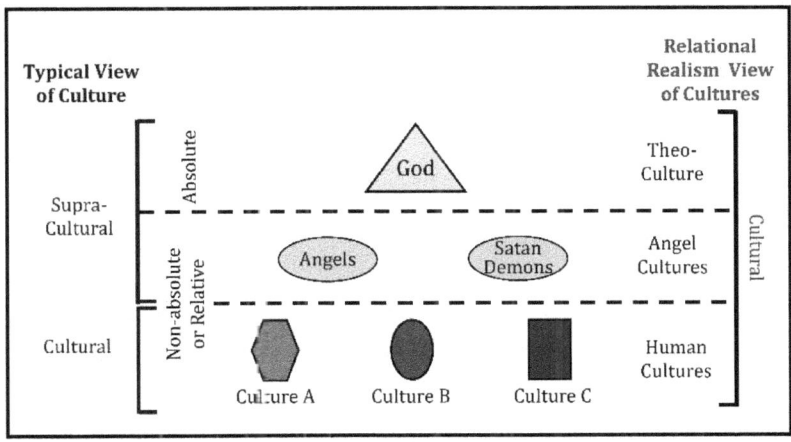

Figure 2. Cultural and Supra-cultural[233]

---

[230] Enoch Wan, *Diaspora Missiology: Theory, Methodology, and Practice*, 2nd ed. (Portland, OR.: Institute of Diaspora Studies, Western Seminary, 2014).

[231] Michael Pocock and Enoch Wan, eds., *Diaspora Missiology: Reflections on Reaching the Scattered Peoples of the World* (William Carey Library, 2015).

[232] Enoch Wan. "The Theological Application of the Contextual Interaction Model of Culture." *His Dominion* (Canadian Theological Seminary) (1, October 1982).

[233] Enoch Wan and Jon Raibley, *Transformational Change in Christian Ministry Second Edition* (Portland, OR.: Western Academic Publishers, 2022), 42.

Relational realism, first introduced by Dr. Wan in an EMS *Occasional Bulletin*,[234] later led to three more relational frameworks as seen below.

FRAMEWORK	KEY ELEMENTS
Relational Realism Paradigm	Reality exists and was created by the Triune God, who is eternally in relationship, and has built relationship into all of creation.
Relational Transformative Paradigm	Transformative change is a result of divine aid, plus godly input, plus positive response. Importance of vertical and horizontal interaction.
Relational Interactionism Paradigm	Transformational vs. transgressional change. Being (who is interacting?), belonging (how are they interacting?), becoming (what influence do they have on each other?)
Relational Transformational Paradigm	Application of the three paradigms by intentionally interacting with others for positive influence.

Figure 3. Relational Frameworks[235]

These relational frameworks have introduced a scriptural foundation for education, communication, leadership, mentorship, discipleship, business as mission, and other areas of Christian ministry.

---

[234] Enoch Wan, "The Paradigm of 'Relational Realism,'" *Occasional Bulletin* of the EMS, 19, no. 2 (2006): 2.

[235] Enoch Wan, Mark Hedinger, and Jon Raibley, *Transformational Growth: Intercultural Leadership/Discipleship/Mentorship* (Western Academic Publishers, 2023), 11.

Conclusion

The conclusion of this biography could be viewed through the lens of Dr. Wan's accomplishments as seen in his bibliography in this book or on his website, enochwan.com.

Yet a more accurate measure of his influence can be seen through his vertical and horizontal relationships with a myriad of people in all walks of life across a wide diversity of human cultures.

Bibliography of Dr. Enoch Wan's Writings

Compiled by Karen Hedinger, Ed.D., & Editorial Team

PUBLICATION LIST - BOOKS

2025

Wan, Enoch, and Mark Hedinger. *Relational Intercultural Communication for Relational Intercultural Education*. Western Academic Publishers, 2025.

Enoch Wan and Jacky Lau. *Chinese Diaspora Kingdom Workers: In Action and With Guidance* (in Chinese). 溫以諾、劉得貴。《神國僑僕：關顧與指引》（香港：Everyone Press Ltd）2025年3月初版（電子版）。免費下載網址：營商事工-書籍 https://www.chinesebam.com/book/

2024

Wan, Enoch. *Oral Discipleship and Leadership Training*. Edited by John Ferch. Western Academic Publishers, 2024.

Wan, Enoch, Mark Hedinger, and Jon Raibley. *Relational Intercultural Education for Intercultural Ministry*. Western Academic Publishers, 2024.

2023

Abdon, Nestor, and Enoch Wan. *Marginality of Visible Minorities in Canada: A Missiological Study*. Western Academic Publishers, 2023.

Wan, Enoch, Mark Hedinger, and Jon Raibley. *Transformational Growth: Intercultural Leadership/Discipleship/Mentorship*. Western Academic Publishers, 2023.

Wan, Enoch, and Ria Martin. *Diaspora Missions Engagement in the Global North through Intercultural Campus Ministry: 'By and Beyond' Filipinos*. Western Academic Publishers, 2023.

2022

Chiu, Noel, and Enoch Wan. *Establishing Frontline LGBTQ Outreach: An Exploratory Study*. Western Academic Publishers, 2022.

Wan, Enoch, and Joshua Paxton. *Relational Partnerships for Missions Mobilization*. Western Academic Publishers, 2022.

Wan, Enoch, and Tom Steffen, eds.. *Reflections on 21st Century Orality*. Western Academic Press, 2022.

Wan, Enoch, and Jon Raibley. *Transformational Change in Christian Ministry Second Edition*. Western Academic Publishers, 2022.

Wan, Enoch, and Natalie Kim. *Relational Intercultural Training for Practitioners of Business As Mission: Theory and Practice*. Western Academic Publishers, 2022.

Wan, Enoch, and Tin Nguyen. *A Holistic and Contextualized Mission Training Program: Equipping Lay Leaders for Local Mission in Vietnam*. Western Academic Publishers, 2022.

Wan, Enoch, and Rob Penner. *Missionary Preparation in The Gospel of Matthew in Light of 28:16-20: A Narrative and Relational Study*. Western Academic Publishers, 2022.

Wan, Enoch, and Jace Cloud. *Doxological Missiology: Theory, Motivation, and Practice*. Western Academic Publishers, 2022.

Wan, Enoch, and John Ferch. *Relational Leadership Development: An Ethnological Study in Inuit Contexts*. Western Academic Publishers, 2022.

Wan, Enoch, and Christopher M. Santiago. *Motivations for Mission: A Relational-Covenantal Perspective*. Western Academic Publishers, 2022.

2021

Early, Alex, and Enoch Wan. *The Cross and the Kaleidoscope: Substitutionary Atonement and Our Relationships*. Western Academic Publishers, 2021.

Gimple, Ryan, and Enoch Wan. *Covenant Transformative Learning: Theory and Practice for Mission*. Western Academic Publishers, 2021.

Wan, Enoch, and J. David Lopez. *The Hispanic Hybrid Identity in Miami: Ethnographic Description and Missiological Implications*. Western Academic Publishers, 2021.

Wan, Enoch, and John Jay Flinn. *Holistic Mission through Mission Partnership: An Instrumental Case Study in La Ceiba, Honduras*. Western Academic Publishers, 2021.

Wan, Enoch, and Howard Shauhau Chen. *Marketplace Transformation: Motivating and Mobilizing Chinese Churches in the Silicon Valley for Gospel Transformation*. Western Academic Publishers, 2021.

2020

Wan, Enoch, and Shane Mikeska. *Engaging the Secular World through Life-on-Life Disciple-Making in the British Context: Relational Paradigm in Action*. Western Seminary Press, 2020.

Wan, Enoch and Robert Penner. *Missionary preparation in the Gospel of Matthew in light of 28:16-20*. Western Seminary Press, 2020.

Wan, Enoch and Tin Nguyen. *A Holistic and Contextualized Mission Training Program: Equipping Lay Leaders for Local Mission in Vietnam*. Western Seminary Press, 2020.

Wan, Enoch and J. David Lopez. *The Hispanic Hybrid Identity in Miami: Ethnographic Description and Missiological Implications*. Western Seminary Press, 2020.

2019

Wan, Enoch, ed.. *Diaspora Missions to International Students*. Western Seminary Press, 2019.

Wan, Enoch, and Mike Hung Lei. *Missions Beyond the Diaspora: Local Cross-Cultural Ministry of Chinese Congregations in the San Francisco Bay Area*. Western Seminary Press, 2019.

Wan, Enoch, and Jacky Lau. *Chinese Diaspora Kingdom Workers: In Action and With Guidance*. Western Seminary Press, 2019.

Wan, Enoch, and John Kuo. *Multiethnic Ministry and Diaspora Missions in Action: A Case Study of the Wu Chang Church of Kaohsiung, Taiwan*. Western Seminary Press, 2019.

Wan, Enoch, and Mathew Karimpanamannil. *A Theology of Spirit-Anointed Witness in Holistic Christian Mission Framed in the Relational Paradigm*. Western Seminary Press, 2019.

Wan, Enoch, and Jeremiah Chung. *Engaging Chinese Diaspora in the Ministry of Bible Translation*, 2019.

Wan, Enoch, Dennis C. Bradford, Leiton E. Chinn, Lisa Espineli Chinn, Sam Green, William Murrel, Katie J. Rawsom, Christopher D. Sneller, Florence PL Tan, and Chin T. Wang. *Diaspora Missions to International Students*. Western Seminary Press, 2019.

2017

Enoch Wan & Mark Hedinger. *Relational Missionary Training: Theology, Theory and Practice* Sky Forest, CA: Urban Loft Publishers, 2017.

2016

Wan, Enoch. *Theology of Unmerited Relationship* (in Chinese) Hong Kong: TienDao Publisher, 2016.

Wan, Enoch, and Anthony Casey. *Church Planting among Immigrants in US Urban Centers (Second Edition): The "Where", "Why", And "How" of Diaspora Missiology in Action*. 2nd edition. Portland, OR: CreateSpace Independent Publishing Platform, 2016.

2015

Pocock, Michael and Enoch Wan (editors). *Diaspora Missiology: Reflections on Reaching the Scattered Peoples of the World*. EMS Series no. 23, Pasadena, CA: William Carey Library, 2015.

Wan, Enoch and Wen Hui Gong. *Relational Theology: An Exploratory Study*. (in Chinese). Hong Kong: TienDao Publisher, 2015. (溫以諾、龔文輝。《散聚宣教學：北美個案研究》（香港天道），2015。)

Wan, Enoch and Abigail Au. *Diaspora Missions to Pakistani in Hong Kong,* (in Chinese). Hong Kong: TienDao Publisher, 2015. (溫以諾、區寶儀。《在港巴裔散聚宣教事工》（香港天道），2015。)

2014

Wan, Enoch. *Diaspora Missiology: Theory, Methodology, and Practice*, rev. ed. Portland, OR: Institute of Diaspora Studies, 2014.

Enoch Wan and Thanh Trung Le, *Mobilizing Vietnamese Diaspora for the Kingdom*. Portland, OR: Institute of Diaspora Studies, 2014.

Enoch Wan and Ted Rubesh, *Wandering Jews and Scattered Sri Lankans: Viewing Sri Lankans of the Gulf Cooperative Council through the Lens of the Old Testament Jewish Diaspora*. Portland, OR: Institute of Diaspora Studies, 2014.

Enoch Wan and Elton S. L. Law. *The 2011 Triple Disaster in Japan and the Diaspora: Lessons Learned and Ways Forward*. Portland, OR: Institute of Diaspora Studies, 2014.

Enoch Wan and Anthony Francis Casey. *Church Planting among Immigrants in US Urban Centers: The Where, Why, and How of Diaspora Missiology in Action*. Portland, Oregon: Institute of Diaspora Studies, 2014.

2013

Yaw Attah Edu-Bekoe and Enoch Wan, *Scattered Africans Keep Coming*. Portland, OR: Institute of Diaspora Studies, 2013.

Wan, Enoch, and Michael Pocock, eds.. *Missions from the Majority World: Progress, Challenges, and Case Studies*. Pasadena, CA: William Carey Library, 2013.

2012

Wan, Enoch and Joy Tira, eds.. *Missions in Action in the 21st Century*. Canada: FIN & Institute of Diaspora Studies, 2012.

2011

Wan, Enoch. *Diaspora Missiology: Theory, Methodology, and Practice, Revised Edition*. Portland, OR: Institute of Diaspora Studies, 2014.

2009

Wan, Enoch. *Missions Practice in the 21st Century*, ed. Sadiri Joy Tira. Pasadena, CA: William Carey International University Press, 2009.

2008

Wan, Enoch, Mary Wan, Wai Suet Chan, and Wai Wen Chan (ed.). *Perspectives on the World Christian Movement – Student Manual* （In Chinese）, CA: Great Commission Center International, May 2008. (溫以諾、溫陳鳳玲、陳惠雪、陳惠文 (主編)。《普世宣教課程—學生本》,（加洲: 大使命中心）, 2008年5月。)

2004

Wan, Enoch. *Christian Witness in Pluralistic Contexts in the 21st Century,* Pasadena, CA: William Carey Library, 2004.

Wan, Enoch and Tuvya Zaretsky. *Jewish-Gentile Couples: Trends, Challenges, and Hopes*, Pasadena, CA: William Carey Library, 2004

Pantoja, Jr., Luis, Sadiri Joy Tira, and Enoch Wan, eds. *Scattered: The Filipino Global Presence.* Manila: LifeChange Publishing, 2004.

2000

Wan, Enoch. *Questions and Answers about Marriage* (in Chinese). Lomita, CA: Great Commission Center International & Overseas Campus Magazine, 2000. (Chinese Title: 溫以諾。《婚姻問題解答 - 實用基督徒家庭生活指南》（美國加州: 海外校園雜誌）2000年8月。)

1999

Wan, Enoch. *Sino-theology: A Survey Study* (in Chinese), Ontario, Canada: Christian Communication Inc. of Canada (1999).
(溫以諾。《中色神學綱要》(加拿大恩福協會)。1999年12月。)

1998

Wan, Enoch. *Banishing the old and building the new: An Exploration of Sino-theology* (In Chinese), Ontario, Canada: Christian Communication Inc. of Canada, September 1998. （温以诺。《破旧与立新 － 中色基督教神学初探》(加拿大恩福协会), 1998年9月)

1995

Enoch Wan, ed., *Missions within Reach: Intercultural Ministries in Canada,* Hong Kong: China Alliance Press, 1995.

1992

Wan, Enoch. *Mission Resource Manual.* Edmonton, Canada: China Alliance Press of Canada, 1992.

PUBLICATION LIST - ARTICLES

2023

Wan, Enoch, and Siu Kuen Sonia Chan. "Contextualization the Asian Way: Relational Contextualization." *Asian Missions Advance*, no. 78 (Winter 2023). https://www.asiamissions.net/asian-missions-advances/amadvance-52-60/asian-missions-advance-78/.

2022

Wan, Enoch. "Application of Relational Interactionism in the Context of Relational Outreach to Diaspora Chinese in North America." *Global Missiology-Chinese Edition* 7, no. 2 (July 2022), www.globalmissiology.org.

2021

Wan, Enoch. "Relational Transformation Leadership - An Asian Christian Perspective." *Asian Missions Advance* (April 2021). http://www.asiamissions.net/relational-transformational-leadership-an-asian-christian-perspective/.

2020

Wan, Enoch. "AfriLink: A Case Study of Glo-cal Diaspora Mission in Hong Kong, Reaching Africans Locally." *Global Missiology-Chinese Edition* 5, no. 1 (January 2020), www.globalmissiology.org.

Wan, Enoch, and Karen Hedinger. "Relational Language Acquisition: The Foundation for Global Kingdom Language Learners." *Occasional Bulletin of EMS* 33, no. 2 (Spring 2020): 23–31.

2018

Wan, Enoch, and Mark Hedinger. "Transformative Ministry for the Majority World Context: Applying Relational Approaches." *EMS Occasional Bulletin* (Spring 2018).

2017

Wan, Enoch. "The Practice of Diaspora Missions in Local Congregation: From Beginning to Base." *Global Missiology* (January 2017), www.globalmissiology.org.

Wan, Enoch. "The Importance and Significance of Missiological Research – Christian Stewardship in Leadership," *Global Missiology* (January 2017), www.globalmissiology.org.

Wan, Enoch and Samuel Wang. "Conflict Paradigm for Theology of Religions." *Global Missiology* (January 2017), www.globalmissiology.org.

Wan, Enoch. "Inter-Disciplinary and Integrative Missiological Research: The 'What,' Why," and 'How.'" *Global Missiology* (July 2017), www.globalmissiology.org.

2016

Wan, Enoch and Joe Dow. "Serving China's Internal Diaspora: Motive, Means And Methods." *Global Missiology* (January 2016), www.globalmissiology.org.

2015

Wan, Enoch. "Is Allah of the Koran the same as Jehovah of the OT? --- Reflection from a Chinese practitioner's perspective." Unpublished paper NW EMS meetings, (2015).

2014

Wan, Enoch and Chandler H. Im, "New Opportunities and Strategic Practices of Diaspora Missions in South Korea." In *Global*

Diasporas and Mission by Chandler Im & Amos Yong (eds.) University of Edinburgh Century Series. (2014).

Wan, Enoch. "Relationship in the 21st Century: Theory and Practice." EVANGELVISION, (March 7, 2014), http://www.gospel-life.net/relationship-in-the-21st-century-theory-and-practice/

Wan, Enoch. "Diaspora Missiology and Beyond: Paths Taken and Ways Forward." Atlanta, GA EMS National Conference, (Sept. 2014).

Wan, Enoch and Tin V. Nguyen. "Towards a Theology of Relational Mission training - an Application of the Relational Paradigm." *Global Missiology* (January 2014), www.globalmissiology.org.

2013

Wan, Enoch. "A Warm, but Empty Voice? Reflections on Face-to-Face Interactions." EVANGELVISION, (December 2, 2013), http://www.gospel-life.net/a-warm-but-empty-voice-reflections-on-face-to-face-interactions/

Wan, Enoch. "New Opportunities and Strategic Practices of Diaspora Missions in South Korea," with Chandler H. Im in *Global Diasporas and Mission:* Edinburgh: Regnum Centenary Series. Chandler H. Im and Amos Yang (2013).

2011

Wan, Enoch & Narry Santos, "Missio-relational Reading of Mark," Evangelical Missiological Society *Occasional Bulletin*, Volume 24, #2 - Spring, 2011

Wan, Enoch. "Missio-relational Reading of Mark," *EMS Audio* interview http://www.emsweb.org/home

Wan, Enoch and John Mark (pseudonym). "Ministering in Turkish context: proposing a five-stage model for church planting," *Global Missiology* (January 2011), www.globalmissiology.org.

Wan, Enoch and Mark Hedinger. "Missionary Training for the Twenty First Century: Biblical Foundations." *Global Missiology* (July 2011), www.globalmissiology.org.

Wan, Enoch. "A Comparative Study of Sino-American Cognitive & Theological Pattern & Proposed Alternative," *Global Missiology* (April 2011), www.globalmissiology.org.

Wan, Enoch. "'Mission' and *Missio Dei*: Response to Charles Van Engen's 'Mission' Defined and Described." *Global Missiology* (April 2011), www.globalmissiology.org.

Wan, Enoch. "Diaspora Ministry Opportunity and Challenge: The Case of Refugee in Italy." *Global Missiology* (April 2011), www.globalmissiology.org.

Wan, Enoch and John Mark (pseudonym). "Ministering in Turkish Context: Proposing a Five-Stage Model for Church Planting." *Global Missiology* (January 2011), www.globalmissiology.org.

Wan, Enoch. "Relational Tree." *Global Missiology* (January 2011), www.globalmissiology.org.

Wan, Enoch. "Diaspora Mission Strategy in the Context of the United Kingdom in the 21st Century." In *Transformation: An International Journal of Holistic Mission Studies,* OCMS (http://trn.sagpub.com). 28(1) (January 2011):3-13.

Wan, Enoch and Yaw Attah Edu-Bekoe. "Diversity of Ghanaian Diaspora in the U.S.A.: Ministering to the Divers Ghanaian Communities through Ghanaian Congregation." In *EMS* series, (2011).

Wan, Enoch. "Korean Diaspora: From Hermit Kingdom to Kingdom Ministry." In *Korean Diaspora and Christian Mission,* eds. Won Suk Ma and S. Hun Kim, UK: Regnum Studies in Missions, (2011):85-102.

Wan Enoch & Mark Hedinger, "El Entrenamiento de Missioneros para el 21 Siglo Fundamentos Bíblicos." *Global Missiology (Spanish)* (January 2011), www.globalmissiology.org.

Wan, Enoch. "Rethinking Missiology in the Context of the 21st Century: Global Demographic Trends and Diaspora Missiology." *Great Commission Research Journal*, Vol.2 no. 1. (Summer 2010): 7-20.

2010

Wan, Enoch. "Celebration and Consultation: From Edinburgh 1910 to Tokyo 2010." In *Evangelical and Frontier Mission Perspectives on* the *Global Progress of the Gospel,* eds. Beth Snodderly and A. Scott Moreau, (UK: Regnum Press 2011)

Wan, Enoch. "Partnerships Should Mimic the Trinity." *Faith Today*, (July/August 2010.)

Wan, Enoch. "A Missio-Relational Reading of Romans." Evangelical Missiological Society *Occasional Bulletin*, (Winter 2010).

Wan, Enoch & Johnny Yee-chong Wan. "Partnership in Action - #2." *Global Missiology* (July 2010), www.globalmissiology.org

Wan, Enoch. "Three Steps Engaging the Diaspora in Canada in Christian Missions." *Global Missiology* (July 2010), www.globalmissiology.org

Wan, Enoch & Johnny Yee-chong Wan. "Relational Study of the Trinity and the Epistle to the Philippians." *Global Missiology* (April 1, 2010), www.globalmissiology.org

Wan, Enoch & Kevin P. Penman. "The 'Why,' 'How' and 'Who' of Partnership in Christian Missions." *Global Missiology* (April 2010), www.globalmissiology.org

Wan, Enoch. "A Missio-Relational Reading of Romans: A Complementary Study to Current Approaches." *Global Missiology* (April 2010), www.globalmissiology.org

Wan, Enoch and Geoff Baggett, "A Theology of Partnership: Implications for Implementation by a Local Church." *Global Missiology* (April 2010), www.globalmissiology.org.

Wan, Enoch. "Rethinking Missiology in the context of the 21st Century: Global Demographic Trends and Diaspora Missiology," Lausanne Diaspora Educators Consultation in Europe, (April 16, 2010), Oxford, UK: OCMS,

Wan, Enoch. "Global People and Diaspora Missiology, From Edinburgh 2010 to Tokyo 2010." In the *Handbook of Global Mission: Consultation, Celebration, May 11th-14th, 2010,* 92-106

Wan, Enoch & Sadiri Joy Tira. "Diaspora Missiology and Mission in the Context of the 21st Century," Seoul, Korea: *Torch Trinity Journal*, (May 30, 2010), Volume 13, No.1, 46-6. Also published in *Global Missiology* (October 2010), www.globalmissiology.org.

Wan, Enoch. "Rethinking Missiology in the Context of the 21st Century: Global Demographic Trends and Diaspora Missiology." *Great Commission Research Journal,* Volume 2, Issue 1, Summer 2010 Biola University. http://apps.biola.edu/gcr/volumes/2/issues/1/articles/7

Wan, Enoch. ""Mission" and "*Missio Dei*": Response to Charles Van Engen's "Mission Defined and Described." In *Missionshift: Global Mission Issues in the Third Millennium,* eds. David J. Hesselgrave and Ed Stetzer, 2010:41-50.

Wan, Enoch. "Three Steps Engaging the Diaspora in Canada in Christian Missions." *Global Missiology,* (July 2010), www.globalmissiology.org.

2009

Wan, Enoch and Mark Vanderwerf. "A Review of the Literature on Ethnicity, National Identity and Related Missiological Studies." *Global Missiology* (April 2009), www.globalmissiology.org.

Wan, Enoch. "Diaspora Couple Priscilla and Aquila: A Model Family in Action for Mission." *Global Missiology* (April 2009), www.globalmissiology.org.

Wan, Enoch. "Meditation (Lent Season) and Christian Missions." *Global Missiology* (April 2009), www.globalmissiology.org.

Wan, Enoch. "Book Review: *The Concept of Ethnicity in the Bible: A Theological Analysis* by Mark Kreitzer." *Global Missiology* (April 2009), www.globalmissiology.org.

Wan, Enoch. "Core Values of Mission Organization in the Cultural Context of the 21st Century." *Global Missiology* (January 2009), www.globalmissiology.org.

Wan, Enoch & Paul Hiebert. "Missional Narrative and Missional Hermeneutic for the 21st Century." *Global Missiology* (January 2009), www.globalmissiology.org.

Wan, Enoch. "Ethical Issues of Conducting Cross-Cultural Field Research." In *Transcending Borders*. Logos Evangelical Seminary. Volume 2.

Wan, Enoch. "A Comparative Study of Sino-American Cognitive & Theological Pattern & Proposed Alternative." In *East-West Cultural*

Exchange: Review & Preview, Edited by Li Lin et al. Shanghai: People's Press, 2009:27-52.

Wan, Enoch. "The Phenomenon of the Diaspora: Missiological Implications for Christian Missions." *Asian American Christianity Reader*. Viji Nakka-Cammauf and Timothy Tseng (editors). ISAAC (Institute for the study of Asian American Christianity). 2009:153-163. Originally published in Chinese: *Great Commission Bi-monthly* 79 (April 2009).

2008

Wan, Enoch & Linda Gross. "Christian Missions to Diaspora Groups: A Diachronic General Overview and Synchronic Study of Contemporary USA." *Global Missiology* (April 2008), www.globalmissiology.org.

Wan, Enoch and Geoff Hartt. "Complementary Aspects of Short-term Missions and Long-term Missions: Cast Studies for a Win-win Situation," in *Effective Engagement in Short-term Missions: Doing it Right!*, ed. Robert J. Priest, EMS series #16, (2008):62-98.

2007

Wan, Enoch. "So Send I You (Melody & Lyric)." *Global Missiology* (October 2007), www.globalmissiology.org.

Wan, Enoch. "Defending or Defrauding the Faith: A Pradigmatic Comparison of the 'Theology of Religions' of Hendrik Kraemer and John Hick." *Global Missiology* (October 2007), www.globalmissiology.org.

Wan, Enoch. "Diaspora Missiology." *Global Missiology* (July 2007), www.globalmissiology.org.

Wan, Enoch. "Sample Books Helpful for Church Planting." *Global Missiology* (July 2007). www.globalmissiology.org.

Wan, Enoch. "Relational Theology and Relational Missiology," *Occasional Bulletin,* Evangelical Missiological Society. (Winter 2007), 21:1, 1-7.

Wan, Enoch. "Explanation and Reflection," (April 2007), on the occasion of Paul Hiebert's passing. http://paul-timothy.net/pages/gm/wan_reflections_on_paul_hiebert_4_2007.pdf

Wan, Enoch. "Ministry in the Context of Suffering: A Case Study of Southern Sudan." In *Missions in Contexts of Violence,* ed. Keith E. Eitel, Evangelical Missiological Society Series, Number 15: 283-310, (2007).

Wan, Enoch. "Diaspora Missiology". *Occasional Bulletin.* Evangelical Missiological Society, Vol. 20 No. 2, (2007).

2006

Wan, Enoch. "Diaspora Missiology" & "Global Diaspora Missiology Consultation." *Global Missiology* (October 2006), www.globalmissiology.org.

Wan, Enoch. "Use of Technology by Mission Workers." *Global Missiology* (January 2006), www.globalmissiology.org.

Wan, Enoch and Mark Hedinger. "Understanding 'relationality' from a Trinitarian Perspective." *Global Missiology* (January 2006), www.globalmissiology.org.

Wan, Enoch. "The Paradigm of 'relational realism'," *Occasional Bulletin,* Evangelical Missiological Society. (Spring 2006), 19:2, p.1-4.

2005

Wan, Enoch. "Holistic Ministry/Missions: Reflections & Resource Material." *Global Missiology* (October 2005), www.globalmissiology.org.

Wan, Enoch. "Social Sciences and Mission." *Global Missiology* (April 2005), www.globalmissiology.org.

Wan, Enoch. "The Paradigm & Pressing Issues of Inter-disciplinary Research Methodology." *Global Missiology* (January 2005), www.GlobalMissiology.org.

Wan, Enoch "Missionary strategy in the Epistle to the Romans," (in Chinese) *To the End of the Earth*, Hong Kong: Association of Christian Missions Ltd. (July-Sept. 2005): 1-2.

Altstadt, Robert and Enoch Wan. "The Salvation of the Unevangelized: What the Literature Suggests." *Global Missiology* (January 2005), www.globalmissiology.org.

2004

Wan, Enoch. "Spiritual Warfare: What Chinese Christians Should Know and Do." (2004), http://www.feca.org/bulletin_07/bulletin

Wan, Enoch and Marty Shaw, Jr.. "The Future of Globalizing Missions: What the Literature Suggests." *Global Missiology* (April 2004), www.GlobalMissiology.org.

Wan, Enoch, "Book Review: *The Fundamentalist Movement Among Protestant Missionaries in China, 1920-1937*, by Kevin Xiyi Yao", *Evangelical Missions Quarterly* 40:4, pp528-530.

Wan, Enoch. "Missionary anthropology = Cultural anthropology + Theology?" in *Pastoral Journal,* Issue 16, (May 2004): 115-130

Wan, Enoch. "Traditional mission theology and contextual mission theology," in *Pastoral Journal,* Issue 16, (May 2004): 149-158.

Wan, Enoch. "A Critique of Charles Kraft's Use/Misuse of Communication and Social Sciences in Biblical Interpretation and Missiological Formulation." *Global Missiology* (October 2004), www.globalmissiology.org.

Wan, Enoch "Ethnic Receptivity and Intercultural Ministries." *Global Missiology* (October 2004), www.globalmissiology.org.

Wan, Enoch and T.V. Thomas. "What Denominational Leaders Should Know But Have Never Been Told Regarding Intercultural Ministries." *Global Missiology* (October 2004), www.globalmissiology.org.

Wan, Enoch. "The Phenomenon of the Diaspora: Missiological Implications for Christian Missions," Chapter 13 of *Asian American Christianity: A Reader*, Edited by Viji Nakka-Cammauf and Timothy Tseng, The Pacific Asian American and Canadian Christian Education project (PAACCE) and the Institute for the Study of Asian American Christianity (ISAAC), (2004).

Wan, Enoch. "Ethnohermeneutics: Its Necessity and Difficulty for All Christians of All Times." *Global Missiology* (January 2004), www.globalmissiology.org.

Wan, Enoch. "Christianity in the East and the West. Article Two Christianity in the Eye of Traditional Chinese." *Missiology.org,*
< http://www.missiology.org> Accessed July 24, 2004.

Wan, Enoch. "Christianity in the East and the West. Article Four. Practical Contextualization: A Case Study of Evangelizing Contemporary Chinese," *Missiology.org*, <http://www.missiology.org> Accessed July 24, 2004.

Wan, Enoch. "Christianity in the East and the West". Article Five. Theological Contributions of Sino-theology to the Global Christian Community (Part One)." *Missiology.org*, <http://www.missiology.org> Accessed July 24, 2004.

2003

Wan, Enoch. "Christianity in the Eye of Traditional Chinese." *Global Missiology* (October 2003), www.globalmissiology.org.

Wan, Enoch. "Critiquing the Method of Traditional Western Theology and Calling for Sino-Theology." *Global Missiology* (October 2003), www.globalmissiology.org.

Wan, Enoch. "Jesus Christ for the Chinese: A Contextual Reflection." *Global Missiology* (October 2003), www.globalmissiology.org.

Wan, Enoch. "Exploring Sino-Spirituality." *Global Missiology* (October 2003), www.globalmissiology.org.

Wan, Enoch. "Practical Contextualization: A Case Study of Evangelizing Contemporary Chinese." *Global Missiology* (October 2003), www.globalmissiology.org.

Wan, Enoch. "Sailing in the Western Wind." *Global Missiology* (October 2003), www.globalmissiology.org.

Patterson, George, Galen Currah, and Enoch Wan. "Classroom Instruction and Mentoring Compared." *Global Missiology* (October 2003), www.globalmissiology.org.

Wan, Enoch. "Spiritual Warfare: Understanding Demonization." *Global Missiology* (Oct. 2003), www.globalmissiology.org.

Wan, Enoch. "Spiritual Warfare: Overcoming Demonization." *Global Missiology* (Oct. 2003), www.globalmissiology.org.

Wan, Enoch. "Pastor As Servant-Leader" *Christian Living Quarterly*, vol. 1, no. 3 (2003), 1.

Wan, Enoch. "Mission Among the Chinese Diaspora: A Case Study of Migration and Mission." *Missiology: An International Review,* Vol. XXXI., No. 1, (January 2003):35-43.

Wan, Enoch. "Exploring Sino-Spirituality." *Christianity in China.* (February 2003).

Wan, Enoch. "The magnificent Christ and human culture." In *The Glorious Christ and the Contemporary Christian.* ed. Lawrence Chan, Concord, CA: Christian Witness Theological Seminary, 268-286.

Wan, Enoch. "Rethinking Missiological Research Methodology: Exploring a New Direction." *Global Missiology* (Oct 2003), www.globalmissiology.org.

Wan, Enoch. "Spiritual Warfare: What Chinese Christians Should Know and Do". *Global Missiology.* (Oct. 2003). www.GlobalMissiology.org

Wan, Enoch. "Sino-Spirituality: A Case Study of Trinitarian Paradigm." *Global Missiology* (Oct. 2003), www.globalmissiology.org.

2001

Wan, Enoch. "21st Century Religious Mega-trend and Challenge – Part Three." *Chinese Church Today* (April: 2001) 48-51.

Wan, Enoch. "21st Century Religious Mega-trend and Challenge – Part Two." *Chinese Church Today* (February 2001) 36-39.

Wan, Enoch. "Ethnocentrism." *Evangelical Dictionary of World Missions*, edited by A Scott Moreau. Baker Books, 2001, 324-325.

2000

Wan, Enoch. "Theological contribution of Sino-theology to global Christian community." *Chinese Around the World,* (July 2000).

Wan, Enoch. "Jesus Christ for the Chinese: A Contextual Reflection." *Chinese Around the World* (November 2000).

Wan, Enoch. "Practical contextualization: A case study of evangelizing contemporary Chinese." *Chinese Around the World* (March 2000), 18-24.

Wan, Enoch. "Theological contribution of Sino-theology to global Christian community." *Chinese Around the World* (July 2000).

Wan, Enoch. "21st Century Religious Mega-trend and Challenge – Part One." *Chinese Church Today* (December 2000), 13-17.

1999

Wan, Enoch. "Christianity in the eye of traditional Chinese." *Chinese Around the World* (July 1999), 17-23.

Wan, Enoch "Critique of Traditional Western Theology." *Chinese Around the World* (October 1999), 19-25.

Wan, Enoch. "Cultural Differences and Conflicts: A Comparative between Local-born Chinese and Overseas-born Chinese." *First Evangelical Church Association Bulletin,* (August:18-20, 1999).

Wan, Enoch. "Sailing in the Western Wind." *Chinese Around the World.* (March:18-21, 1999).

Wan, Enoch. "Cults and Missions." *Great Commission Quarterly* (May 9-11, 1999).

Wan, Enoch. "Systematisation of the Theological Pursuit for the Chinese: An Exploration." In *Modernity, Change in Tradition and Theological Reflection,* edited by Eddie Chung. Hong Kong: Tao Fong Shan Christian Centre Ltd., 1999, 183-203.

Wan, Enoch. "Spiritual Warfare – What Chinese Christian Should Know And Do." *First Evangelical Church Association Bulletin* (December:6-9, 1999).

Wan, Enoch. "Exploring Sino-Spirituality." *First Evangelical Church Association Bulletin (*December 1999), 16–21.
<http://www.christianityinchina.org> Accessed July 24, 2004.

1997

Wan, Enoch. "A Case Study of Comparative Analysis of Three Religious Movements in Latin America." *Evangelical Theological Society* (March 1997).

1996

Wan, Enoch. "Horizon of Inter-philosophical Dialogue: A Paradigmatic Comparative Study of the Ameri-European & The Sino-Asian Cognitive Patterns/Processes." (In Chinese) *Cultural Revitalization for China* (1996:1-5).

Wan, Enoch. "A critique of Charles Kraft's use /misuse of communication and social science in biblical interpretation and missiological formulation." In *Missiology and the social sciences:*

contributions, cautions and conclusions, eds. Edward Rommen and Gary Orwin, Pasadena: William Carey Library (1996), p.121-164.

Wan, Enoch. "Spiritual Dynamics in Trinitarian Missiology." *Reformed Theological Seminary,* EMS SE Meeting (March 1996).

1995

Wan, Enoch. "Protestant Ethic and Chinese Culture: A Reflection of Max Weber's Theory and Methodology." In *East & West: Religious Ethics and Other Essays,* eds. Zhang Zhigang & M.Y. Stewart, Beijing: Central Translation & Publication of China.

Wan, Enoch, ed.. *Missions Within Reach: Intercultural Ministries in Canada*, Hong Kong: China Alliance Press, 1995.

1994

Wan, Enoch. "Horizon of Inter-philosophical Dialogue: A Paradigmatic Comparative Study of the Ameri-European & The Sino-Asian Cognitive Patterns/Processes." (In Chinese) *Cultural Revitalization for China.* (1996:1-5)

1992

Wan, Enoch. "Scriptural Spirituality." *Chinese in North America* (July-August 1992: 2-4).

1991

Wan, Enoch. "The Theology of Family: A Chinese Case Study of Contextualization." *Chinese in North America* (March - April 1991).

Wan, Enoch. "The Theology of Spiritual Formation: A Case Study of Contextualized Chinese Theology." *Chinese in North America*, California: Chinese Coordination Centre of World Evangelism - North America (March-April 1991), 2-7.

1990

Wan, Enoch. "Ethnic Receptivity Factors." In *Reclaiming a Nation*, ed. Arnell Motz, Richmond, B.C., Canada: Church Leadership Library, 117-132.

1989

Wan, Enoch. "Deliverance from Demonization." *Alliance Family* (1989 Spring: 8-12), Manila, Philippines: CAMACOP.

1988

Wan, Enoch. "Spiritual Warfare: Understanding Demonization," *Alliance Family* (1988 Summer: 6-18), Manila, Philippines: CAMACOP.

Wan, Enoch. "The Confucian Ethic and the Chinese Cultural Attitudes Towards Work." *Crux*, Vol. XXIV, No. 3, (September 1988).

Wan, Enoch. "The Worldview of Overseas Chinese." (In Chinese) *Chinese Churches Today,* Hong Kong: Chinese Coordination Centre of World Evangelism (December 1988: 23ff).

1985

Wan, Enoch. "Tao - The Chinese Theology of God-Man," *His Dominion*, (Spring 1985: 24-27), Regina, Saskatchewan: Canadian Theological Seminary.

1983

Wan, Enoch. "The Strength and Weakness of Chinese Culture." (In Chinese) *Chinese Churches Today* (January 1983: 8ff), Hong Kong: Chinese Coordination Centre of World Evangelism.

Wan, Enoch. "Know Thyself." *Intouch,* Canadian Theological Seminary, Vol. 12 Number 2, (1983).

1982

Wan, Enoch. "Critique of Functional Missionary Anthropology." *His Dominion*, Vol. 8, No. 3, (Spring 1982):18-22.

Wan, Enoch. "The Theological Application of Contextual-Interaction Model of Culture." *His Dominion*, Vol. 9 Number 1, (October 1982).

1979

Wan, Enoch. "The Theological Application of the Contextual-Interaction Model of Culture." *His Dominion*, Regina, Saskatchewan: Canadian Theological Seminary, 1979.

Wan, Enoch "Faith and Culture," *The Alliance Quarterly*, (June 1979): vol. 28: 3ff.

1978

Wan, Enoch. "The Dynamics of Ethnicity: A Case Study on the Immigrant Community of New York Chinatown." Unpublished doctoral dissertation, State University of New York at Stony Brook, 1978.

CHINESE PUBLICATION LIST 中文著作目錄 [236]

2025

溫以諾、李曙明。<恩縱靈修法>《環球華人宣教學期刊》第八十一期，2025 年 7 月。

溫以諾。<懷念恩師：章力生老師>《環球華人宣教學期刊》第八十期，2025 年 4 月。

溫以諾、劉得貴。《神國僑僕：關顧與指引》（香港：Everyone Press Ltd）2025 年 3 月初版（電子版）。(Chinese version of *Chinese Diaspora Kingdom Workers: In Action and With Guidance*, by Enoch Wan & Jacky Lau, Portland, Oregon: Western Seminary Press, 2019)。

免費下載網址：營商事工-書籍
https://www.chinesebam.com/book/

2024

溫以諾。《實用恩情神學簡介》(Chinese version of *Introduction to Relationship of Grace*, by Enoch Wan, OR: Western Academic Publishers, 2024)。 中文版的免費下載網址：《環球華人宣教學期刊》第七十九期，2025 年 1 月。

溫以諾、鄧明慧。<從使徒行傳「見證」一詞重探「宣教」的定義>《環球華人宣教學期刊》第七十七期，2024 年 7 月。

---

[236] This Chinese list, including Dr. Wan's Chinese books and articles, was compiled based on the information extracted from *Global Missiology - Chinese Edition*《環球華人宣教學期刊》and from Dr. Wan's webpage <https://www.enochwan.com/chinese/full/(1.5)%20articles.html and the Chinese section> Accessed on 2025-08-14.
Editorial note: some Chinese publications in this list may have appeared in the English list.

溫以諾。<跨文化教育與跨文化門徒訓練>《環球華人宣教學期刊》第七十六期，2024年4月。

溫以諾、不記名。<「關係式更新營商宣教」Relational "Business for Transformation" (R-B4T)>《環球華人宣教學期刊》第七十五期，2024年1月。

溫以諾、龔文輝。《北美散聚華人教會：宣教事工個案研究》(Chinese version of *Diaspora Missions of Chinese Diaspora Congregationsin North America,* by Enoch Wan & W. Gong, OR: Western Academic Publishers, January 2024)。 免費下載網址：《環球華人宣教學期刊》第七十八期，2024年10月。

2023

溫以諾主編。《實用關係神學簡介》(Chinese version of *Introduction: Practical Relational Theology,* ed. Enoch Wan, OR: Western Academic Publishers, December 2023)。 中文版的免費下載網址：《環球華人宣教學期刊》第七十九期，2025年1月。

溫以諾。<宗教改革五百週年慶典：馬丁‧路德（Martin Luther)範式轉移對現代福音事工的啟迪>《環球華人宣教學期刊》第七十四期，2023年10月。

溫以諾。<夫妻互動顯恩情>《環球華人宣教學期刊》第七十二期，2023年1月。

2022

溫以諾主編。《馬來西亞散聚宣教事工》(Chinese book：*Malaysia Diaspora Missions,* ed. Enoch Wan, OR: Western Academic Publishers, June 2022)。 中文版的免費下載網址：《環球華人宣教學期刊》第七十八期，2024年10月。

溫以諾、郭麗輝。<「關係互動論」的應用：北美華人文化處境下的恩情佈道>《環球華人宣教學期刊》第六十九期，2022年7月。

溫以諾。<悼念梁偉材牧師>《環球華人宣教學期刊》第六十八期，2022年4月。

溫以諾。<從「關係互動論」 反思「靈性轉化」及「社會轉化」>《環球華人宣教學期刊》第六十七期，2022年1月。

2021

溫以諾。<連牧師在香港推動「本地跨文化宣教事工」>《環球華人宣教學期刊》第六十五期，2021年7月。

溫以諾。<連達傑牧師著作簡介>《環球華人宣教學期刊》第六十五期，2021年7月。

朱內萍、溫以諾。<宣教實踐初探：從「恩情神學」到「讀畫心理分析」>《環球華人宣教學期刊》第六十四期，2021年4月。

2020

溫以諾、陳小娟。<關係宣教學的真、善、美："missio Dei" 的認識與實踐>《環球華人宣教學期刊》第六十二期，2020年10月。

溫以諾、林銀姬。<探討向沙縣小吃餐飲業人員傳福音的散聚宣教方案>《環球華人宣教學期刊》第六十一期，2020年7月。

溫以諾。<「環球/本地模式」(glo-cal) 散聚宣教個案研究：「愛非連 AfriLink」(在香港向非洲人跨文化宣教)>《環球華人宣教學期刊》第五十九期，2020年1月。

2019

溫以諾。<宗教改革五百週年慶典：從馬丁．路德到今時的隔代範式轉移 (上)>《環球華人宣教學期刊》第五十八期，2019年10月。

溫以諾、黃翠嫩。<關係導向宣教在台灣基層宣教的應用>《環球華人宣教學期刊》第五十七期，2019年7月。

溫以諾、周新生。<淺談唐朝景教來華之因由及沒落>《環球華人宣教學期刊》第五十七期，2019年7月。

溫以諾、Joe Dow。<服侍中國國內遷徙人群：動機、途徑與方法>《環球華人宣教學期刊》第五十五期，2019年1月。

溫以諾、梁永昌。<從旅遊業探討跨文化傳福音的策略>《環球華人宣教學期刊》第五十五期，2019年1月。

溫以諾、林志明。<西馬尼泊爾散聚宣教事工>《環球華人宣教學期刊》第五十五期，2019年1月。

2018

溫以諾、溫陳鳳玲合編。《意大利散聚宣教事工》(Chinese book: *Italian Diaspora Chinese & Diaspora Missions*, Enoch Wan & Mary

Wan (editors), OR: Western Seminary Press, Center for Diaspora & Relational Research, December 2018)。 免費下載網址:《環球華人宣教學期刊》第七十八期,2024 年 10 月。

溫以諾、阮慧珍。<評汪維藩的中國神學及其文化淵源>《環球華人宣教學期刊》第五十四期,2018 年 10 月。

溫以諾、謝貴芳。<評吳雷川在中色神學方面的努力>《環球華人宣教學期刊》第五十四期,2018 年 10 月。

溫以諾、黃翠嫩。<關係導向宣教在台灣基層宣教的應用>《環球華人宣教學期刊》第五十四期,2018 年 10 月。

溫以諾、王良碧。<評趙紫宸在中色神學方面的努力>《環球華人宣教學期刊》第五十四期,2018 年 10 月。

溫以諾、黃靖斌。<網絡宣教動力的來源及具體運作>《環球華人宣教學期刊》第五十三期,2018 年 7 月。

溫以諾、張軍玉。<從綜合研究法反思:全球化、處境化、全球在地化及華人散聚現象>《環球華人宣教學期刊》第五十一期,2018 年 1 月。

張軍玉、溫以諾。<跨科際綜合研究法的宗教比較應用:諾亞方舟史實、異教故事及 "送子觀音" 個案探討>《環球華人宣教學期刊》第五十一期,2018 年 1 月。

2017

連達傑、溫以諾。<從《咫尺宣教:動員香港華人教會服侍在港印尼家傭》一書談起>《環球華人宣教學期刊》第五十期,2017 年 10 月。

廖少舫、溫以諾。<全球人口流動趨勢、散聚宣教學的聖經基礎、烏克蘭散聚華人宣教的呼聲>《環球華人宣教學期刊》第五十期,2017 年 10 月。

溫以諾、賴顯光。<華人猶宣歷史的第一頁及近期動態>《環球華人宣教學期刊》第四十九期,2017 年 7 月。

溫以諾。<從宣教神學反思「選民」— 猶太人>《環球華人宣教學期刊》第四十九期,2017 年 7 月。

溫以諾。<屬靈爭戰的認識與事奉>《環球華人宣教學期刊》第四十八期,2017 年 4 月。

溫以諾。<堂會落實參與散聚宣教事工:實踐始點 -》 外展基地>《環球華人宣教學期刊》第四十七期,2017 年 1 月。

2016

溫以諾。《恩情神學 – 跨科研究與應用際》（香港：徒。書館 eLibrary），2016。

溫以諾。〈從關係論反思宣教的動力〉《環球華人宣教學期刊》第四十六期，2016年10月。

溫以諾。〈貫連「神學」與「宣教學」的「恩情神學」（專刊出版前的濃縮版）〉《環球華人宣教學期刊》第四十三期，2016年1月。

溫以諾。〈恩情神學及關係論參考書目〉《環球華人宣教學期刊》第四十三期，2016年1月。

溫以諾。〈天道新近推出的電子「徒」書館〉《環球華人宣教學期刊》第四十三期，2013年1月。

2015

溫以諾。〈「關係神學論」在漢語語境中的個案：中色神學舉隅〉《環球華人宣教學期刊》第四十一期，2015年7月。

溫以諾。〈恩情關係勝於虛擬世界的模擬關係〉《環球華人宣教學期刊》第四十一期，2015年7月。

溫以諾。〈各按其時成為美好〉《環球華人宣教學期刊》第四十一期，2015年7月。

溫以諾。〈教會宣教動力的來源、分類及具體運作〉《環球華人宣教學期刊》第四十期，2015年4月。

溫以諾。《關係神學初探》（香港：徒。書館 eLibrary），2015。

溫以諾、龔文輝。《散裔宣教學：北美個案研究》（香港天道），2015。

溫以諾、區寶儀。《在港巴裔散聚宣教事工》（香港天道），2015。

2014

溫以諾、納里・桑托斯。〈馬可福音的宣教-關係式讀解〉《環球華人宣教學期刊》第三十八期，2014年10月。

溫以諾。〈超乎「唯獨恩典」〉《環球華人宣教學期刊》第三十七期，2014年7月。

溫以諾。〈「關係神學」與「關係宣教」〉《環球華人宣教學期刊》第三十六期，2014年4月。

溫以諾。〈教會宣教動力的來源、分類及具體運作〉《環球華人宣教學期刊》第三十五期，2014年1月。

溫以諾。〈工人事奉的模式〉《環球華人宣教學期刊》第三十五期，2014年1月。

2012
溫以諾。〈從「關係論」的角度解讀大衛的兩首詩篇（詩16, 23）〉《環球華人宣教學期刊》第三十期，2012年10月。

2011
溫以諾。〈羅馬書的「宣教-關係式」解讀〉《環球華人宣教學期刊》第二十六期，2011年10月。

溫以諾、黃建輝。〈澳洲華人現況及澳洲華人教會宣教現況〉《環球華人宣教學期刊》第二十三期，2011年1月。

2010
溫以諾。〈從散聚看香港的宣教角色〉宣教專題講座，香港浸信會神學院應用神學教育中心，2010年12月13日。

溫以諾、林玉香。〈《監獄書信》中的「關係神學 —人論」〉《環球華人宣教學期刊》第十四期，2008年10月。

溫以諾。〈莫效世俗_甘於為僕〉《大使命雙月刊》2010年10月第88期5-10頁。

2009
溫以諾。〈變幻世界中信徒的資源及見証〉《環球華人宣教學期刊》第十五期，2009年1月。原載於《華傳路81期2008年》。

溫以諾。〈中國色彩神學系統化的探討〉《環球華人宣教學期刊》第十六期2009年4月。

溫以諾。〈模範宣教家庭〉《環球華人宣教學期刊》 第十七期，2009年7月。

溫以諾。〈模範宣教家庭〉《環球華人宣教學期刊》第十六期，2009年4月。（本文原載於《大使命》雙月刊第七十九期二零零九年四月）。

2008
溫以諾。〈從《監獄書信》探討「關係神學論」〉《環球華人宣教學期刊》第十四期，2008年10月。

溫以諾、溫陳鳳玲、陳憲雪、陳惠文（主編）。《普世宣教課程—學生本》，（加洲：大使命中心）2008年5月。

溫以諾。〈「關係實在論」簡介〉《環球華人宣教學期刊》第十一期 2008年1月。

何和平、溫以諾。〈論「超越」關係〉《環球華人宣教學期刊》第十二期，2008年4月。

2007

溫以諾。〈宣教的「落實」〉《環球華人宣教學期刊》第十期，2007年10月。（本文原載於《今日華人教會》2007年4月號6-9頁）

溫以諾。〈福音使者：「變色龍」或「賺錢蟲」〉《環球華人宣教學期刊》第十期，2007年10月。

溫以諾。〈照樣差你 – 詞和曲〉《環球華人宣教學期刊》第十期，2007年10月。

溫以諾。〈「家」的文化傳統：華人基督徒的信仰及實踐〉《環球華人宣教學期刊》第八期 2007年4月。

溫以諾。〈萬世戰爭〉《環球華人宣教學期刊》第七期，2007年1月。

溫以諾。〈我的夢 – 普世福音遍傳〉《大使命雙月刊》。

溫以諾。〈散聚宣教學〉《大使命雙月刊》2007年10月第70期24-28頁。

溫以諾。〈「關係實在論」模式 簡介〉《環球華人宣教學期刊》Dec13 2007。（本文原稿為英文，專文題目是 "The Paradigm of 'Relational Realism,'" 刊載於 *Occasional Bulletin*, vol. 19 No.2, Spring 2006. The Evangelical Missiological Society EMS）

溫以諾。〈從華人信徒角度看猶太人福音事工〉《大使命雙月刊》第七十一期。2007.12:22-24。

2006

溫以諾。〈西風東漸〉《環球華人宣教學期刊》 第四期，2006年4月。

溫以諾。〈「多元化中華民族」及「一元化華夏文化」背景中的基督教〉《環球華人宣教學期刊》第三期，2006年1月。

2005

溫以諾。〈從羅馬書略談宣教策略〉《環球華人宣教學期刊》第二期，2005年10月。（經香港差傳事工聯會允准，轉載自《往普天下去》2005年7-9月號，頁1-3。）

溫以諾。〈中華文化與中色神學舉偶〉《環球華人宣教學期刊》第二期，2005年10月。

溫以諾。〈講題：《中色神學綱要》一書的簡介與個人對「中色神學」的期盼〉《環球華人宣教學期刊》第一期，2005年7月。

2004

溫以諾。〈宣教文化人類學 = 文化人類學 + 神學〉《教牧期刊》第十六期. 2004.5:118-156。

溫以諾。〈傳統式神學與處境化神學論宣教〉《教牧期刊》第十六期. 2004.5:149-158。

溫以諾。〈對處境化宣教神學的回應〉《教牧期刊 — 2003年5月8日專題研討輯錄專文》第十六期. 2004.5:115-192。

2003

溫以諾。〈榮耀的基督與人類文化〉《榮耀的基督與當代信徒》陳若愚主編，基督工人神學院，2003:269-286。

2000

溫以諾。《婚姻問題解答 – 實用基督徒家庭生活指南》（美國加州：海外校園雜誌），2000年8月。（免費下載網址：《環球華人宣教學期刊》第七十九期，2025年一月）

溫以諾。〈屬靈戰爭的認識與實踐〉《事奉問題解答第四課》。（美國加州）海外校園雜誌，2000年8月26-33頁。

1999

溫以諾。〈異端與差傳〉《大使命季刊》1999.5:9-11。

溫以諾。〈中國色彩神學系統化的探討〉《現代性、傳統變遷與神學反思：第一、二屆漢語神學圓桌會議論文言集》劉小楓、謝品然、曾慶豹編，1999:183-204。

溫以諾。〈屬靈戰爭：華人信徒須知〉《羅省基督教聯會會訊》。1999年12月6-9頁。

溫以諾。《中色神學綱要》（加拿大恩福協會）。1999年12月。

1998

溫以諾。〈中色屬靈觀〉《羅省基督教聯會會訊》。1998年12月16-22。

溫以諾。《破旧与立新：中色基督教神学初探》（加拿大恩福协会），1998年9月。

溫以諾。〈海外華人、華僑的意識〉《海外華人教會》1988：12-23-24。

1979

溫以諾。〈有關信仰與文化的我見〉《建道通訊》第廿八期，1979：4-7。

Tributes

I had the good fortune to be a student under Dr. Enoch Wan, and this relationship has shaped my work as a missionary both directly and indirectly. The first day of class in the Intercultural Studies program at Reformed Theological Seminary (RTS), I found a seat next to Sadiri Joy Tira who was soon to be appointed the Senior Associate for Diasporas of the Lausanne Movement. Joy was at RTS because of the mentorship of Dr. Wan, an early pioneer in the field of diaspora studies. Joy was already a leader in the Filipino diaspora, and I recently had been appointed by my mission board to serve in the Philippines. I was soon drawn into this diaspora world. Dr. Wan encouraged his students at RTS to recognize the importance of God's design for global migration and to map these new insights into the emerging field of diaspora missiology.

Because of this influence, once in the Philippines, I began to work with the local chapter of the Philippines Missions Mobilization Movement of the Philippines Missions Association. The PM3 helped local churches send their members who found work overseas in a healthy and missional manner. The growing importance of diaspora missions for the Philippine church was greatly aided by the 2004 publication of Scattered: The Filipino Global Presence, edited by Drs. Wan, Tira, and Pantoja. In 2006, as a faculty member of the Cebu Graduate School of Theology, I hosted Dr. Wan and Dr. Tira as they taught the first diaspora missions course at the seminary.

In 2009 at the Lausanne diaspora missions educators gathering in Seoul, South Korea, I witnessed the gracious influence of Dr. Wan on the delegates. Those delegates crafted the resolutions that became the basis for the Lausanne statements on missions and migration, having grown from the Cape Town Congress in 2010 and the 2011 establishment of the Global Diaspora Network (GDN). As a representative for GDN in North and South America, I witnessed how our work to establish diaspora missiology globally within mission training schools and centers was built upon the foundation laid by Dr. Wan.

My subsequent work with encouraging mission sending organizations to embrace diaspora missions and to assist in mobilizing the migrating Majority World Christian populations in the Middle East and North Africa has been greatly aided by Dr. Wan's encouragement and wisdom. The Institute of Diaspora Studies he established at Western Seminary provided valuable resources, and more than once I found myself in extremely beneficial ministry partnerships with students he mentored at Western. From personal experience, I have seen how his global influence continues to shape the world of diaspora missions.

It has been a great privilege to be his student and now fellow laborer for the gospel among the people moving around the globe. His insights and commitment to diaspora missions have had a profound impact on my thinking and ministry. I am deeply grateful for his life and work.

John Baxter, D. Min.
Director of Diaspora Initiatives, Converge International Ministries

I was a young candidate preparing to go to Africa when I ended up in Dr Enoch Wan's class at Canadian Theological Seminary in Regina, Canada. I'm not sure I remember much from the class content, but what stuck with me was this humble man of God - I said to myself, I would like to be like that. Then many years later when I was working back in Canada as a missions mobilizer I frequently attended the annual Missio Nexus gatherings and I would intersect with Dr Wan who recommended new missiological resources and publications (EMS) - most of which I bought and read - and in a unique way Dr Wan continued to build into my missiological understanding.

Ronald Brown, D.Min.
Missions Mobilizer & Former VP for Global Ministries,
The C&MA in Canada,

I have known Dr. Enoch Wan since he served as the Founding Director of the Mission Department at the Hong Kong Alliance Bible Seminary by the invitation of Dr. Philip Teng in the late 1970's. For all these years, God has greatly used Dr. Wan in various ministries, such as pastoral, missional, academic, publishing etc., all around the world. He is one of the few Chinese church leaders recognized by the global church especially in mission arena. Because of his up-bringing background, he sensed the importance of personal relationship among the developing peoples and promote the Relational Theology and Missiology. Before the concept of "missions at our doorstep" was popularized, he had already participated in the mission to the ethnic peoples among North American churches. Dr. Wan and his colleagues convened the first Intercultural Ministries National Conference of Canada (1993), which was attended by over 100 representatives from over 30 denominations and mission agencies. He edited and published the compendium of the conference, *Missions Within Reach: Intercultural Ministries in Canada.*[237]

In pattern after the CCCOWE Movement[238], a network among diaspora Chinese churches for mission which was established by Dr. Thomas Wang in 1976, Dr. Wan encouraged and helped the Filipino churches to form their own worldwide network. Gradually, through his writing and speaking, the importance of Diaspora Missiology was acknowledged by mission leaders and becomes one of the key strategies in reaching the unreached.

I would like to take this opportunity to express my personal gratitude for Dr. Wan's precious contribution to the Board of the Great Commission Center International (GCCI) for over a decade. In addition, when I hesitated whether to accept the invitation of serving as the President of GCCI in 2008 succeeding Dr. Thomas Wang, Dr. Wan voluntarily offered to be my deputy in order to boost my confidence. Although he served in a no-pay and voluntary capacity, he faithfully involved in GCCI ministries in many ways whenever he could and was very supportive to me personally.

Let me sum up briefly how I know Dr. Wan in the followings:

---

[237] Wan, Enoch, ed., *Missions Within Reach: Intercultural Ministries in Canada*, Hong Kong: China Alliance Press.
[238] Chinese Coordination Centre of World Evangelization 世界華福中心

On the Academic Level
A prolific scholar with pastoral heart.
A mission strategist with field experience.
A passionate educator with Kingdom mind-set.
A traditional Chinese with global insight.
On the Personal Level
He is humble and easy going.
He is energetic and hard working.
He is considerate and caring.
He is inspiring and encouraging.

Dr. Wan, Happy 78th Birthday! Next time when we get together in the San Francisco Bay Area, we will have In-N-Out Burger and beef/mutton with preserved vegetable hot pot （牛／羊肉酸菜砂鍋） plus Chinese pizza covered with lots of sesame （芝麻大餅） again.

Sharon Wai Man Chan, Ph.D.
Former President, Great Commission Center International

It is a rare gift to serve alongside someone whose life and ministry have left a global imprint—and rarer still when that person is also a friend. Dr. Enoch Wan has been such a gift to Western Seminary, to the global Church, and to me personally.

Enoch's contributions to the field of Intercultural Studies have been nothing short of foundational. As the architect of Diaspora Missiology, he charted new territory in how we understand and engage the global movement of peoples for the sake of the gospel. His development of the Relational Paradigm offered a holistic corrective to individualistic and reductionist models of theology and ministry. Through more than a dozen books, scores of scholarly articles, and editorial leadership in missiological publications, Enoch has shaped the thinking and practice of missionaries, scholars, and church leaders across the globe.

But Enoch is not only a prolific scholar—he is a faithful servant. Whether teaching in the classroom, mentoring students, leading missional initiatives, or engaging in cross-cultural ministry firsthand, he has embodied the very principles he teaches. His work has never been an academic exercise alone. It has been a lived expression of obedience to the Great Commission.

At Western Seminary, we have been blessed by Enoch's leadership, collegiality, and tireless devotion to training men and women for gospel-centered transformation. He has served not only as a professor but also as a missionary, anthropologist, and pioneer. His name has become synonymous with integrity, innovation, and intercultural intelligence.

And on a personal note, I have always appreciated Enoch's humility, humor, and unwavering loyalty to Christ. He is both a man of deep convictions and warm friendship—a rare and beautiful combination.

This Festschrift is a fitting tribute to a man whose legacy will continue through the generations of students, scholars, and gospel workers he has influenced. Enoch, thank you for your life of faithful service. You have run the race well—and we are all better for it.

With deep respect and gratitude,

Charles J. Conniry, Jr., Ph.D.
President, Western Seminary, Portland, Oregon

The trajectory of my personal and professional formation is rooted in humble beginnings, marked by an enduring pursuit of knowledge and intellectual growth. My first encounter with the transformative power of learning came unexpectedly, upon discovering a discarded book — History of Civilizations — in an abandoned piece of furniture behind the house where my family lived. From that moment, my passion for books and the individuals who authored them became a guiding force in my life.

Through years of study and travel, both physical and intellectual, I developed the discernment to differentiate between works of varying depth and impact, as well as between authors whose contributions transcend mere publication. Among those who most profoundly influenced my intellectual and vocational journey, Dr. Enoch Wan (Ph.D. in Anthropology, State University of New York) stands as a singular figure — a scholar who embodies the integration of rigorous academic discipline with a rich Anglophone Chinese cultural heritage.

I had the distinct privilege of studying under and living in close association with Dr. Wan during my time at Reformed Theological Seminary in Jackson, Mississippi. Our engagement extended beyond the classroom, as I later hosted him in Brazil, during which we traveled extensively and shared numerous substantive conversations that further deepened my understanding of his scholarship and character.

At Reformed Theological Seminary, I was mentored by distinguished faculty, including Elias Medeiros, Samuel Larsen, Michael Paine, and, most notably, Enoch Wan. Under Dr. Wan's instruction, I pursued advanced studies in Anthropology, Missiology, and Methodology. His intellectual influence proved pivotal, shaping not only my academic trajectory but also my approach to ministry, life, and professional endeavors.

Dr. Wan instilled in me an enduring appreciation for the centrality of method — both as the foundation for constructing and validating theoretical frameworks and as the instrument through which such frameworks exert influence over societal and intellectual domains. His mentorship cultivated in me an affinity for theory-building methodologies, particularly Grounded Theory as articulated by Barney Galland Glaser and Anselm Leonard Strauss.

The practical implications of his influence have been far-reaching:
- In academic research, I have adopted a methodologically rigorous, theory-driven approach.
- In ministry, I have learned to observe human behavior with analytical precision.
- In life, I have embraced strategic long-term planning.
- In business, I have applied methodological principles to the study and interpretation of currency behavior and economic patterns.

Dr. Enoch Wan remains, in my estimation, not only a scholar of remarkable depth but also a methodological architect whose legacy continues to shape those he mentored. His insistence that methodology serves as the decisive measure of process — the determinant of success or failure — remains a cornerstone of my intellectual framework. His commitment to relational theory, academic integrity, and the advancement of knowledge is amply demonstrated in his professional corpus and in the ongoing impact of his teaching and mentorship.

Rev. Sirgisberto de Costa, Ph.D.
Senior Pastor, Bethesda Presbyterian Church, Brasilia, Brazil

Dr. Enoch Wan is arguably the authority in diaspora missiology. It has become his lifelong passion and commitment as he embodies the "scattered people." The strength of his scholarship is twofold. Firstly, he is a practitioner-scholar. I planted churches in two metropolitan areas in North America and served as a missionary teacher in Asia. Consequently, his research incorporates traditional literary knowledge, critically tested on the ground. Secondly, his diaspora missiology is firmly evangelical; hence, he carefully discerns God's plan among the people on the move. This providential perspective, however, does not gloss over the challenging realities of immigrants, refugees, transnational workers, and the like. There are so many facets in his scholarship. Therefore, it is fitting that this volume celebrates his life, ministry, and scholarship, and I add my congratulations to this fellow Asian who has found a "strange land" as God's destiny.

Wonsuk Ma, Ph.D.
Distinguished Professor of Global Christianity
Executive Director of the Center for Spirit-Empowered Research
Oral Roberts University, Tulsa, OK, USA

For thirty-five years, I have watched Rev. Dr. Enoch Wan serve the church with a scholar's mind, a pastor's heart, and a missionary's footsteps. We first connected within the Canadian Chinese Alliance family, where his teachings and counsel helped many of us anchor our ministry in Scripture while engaging diverse cultures with humility and courage. Long before "diaspora" became a common term in mission discussions, Dr. Wan encouraged us to reread Acts 17 and see human mobility as a divine opportunity for the spreading of the gospel rather than just a social trend.

Over decades of dialogue, classrooms, and field collaboration, he kept the focus on Christ and people. He avoided academic distance and asked better questions related to daily life. Under his guidance, many of us shifted from "mission to migrants" to "mission through migrants," learning to see the Chinese diaspora not as a problem to manage but as partners to equip many and ready to bless both neighbours and nations.

I remember conference hallways where he lingered to listen, to pray, and to connect emerging workers with mentors. I recall emails filled with articles, carefully chosen footnotes, and quiet encouragement: "Press on; the church needs this." I think of intercessions that name cities and people one by one. His anthropology served his doxology; his research consistently led to worship, witness, and wise practice. Under his influence, my own preaching and teaching learned to cross cultures without ever losing the cross.

Many were shaped by his writings and by the way he trained leaders to be bilingual and bicultural, enabling them to preach in Cantonese or Mandarin while discipling youth in English. In classrooms, church basements, and prayer rooms, he called congregations to unite and welcome the nations already at our doorstep. His vision helped Chinese churches shift their focus from maintenance to mission, from scarcity to faith.

In recent years, it has been my joy to collaborate with Dr. Wan in mobilizing Chinese diaspora missions around the world. Together, we have brought together pastors, seminarians, and marketplace leaders to envision ways in which local churches can send and receive, learn, and lead both here and abroad. He builds bridges between the academy and the congregation, mission agencies and seminaries, generations, and different places. He demonstrates a generous orthodoxy that stays true to the gospel, is eager to work collaboratively, and is quick to celebrate God's work through others.

The Festschrift theme "Missionary, Anthropologist, Professor" suits him well, yet the common thread linking these roles is simple obedience: "Here am I. Send me." May the Lord grant Dr. Wan renewed strength to continue shepherding the global Chinese church toward wise and loving witness among all peoples. "Your labour in the Lord is not in vain" (1 Cor 15:58).

To God be the glory!

Rev. Francis Tam, D.Min.
Executive Director, CCCOWE Canada [239]
Interim Principal, Canadian Chinese School of Theology Calgary

When I think of Dr Wan, I am convinced that **God is love** (1 John 4:8). For me, the most prominent impression of Dr Wan is his voice, always calm, gentle, patient, and full of grace. Ever since fourteen years ago when God blessed me with the first opportunity to communicate with Dr Wan, the time accumulated from phone calls has far surpassed the three times we briefly met in person. Back then I was spiritually an infant and mentally suffering from severe depression. Dr Wan, guided by the Holy Spirit and over many years, spent incalculable amount of his precious time, energy, phone bills, and even sacrificed his sleep to walk with me through that dark valley—even though I was a nobody he'd never met before. Once, my father cried out, "Dr Wan, how can we ever pay you back for such kindness? Even if we were to sell all of our possessions, that would still be useless compared to what we owe you— it's like a drop in the ocean." To which Dr Wan replied, "You don't owe me anything, and there's no need to pay me back, for what I am doing is a kingdom investment."

---

[239] CCCOWE Canada – 加拿大華福中心, Chinese Coordination Centre of World Evangelization Canada

During one phone call, I was overwhelmed by Dr Wan's unbelievable patience and generosity, and I couldn't fathom why anyone could be so selfless and loving towards a complete stranger! So, in tears I asked, "Dr Wan, how can you show me so much love when I am full of negativity and we're not even blood-related?" I will never forget Dr Wan's voice when he answered me which was full of joy and a little laughter. He smiled and said, "Mandy, **we love because God first loved us** (1 John 4:19)! I have received so much love from God; if I don't give that love out, I will burst! God's love multiplies when you give to others what you have received. That is how God's kingdom works. One day, when God has healed you, don't be selfish; make yourself available to others who need God's love just like you do today. Remember, **it is more blessed to give than to receive** (Acts 20:35)."

When I think of Dr Wan, God's word becomes alive. Whatever the topic of our conversation might be, Dr Wan ALWAYS points me to the most appropriate Bible verse or passage for that particular situation; then he will open God's word for me. When Dr Wan speaks, I am often reminded of those people listening to Jesus and how they were "**amazed at the gracious words that came from his lips**" (Luke 4:22). It is through Dr Wan's life example that God has shown me why the Bible, unlike any other book, is the living word of God!

When I think of Dr Wan, I see a true prayer warrior. From our first phone call in 2011, every conversation we've had was always concluded in prayer, no matter how brief–like Dr Wan was queuing to board a flight. During my many years struggling with depression, numerous times my storms and tsunamis were miraculously calmed down by Dr Wan's phone call and prayer which is infused with the Scripture. Hearing Dr Wan's still voice declaring God's truth, promises and steadfast love will flush away my fear and anxiety; and refill my heart with joy and hope instead. The most touching prayer was with my husband and me on our wedding night, as we knelt down in front of the phone in England, Dr Wan, far away in the States, blessed our marriage and prayed that we shall be "**heirs of the gracious gift of life**" (1 Peter 3:7). Nine years on, we are only increasingly more grateful towards Dr Wan for his continuous love and care for us.

When I think of Dr Wan, my heart is always filled with deep awe, respect and gratitude. My prayer is that may the Lord multiply his blessings upon Dr Wan, Mrs Wan and their family, and that more and more people will be drawn to the Lord Jesus through encountering Dr Wan and his irresistible gentleness and graciousness—for **the fragrance of Christ** (2 Corinthians 2:15) oozes out of him.

Mandy Tao, Ph.D.
An academic and social scientist in the UK

Afterword

Miriam Adeney, Ph.D.

What if Enoch had not been here? Between the pointed pine-scented evergreens and blue Pacific and snowy white mountains, Enoch Wan has been the man in the gap in this northwest corner of the country. As Director of Intercultural Studies at Western Seminary in Portland Oregon, he has shaped the minds of generations of graduate students. It might have been easier for him to remain a church-planter and pastor. That would have used his gifts and blessed communities. But there was a need for someone to help church leaders understand their cultural contexts and serve them wisely, to grasp the big picture and its complex, systematic dynamics. Enoch was that man. He stepped up.

In so doing, Enoch shouldered the program that began in 1925 when Walter Hinson founded Portland Baptist Bible Institute, the forerunner of Western Seminary. On the edge of Mt. Tabor but also right in the thick of the city, this school was blessed by the visionary African expert Donald K Smith, who developed a rich missiology program. Other scholars like Pakistan specialist Mary Wilder, M.D., expanded the robust offerings. Graduate students came from across the region, and beyond. A Worldview Center emerged to house international and local student families in community. Churches throughout the state sent construction and electric teams to whip the Center building into shape.

Enoch Wan became the steward of this resource. Meanwhile, the internet revolution was exploding. For a variety of reasons, fewer bodies were showing up on seminary campuses. COVID delivered the ultimate clamp down. How could the seminary respond? A vigorous online program was developed, with Enoch at the forefront in his area.

Now students around the world could enroll in Western Seminary's graduate intercultural studies programs. Enoch greeted each of these Master's and Doctoral students with enthusiastic personal interest. Since "Relational Theology" is one of his theoretical emphases, he put this into practice with his own classes. Not only did he prod students toward academic rigor but also nurtured them as human beings facing challenges and experiencing joys as they grew into Christ's likeness.

Remarkably, Enoch also set up a system so that graduates could publish their own books, often adaptations of their academic dissertations. These volumes vibrate with maps, tables, and statistics, as well as cultural and theological background, cases, and applications. For example, two of his Vietnamese doctoral students, Thanh Trung Le and Tin Nguyen, published *Mobilizing Vietnamese Diaspora for the Kingdom* and *A Holistic and Contextualized Mission Training Program: Equipping Lay Leaders for Local Mission in Vietnam.* Sometimes Enoch would join as co-author, as he did with these Vietnamese books.

One of the most powerful social realities in our time is the global flow of people pouring across the world. At least 200 million individuals live outside the countries where they were born. Enoch is one of those. Born in China, raised in an orphanage in Hong Kong, educated in Hong Kong and the USA, and serving in various cities inside and outside the USA, Enoch knows the life of a migrant. It is no wonder that he has been one of the pioneers in the subdiscipline of missiology known as diaspora studies.

Diaspora movements are a major mission opportunity, making the gospel accessible to formerly unreached peoples, like Afghans who now worship Jesus in more than thirty countries. Diaspora movements also propel streams of fellow believers into our communities, providing us with new partners and teachers. Today there are 700 languages spoken in New York City, many in that city's ethnic churches. Unquestionably, uprooting is painful. Still, on the positive side, it can detach us from a false sense of security and lead us into unexpected blessings. Enoch Wan's life experiences have honed his expertise here, informing and guiding other Christians who find ourselves swirling in new maelstroms.

This is a book that honors Professor Enoch Wan, a key missiologist in the Pacific Northwest. He has been willing to stand in the gap, holding out wisdom to inquiring minds who want to know what is happening, who hope to serve people more faithfully, who need counsel and likeminded community. From his quick smile and dancing eyes it is clear that he has enjoyed this challenge of mentoring those who migrate into his orbit. He has reveled in building relationships for the Kingdom of God.

Editors & Contributors

Editors (& Contributors)

Mark R. Hedinger, D.I.S., served as a Bible School director and teacher in Mexico for 12 years, and then as an International Director for his sending organization (Crossworld). Seeing a need for better training of missionary workers led him to Western Seminary for his Doctor of Intercultural Studies degree. He currently serves as Executive Director and Culture Trainer for a not-for-profit called CultureBound and as adjunct faculty for the intercultural programs at Western Seminary. He is a medical interpreter helping English and Spanish speakers to communicate in medical contexts. He enjoys being husband to Karen and father and grandfather within their family.

Jacky Lau, Ph.D., is an adjunct Professor of Misson at the Ambrose Seminary in Canada and a board member with the International Student Ministries Canada. He is Worker Emeritus with the Christian & Missionary Alliance in Canada and had served as Pastor, Church Planter, Team Leader and Global Track Leader. Jacky was the founding pastor of the Chinese Christian Church of Dubai in UAE. He and his wife, Anne, have collaborated in ministry for over 25 years. God bless them with two children and six grandchildren.

Sadiri Joy Tira, D.Min., D.Miss., is diaspora missiology specialist at the Jaffray Centre for Global Initiatives at Ambrose University in Canada. A reflective-practitioner, Sadiri Joy Tira served as catalyst for diasporas (formerly, senior associate for diasporas) for the Lausanne Movement from 2007–2019, founding chairperson of the Global Diaspora Network (2010–2015), and as senior pastor of First Filipino Alliance Church in Edmonton, Canada's "Gateway to the North" for over two decades.

Contributors

Miriam Adeney, Ph.D., is an anthropologist, missiologist, and coach for Christian writers worldwide. She has served as President of the American Society of Missiology, Board Member for Christianity Today, participating member of the World Evangelical Alliance and of the Diaspora Task Force of the Lausanne Committee on World Evangelization. She has received Lifetime Achievement Awards from the Christians for Biblical Equality and Media Associates International.

Tereso (Terry) C. Casiño, Th.D., Ph.D., is Executive Director of the D.Min. program and Professor of Missiology and Intercultural Studies at the School of Divinity of Gardner-Webb University in North Carolina, U.S.A. He was chair of the North America Diaspora Educators of the Lausanne Global Diaspora Network, founding Director of Asia Pacific Institute of Missions in Philippines, and founding Vice-President of the International Center for Diaspora Missions in South Korea. Dr. Casino's research and publication focus on intercultural theology, missions anthropology, contextualization, worldviews and world picture, church planting movements, and diaspora missiology.

Matt Cook, Ph.D., is an assistant professor of Bible, Global Missions, and World Religions at Freed-Hardeman University and is the Program Coordinator of the Doctor of Ministry program. Prior to his role at FHU, Matt and his wife Charla were church planters in Cusco, Peru. Matt earned a Ph.D. (2019) in Missions and World Religions from The Southern Baptist Theological Seminary. His research interests include diaspora missiology, contextualization, and missions pedagogy.

Karen R. Hedinger, Ed.D., served as a missionary to Mexico for 12 years. Since that time, she earned a Doctor of Education in Intercultural Education degree from Western Seminary. She is currently the Associate Director of the Doctor of Intercultural Studies and the Ph.D. in Intercultural Education programs at Western Seminary. She is also the director of Second Language Acquisition and the training coordinator for CultureBound, a Christian not-for-profit training organization. Karen and her husband Mark have four grown children and many grandchildren.

J. Nelson Jennings, Ph.D., is the editor of the English online journal *Global Missiology*. He moved his family from the USA to Japan as church-planting missionaries in 1986. Jennings taught at Tokyo Christian University (1996-1999) and at Covenant Theological Seminary (1999-2011), then served at the Overseas Ministries Study Center (2011-2015) and with Global Mapping International (2016-2017). For over six years (2015-2021) Jennings served as Mission Pastor, Consultant, and International Liaison for Onnuri Church, Seoul. Jennings and his wife Kathy have three adult daughters and seven grandchildren.

Elton Siu Lun Law, D.Miss., is the Chief Executive of the Hong Kong Association of Christian Missions and an Associate Professor at Yan Fook Theological Seminary in Hong Kong. An ordained pastor, Dr. Law has extensive experience in missions, having served as a missionary and field director in Japan.

Thanh Trung Le, D.Min., D.Miss., has served as the senior pastor of Edmonton Vietnamese Alliance Church since 1986. He has also coordinated the Worldwide Association of Vietnamese Alliance Churches since 2006 and previously served as Director of the Association of Vietnamese Alliance Churches in Canada (2000–2008). He has taught at the Alliance Theological College and Logos College in evangelism, discipleship, and missions.

Ria Llanto Martin, D.I.S., is a first-generation Filipino immigrant in the USA. She received her Doctor of Intercultural Studies from Western Seminary, Portland, OR. She is an adjunct faculty member at Dallas International University, where she teaches Intercultural Teamwork and serves as the Director of Intercultural and Global Services at Columbia Theological Seminary.

Danyal Qalb, Ph.D., Danyal is a German who grew up in Brazil and works in the Philippines since 2007. He is the first to earn a Ph.D. in Orality Studies and currently serves as Research Director with Orality Collaborators (https:orality.co). Danyal oversees the development of the Global Orality Mapping Project (GOMAP), teaches orality principles and methods around the world, and is the co-founder and editor of the OralityTalks Journal.

Narry Santos, Ph.D., is Associate Professor of Christian Ministry and Intercultural Leadership at the seminary of Tyndale University in Toronto and Vice President of the Evangelical Missiological Society Canada. He also serves as part-time Senior Pastor of Greenhills Christian Fellowship (GCF) Peel and GCF York in Ontario, Canada. He recently planted Saddleback South Manila and was its pastor for three years. Before Saddleback Church, he ministered at GCF in different pastoral responsibilities for 20 years, including helping plant six churches in Canada and four in the Philippines.

Tom Steffen, D.Miss., is professor emeritus of intercultural studies, Cook School of Intercultural Studies, Biola University. Related publications include *Reconnecting God's Story to Ministry*; *Worldview-based Storying*; *New and Old Horizons in the Orality Movement* (co-edited with Cameron Armstrong); *The Return of Oral Hermeneutics* (with Bill Bjoraker); *Character Theology: Engaging God through His Cast of Characters* (with Ray Neu).

Sadiri Tonyvic Tira is the Discipleship Essentials Partnership Development Director with Trans World Radio Canada and the founding planter of Supper Club, a polymorphic church community in Edmonton, Canada. His ministry experience spans inner-city outreach, young adult discipleship, and global yet deeply practical mission, having previously served as Pastor for Young Adults and later for Missions and Church Strategy at Central Edmonton Alliance Church, and as Senior Manager of Homeless Programs at Hope Mission. His work centers on relational discipleship, urban mission, and church innovation. Dr. Enoch Wan and his wife served as marital godparents to Tony and his wife, Zen. Their early conversations on relational mission helped shape the theological vision that now fuels Tony's ministry among emerging generations.

Lorajoy Tira-Dimangondayao is a member of the World Evangelical Alliance Global Migration Task Force and previously, worked closely with the leadership of the Lausanne Movement's Diasporas issue group (2007-2019), after which she served on the board of directors of Lausanne Movement Canada. With intersectional communities close to her heart, Lorajoy serves in fund development for Edmonton-based non-profit, Adeara Recovery Centre, and researches Filipino Christianity in Canada from Tyndale University. Lorajoy is committed to the life of communities and is thankful for engagements that have gifted her the privilege of listening to stories of how people from all over Canada—and the world—work together to make a home.

Juno Wang, D.I.S., is a practitioner, researcher, and trainer of Diaspora Missions. She served at the Great Commission Center International under the leadership of the late Dr. Thomas Wang for nearly eighteen years before pursuing her seminary training. She earned a doctorate in Intercultural Studies from Western Seminary, a master's degree in Intercultural Ministry from Golden Gate Baptist Theological Seminary, and an MBA from Azusa Pacific University. Since 2009, she has been involved in multi-ethnic community outreach in Silicon Valley, California.

Tuvya Zaretsky, D.I.S., is a career missionary with the Jews for Jesus ministry. He began his service among other Jewish people in 1972, initially as a volunteer, and then in 1974 as the first field missionary with Jews for Jesus. For twenty years he was president of the international Lausanne Consultation on Jewish Evangelism. His wife, Ellen, has served as ministry partner since their marriage in 1980. They are incredibly proud parents of three amazing offspring and a lineage that continues to grow.

www.ingramcontent.com/pod-product-compliance
Lightning Source LLC
Chambersburg PA
CBHW06065510O426
42734CB00047B/1814